TUTOR DELIVERY PACK

CHEMISTRY

— GCSE —

HIGHER

Author: Lyn Nicholls

CHEMISTRY HIGHER

Contents

CHEMISTRY HIGHER

Contents

CHEMISTRY HIGHER

How to use this pack

The *Tutors' Guild* AQA GCSE (9–1) Chemistry Tutor Delivery Pack gives you all of the tools you need to deliver effective Chemistry lessons to GCSE students who are sitting the Higher tier papers of AQA GCSE (9–1) Chemistry and AQA GCSE (9–1) Combined Science: Trilogy.

Lessons

There are 38 one-hour, six-page lessons in this Tutor Delivery Pack. Most tutors working for a full year will have around 38 lessons with a student. If you have less contact time, you can choose which lessons are most important to the student. Each lesson is standalone and can be taught independently from those preceding it.

Lesson plans

The first page of each lesson is your *lesson plan*. It is designed specifically for tutors and is intended to guide you through a one-hour session in either a one-to-one or small group setting. It is not designed to be student-facing.

Learning objectives and specification links

At the top of each lesson plan, you will find two lists. The first – *learning objectives* – is a list of your aims for the lesson. The learning objectives will be informed by the specification but may have been rephrased to make sure they are accessible to and useful for everyone. You can discuss these with the student or use them for your own reference when tracking progress. The second list – *specification links* – shows you where in the specification you can find the objectives relevant to the lesson. You can find out more about the specification on pages 7–10.

Activities

The first five minutes of your lesson should be spent reviewing the previous week's homework. You should not mark the homework during contact time: instead, use the time to talk through what the student learned and enjoyed, and any difficulties they encountered.

The final five minutes should be used to set homework for the forthcoming week. There are three ways to do this: using the *end-of-lesson report* on page 16; orally with a parent or guardian; or simply using the *homework activity sheet* on the fifth page of each lesson.

In each lesson plan, you will find four types of activities.

- *Starter activities* are 5–10 minutes each and provide an introduction to the topic.
- *Main activities* are up to 40 minutes long and are more involved, focussing on the main objectives of the lesson.
- *Plenary activities* are 5–10 minutes each, require little to no writing and recap the main learning points or prepare for the homework.
- *Homework activities* can be up to an hour long and put learning into practice.

In the lesson plan, you will find a page reference (where the activity is paper-based), a suggested timeframe and teaching notes for each activity. The teaching notes will help to guide you in delivering the activity and will also advise you on any common misconceptions associated with the topic.

Support and extension ideas

This pack is aimed at students who are targeting grades 4–9, but every student is different: some will struggle with activities that others working at the same level find straightforward. In these sections, you will find ideas for providing some differentiation throughout the activities.

How to use this pack

Progress and observations

This section is left blank for you to use as appropriate. You can then use the notes you make to inform assessment and future lessons, as well as to inform progress reports to parents or guardians.

Activities

There are four student-facing activity sheets for each lesson: one for the starter activities; two for the main activities and one for the homework activity. On each sheet, you'll find activity-specific lesson objectives, an equipment list and a suggested timeframe. All activities are phrased for one-to-one tutoring but are equally as appropriate for small group settings. If you have a small group and the task asks you to work in pairs or challenge each other, ask the students to pair up while you observe and offer advice as necessary. Where appropriate, answers can be found on the sixth page of the lesson.

Diagnostics

The first lesson in this pack is a diagnostic lesson, designed to help you find out more about your student: their likes and dislikes; strengths and weaknesses and personality traits. As well as the diagnostic lesson, the needs analysis section (pages 13–14) allows you, the student and the student's parents or guardians to investigate together which areas of the subject will need greater focus. Together, these sections will help you deliver the most effective, best value tuition.

Progress report

This can be used to inform parents or guardians or for your own planning as frequently or infrequently as is useful for you. Spend some time discussing the statements on the report with the student. Be prepared, though – some students will tell you there isn't anything that they enjoy about the subject!

End-of-lesson report

Parent participation will vary greatly. The end-of-lesson report is useful for efficiently feeding back to parents or guardians who prefer an update after each lesson. There is space to review completed homework and achievements in the lesson, as well as space for the student to explain how confident they feel after the lesson. Finally, there is a section on what steps, including homework, the parent and student can take to consolidate learning or prepare for the following week. The end-of-lesson report may also be useful for communicating with some parents or guardians who speak English as a second language, as written information may be easier to follow.

Certificates

In the digital version of this pack, you will find two customisable certificates. These can be edited to celebrate achievements of any size.

TUTORS GUILD **CHEMISTRY** HIGHER

Information for parents and guardians

Introduction

Your child's tutor will often make use of resources from the *Tutors' Guild* series. These resources have been written especially for the new 9–1 GCSEs, and are tailored to the AQA GCSE (9–1) Chemistry and the AQA GCSE (9–1) Combined Science: Trilogy specifications. The tutor will use their expert knowledge and judgement to assess the student's current needs. This will allow them to target areas for improvement, build confidence levels and develop skills as quickly as possible to ensure the best chance of success.

Just as a classroom teacher might do, the tutor will use lesson plans and activities designed to prepare the student for the 9–1 GCSEs. Each set of resources has been designed by experts in GCSE Chemistry and reviewed by tutors to ensure it offers great quality, effective and engaging tuition.

Getting started

Before tuition can begin, the tutor will need to know more about your motives for employing them in order to set clear, achievable goals. They will also try to learn more about the student to ensure lessons are as useful and as engaging as possible.

To gather this information, the tutor will work through the *needs analysis* pages of this pack with you. It shouldn't take too long, but it will really maximise the value of the tuition time you pay for. You could also take this opportunity to discuss with the tutor any questions or concerns you may have.

Lessons and homework

Each lesson will have the same structure: there will be a starter, which is a quick introduction to the topic; some main activities, which will look at the topic in greater detail; and a plenary activity, which will be used to round off the topic. Throughout the year, the student will become increasingly confident with the content of the specification, but will also improve his or her speaking, writing, reading, listening and co-ordination skills through a carefully balanced range of activities.

At the end of each lesson, the tutor will set some homework, which should take no longer than an hour to complete. If you don't want the tutor to set homework, please let them know. If you are happy for homework to be given, they will either discuss the homework task with you at the end of the lesson or give you an end-of-lesson report. All of the homework activities are designed to be completed independently, but if you would like to help with completion of homework, the tutor will be able to tell you what you can do.

Further support

Parents and guardians often ask a tutor what else they can do to support their child's learning or what resources they can buy to provide extra revision and practice. As a Pearson resource, *Tutors' Guild* has been designed to complement the popular *Revise* series. Useful titles you may wish to purchase include:

- *Revise* AQA GCSE (9–1) Chemistry Higher Revision Guide (ISBN 9781292131283)
- *Revise* AQA GCSE (9–1) Chemistry Higher Revision Workbook (ISBN 9781292131269)
- *Revise* AQA GCSE (9–1) Combined Science: Trilogy Higher Revision Guide (ISBN 9781292131627)
- *Revise* AQA GCSE (9–1) Combined Science: Trilogy Higher Revision Workbook (ISBN 9781292131689)

Using pages 251–252 of this pack, the tutor will be able to tell you which pages of the resources are appropriate for each lesson.

Information for parents and guardians

What's in the test?

You may have heard a lot about the new 9–1 GCSEs from your child's school, from other parents or in the media. Here is a breakdown of the AQA GCSE (9–1) Chemistry exam.

Students will sit two papers that assess learning against the AQA GCSE (9–1) Chemistry specification.

Paper 1: *Topics 1–5: Atomic structure and the periodic table; Bonding, structure, and the properties of matter; Quantitative chemistry; Chemical changes; and Energy changes. (50% of the total marks)*
Students are given 1 hour and 45 minutes to complete Paper 1. It is made up of multiple-choice, structured, closed short answer and open response questions.

Paper 2: *Topics 6–10: The rate and extent of chemical change; Organic chemistry; Chemical analysis, Chemistry of the atmosphere; and Using resources. (50% of the total marks)*
Students are given 1 hour and 45 minutes to complete Paper 2. Again, it is made up of multiple-choice, structured, closed short answer and open response questions.

AQA GCSE (9–1) Combined Science: Trilogy

This pack can also be used to teach AQA GCSE (9–1) Combined Science: Trilogy. A breakdown of the differences between the AQA GCSE (9–1) Chemistry and AQA GCSE (9–1) Combined Science: Trilogy specifications can be found on pages 11–12.

Here is a breakdown of the Chemistry section of the AQA GCSE (9–1) Combined Science exam.

Paper 1: *Topics 8–12: Atomic structure and the periodic table; Bonding, structure, and the properties of matter; Quantitative chemistry; Chemical changes; and Energy changes. (16.7% of the total marks)*
Students are given 1 hour and 15 minutes to complete Paper 1. It is made up of multiple-choice, structured, closed short answer and open response questions.

Paper 2: *Topics 13–17: The rate and extent of chemical change; Organic chemistry; Chemical analysis; Chemistry of the atmosphere; and Using resources. (16.7% of the total marks)*
Students are given 1 hour and 15 minutes to complete Paper 2. It, again, is made up of multiple-choice, structured, closed short answer and open response questions.

Results and grades

GCSE results day is typically the third or fourth Thursday in August. It is the same day across the country, so you can find out the exact date online. On results day, students will be given a slip of paper (or one per exam board, if the school hasn't collated them) with an overall grade for each GCSE. Grades for the 9–1 GCSE in Chemistry are given as numbers (9–1) instead of letters (A*–U). The diagram below shows roughly how the old-style grades translate to the new ones.

	A*		A	B		C	D	E	F	G	U
9		8		7	6	5		4	3	2	1	U

As you can see, the new grade 9 is pitched higher than an A*. There is also a wider spread of grades available for students whose target would previously have been a B/C. GCSE (9–1) Chemistry is a tiered exam, with the Foundation papers aimed at those students targeting grades 1–5, and the Higher papers aimed at students hoping for grades 4–9.

Specification guidance

The new AQA GCSE (9–1) Chemistry qualification was introduced for first teaching in 2016 and first assessment in 2018.

If you have experience in tutoring or teaching the previous curriculum, much of the content and assessment will be familiar. If this is the case, please turn to pages 8–10 for guidance on what has changed.

If you are new to tutoring GCSE Chemistry, this page will give you a brief introduction to the qualification before you move on to pages 8–10. Further guidance on particular areas of the specification – including common misconceptions and barriers to learning – can be found in the lesson plans throughout this book. Full details of the specification can be found on the AQA website.

Key facts

Subject content

There are ten areas of chemistry that will be assessed:

- Atomic structure and the periodic table
- Bonding, structure, and the properties of matter
- Quantitative chemistry
- Chemical changes
- Energy changes
- The rate and extent of chemical change
- Organic chemistry
- Chemical analysis
- Chemistry of the atmosphere
- Using resources

The ten domains are further broken down into smaller content areas. These are set out from page 15 onwards of the AQA specification, which can be found on the AQA website.

Each lesson plan in this pack highlights which areas of the specification are covered. In order to maximise your student's chances of success, the pack covers the most important specification areas and those students struggle with the most; it is intended to supplement and enhance classroom teaching and does not therefore cover the entire specification.

Exam papers

Both Foundation and Higher students will sit two exam papers:

- **Paper 1**
  - Topics 1–5: Atomic structure and the periodic table; Bonding, structure, and the properties of matter; Quantitative chemistry, Chemical changes; and Energy changes
  - 1 hour 45 minutes
  - 100 marks
  - 50% of GCSE
  - Foundation/Higher Tier
  - Multiple choice, structured, closed short answer and open response questions.
- **Paper 2**
  - Topics 6–10: The rate and extent of chemical change; Organic chemistry; Chemical analysis, Chemistry of the atmosphere; and Using resources
  - 1 hour 45 minutes
  - 100 marks
  - 50% of GCSE
  - Foundation/Higher Tier
  - Multiple choice, structured, closed short answer and open response questions.

As the breakdown above shows, each exam paper is given an equal weighting: half of the total available marks are available for each paper. Foundation students will be able to access grades 1–5 and Higher students will be able to access grades 4–9.

At least 15% of marks will be allocated to testing students' experience of practical science, and 20% of marks will be given for maths skills.

CHEMISTRY HIGHER

Specification guidance

What's changed?

Key changes

There are several key changes to the AQA GCSE (9–1) Chemistry course, brought about by new Ofqual requirements. The hope is that increasing the demand of GCSE Chemistry will better prepare students to apply their learning in everyday life, in work and in further studies. The new course will be more demanding in the following ways.

- **The grading system has changed.**

  The A* to G grades will be replaced by 9 to 1 for GCSE Chemistry. Combined Science will have a 17 point grading scale, from 9–9, 9–8 through to 2–1, 1–1.

- **There is more subject content.**

  You'll have more topics to cover with your student, and the topics will be denser. This will change how you teach the course: will you recommend increased contact time, set more independent work or prioritise which content you cover?

- **The level of demand increases.**

  Questions become steadily more demanding within each topic area and throughout the paper, giving students of all abilities the chance to gain marks on each topic.

- **Total exam time has increased.**

  The minimum exam time for GCSE Chemistry is 3 hours 30 minutes. The minimum exam time for Combined Science is 7 hours.

- **There are no controlled assessments.**

  Controlled assessment will no longer be carried out, but will instead be replaced with exam questions testing students' understanding of scientific experimentation, including use of apparatus and techniques. Students are now expected to carry out a number of required practical activities in class, their knowledge of which will then be tested in the exam.

- **Quality of Written Communication (QWC) is no longer assessed.**

  Marks are no longer available for the quality of written communication. However, logical structuring of extended responses is still necessary to achieve a good grade in GCSE (9–1) Science qualifications.

New content

New topics include the following:

- Electrolysis of molten ionic compounds
- Chromatography
- Cells and batteries
- Global climate change.

To make way for this new content, some previously covered content has been omitted from the new specification, including some aspects of the subject areas Hydrocarbon fuels, Metals and Quantitative chemistry.

While this pack will help you to deliver the new content, you should make sure you are familiar and comfortable with the new topics and the best practices for teaching them. A full list of new content can be found on AQA's website.

TUTORS GUILD **CHEMISTRY** HIGHER

Specification guidance

Science and maths skills

The new GCSE (9–1) Chemistry qualification places special emphasis on mathematical skills, and on learning to work scientifically. You need to make sure you are able to help your students develop such skills.

Working scientifically

GCSE (9–1) Chemistry covers a range of scientific skills, including experimenting, observing and analysing results.

1. Development of scientific thinking

This section covers a range of skills related to scientific thought, including: understanding scientific methods and theories; using scientific models; evaluating scientific risks; consideration of ethical issues.

2. Experimental skills and strategies

This section covers a range of skills and strategies, including: developing hypotheses based on scientific theories; applying knowledge to select apparatus; sampling techniques; evaluation of scientific methods.

2. Analysis and evaluation

This section covers skills relating to the collection, presentation and analysis of data, including: translating data from one form to another; mathematical and statistical analysis; interpreting observations; communicating scientific rationale.

4. Scientific vocabulary, quantities, units, symbols and nomenclature

This section includes: using scientific vocabulary; using units correctly; using prefixes and powers of ten for orders of magnitude; using an appropriate number of significant figures.

The lesson plans in this pack indicate where key areas of working scientifically have been covered.

Mathematical skills

In GCSE (9–1) Chemistry, a minimum of 20% of marks will test the student's skills in mathematics. This is compared to 10% in GCSE Biology, and 30% in GCSE Physics.

Students will be required to demonstrate the following maths skills in GCSE (9–1) Chemistry:

- Arithmetic and numerical computation
- Handling data
- Algebra
- Graphs
- Geometry and trigonometry.

These five areas are described in full from page 90 of the AQA specification, which can be found on the AQA website.

In Foundation Tier papers maths skills will be tested up to Key Stage 3 standard. In Higher Tier papers maths skills requirements will not be lower than the requirements for the Foundation Tier in a GCSE qualification in mathematics.

The lesson plans in this pack indicate which areas of maths skills are covered in individual lessons.

CHEMISTRY HIGHER

AQA

Specification guidance

Practical work

Students will carry out eight practicals for each of Biology, Chemistry and Physics, and 16 for Combined Science, which are all outlined in the relevant AQA specifications. This pack will not include practical work in the lessons, but will cover the relevant practical methods and apparatus needed for the exam.

- **Required practical activity 1:**

  Preparation of a pure, dry sample of a soluble salt from an insoluble oxide or carbonate, using a Bunsen burner to heat dilute acid and a water bath or electric heater to evaporate the solution.

- **Required practical activity 2 (Chemistry only)**

  Determination of the reacting volumes of solutions of a strong acid and a strong alkali by titration.

- **Required practical activity 3**

  Investigate what happens when aqueous solutions are electrolysed using inert electrodes. This should be an investigation involving developing a hypothesis.

- **Required practical activity 4**

  Investigate the variables that affect temperature changes in reacting solutions such as, eg acid plus metals, acid plus carbonates, neutralisations, displacement of metals.

- **Required practical activity 5**

  Investigate how changes in concentration affect the rates of reactions by a method involving measuring the volume of a gas produced and a method involving a change in colour or turbidity. This should be an investigation involving developing a hypothesis.

- **Required practical activity 6**

  Investigate how paper chromatography can be used to separate and tell the difference between coloured substances. Students should calculate Rf values.

- **Required practical activity 7 (Chemistry only)**

  Use of chemical tests to identify the ions in unknown single ionic compounds covering the ions from sections Flame tests through to Sulfates.

- **Required practical activity 8 (Chemistry only)**

  Analysis and purification of water samples from different sources, including pH, dissolved solids and distillation.

AQA GCSE (9–1) Combined Science: Trilogy

This pack can also be used to teach the AQA GCSE (9–1) Combined Science: Trilogy specification. This exam will cover the same ten areas of Chemistry as those taught in AQA GCSE (9–1) Chemistry, along with topics from the AQA GCSE (9–1) Biology and Physics specifications. The GCSE (9–1) Combined Science: Trilogy qualification is linear, meaning that students will sit all their exams at the end of the course.

Exam papers

For the Chemistry section of the exam, both Foundation and Higher students will sit two exam papers:

- **Chemistry Paper 1**
  - Topics 8–12: Atomic structure and the periodic table; Bonding, structure, and the properties of matter; Quantitative chemistry; Chemical changes; and Energy changes
  - Written exam: 1 hour 15 minutes
  - 70 marks; 16.7% of GCSE
  - Foundation and Higher Tier
  - Multiple choice, structured, closed short answer and open response questions.

- **Chemistry Paper 2**
  - Topics 13–17: The rate and extent of chemical change; Organic chemistry; Chemical analysis; Chemistry of the atmosphere; and Using resources
  - Written exam: 1 hour 15 minutes
  - 70 marks; 16.7% of GCSE
  - Foundation and Higher Tier
  - Multiple choice, structured, closed short answer and open response questions.

A map for teaching AQA GCSE (9–1) Combined Science: Trilogy using this pack is available on pages 11–12.
Please note that this pack is not intended to be used to teach AQA GCSE (9–1) Combined Science: Synergy.

Mapping of lessons to AQA GCSE (9-1) Combined Science: Trilogy

Lesson	Specification reference		Suggested adaptation for Trilogy
	Chemistry	Combined	
1		Not applicable	This lesson and activities can be used for Combined Science Trilogy, substituting 'Combined Science' for 'Chemistry'.
2	4.1.1.1; 4.1.1.2	5.1.1.1; 5.1.1.2	No change
3	4.1.1.3; 4.1.1.4	5.1.1.3; 5.1.1.4	No change
4	4.1.1.5; 4.1.1.6; 4.1.1.7	5.1.1.5; 5.1.1.6; 5.1.1.7	No change
5	4.1.2.1; 4.1.2.2	5.1.2.1; 5.1.2.2	No change
6	4.1.2.3; 4.1.2.4; 4.1.2.5; 4.1.2.6	5.1.2.3; 5.1.2.4; 5.1.2.5; 5.1.2.6	No change
7	4.1.3.1; 4.1.3.2		Not relevant
8	4.2.1.1; 4.2.1.2; 4.2.1.3; 4.2.2.3	5.2.1.1; 5.2.1.2; 5.2.1.3; 5.2.2.3	No change
9	4.2.1.4; 4.2.1.5	5.2.1.4; 5.2.1.5	No change
10	4.2.2.1; 4.2.2.2; 4.2.2.4	5.2.2.1; 5.2.2.2; 5.2.2.4	No change
11	4.2.2.5; 4.2.2.6; 4.2.2.7; 4.2.2.8; 4.2.3.1; 4.2.3.2; 4.2.3.3	5.2.2.5–5.2.2.8; 5.2.3.1–5.2.3.3	No change
12	4.2.4.1; 4.2.4.2		Not relevant
13	4.3.1.1; 4.3.1.2; 4.3.1.3; 4.3.1.4	5.3.1.1; 5.3.1.2; 5.3.1.3; 5.3.1.4	No change
14	4.3.2.1; 4.3.2.2; 4.3.2.3; 4.3.2.4; 4.3.2.5	5.3.2.1; 5.3.2.2; 5.3.2.3; 5.3.2.4; 5.3.2.5	No change
15	4.3.3.1; 4.3.3.2		Not relevant
16	4.3.4; 4.3.5		Not relevant
17	4.4.1.1; 4.4.1.2; 4.4.1.3; 4.4.1.4	5.4.1.1; 5.4.1.2; 5.4.1.3; 5.4.1.4	No change
18	4.4.2.1; 4.4.2.2; 4.4.2.3	5.4.2.1; 5.4.2.2; 5.4.2.3	This lesson can be used for Combined Science. The practical becomes required practical 8.
19	4.4.2.4; 4.4.2.5; 4.4.2.6	5.4.2.4; 5.4.2.5	Parts of this lesson can be used for Combined Science. The starter, 'Strong and weak acids', the plenary and homework activity can be used. Titrations are not in the Combined Science specification.
20	4.4.3.1; 4.4.3.2; 4.4.3.3; 4.4.3.4; 4.4.3.5	5.4.3.1–5.4.3.5	This lesson can be used for Combined Science. The practical becomes required practical 9.
21	4.5.1.1; 4.5.1.2; 4.5.1.3	5.5.1.1; 5.5.1.2; 5.5.1.3	This lesson can be used for Combined Science. The practical becomes required practical 10.

CHEMISTRY HIGHER

Mapping of lessons to AQA GCSE (9–1) Combined Science: Trilogy

Lesson	Specification reference		Suggested adaptation for Trilogy
	Chemistry	Combined	
22	4.5.2.1; 4.5.2.2		Not relevant
23	4.6.1.1; 4.6.1.2; 4.6.1.3; 4.6.1.4	5.6.1.1; 5.6.1.2; 5.6.1.3; 5.6.1.4	This lesson can be used for Combined Science. The practical becomes required practical 11.
24	4.6.2.1; 4.6.2.2; 4.6.2.3	5.6.2.1; 5.6.2.2; 5.6.2.3	This lesson can be used for Combined Science. The starter will need additional explanation as it refers to rechargeable batteries covered in the single science.
25	4.6.2.4; 4.6.2.5; 4.6.2.6; 4.6.2.7	5.6.2.4; 5.6.2.5; 5.6.2.6; 5.6.2.7	Omit question 5 in the Homework activity.
26	4.7.1.1; 4.7.1.2; 4.7.1.3	5.7.1.1; 5.7.1.2; 5.7.1.3	No change
27	4.7.1.4; 4.7.2.1; 4.7.2.2; 4.7.2.3; 4.7.2.4	5.7.1.4	The Starter activity and Main activity: Cracking and ethene can be used. Omit the rest of the lesson.
28	4.7.3.1; 4.7.3.2; 4.7.3.3; 4.6.3.4		Not relevant
29	4.8.1.1; 4.8.1.2; 4.8.1.3	5.8.1.1; 5.8.1.2; 5.8.1.3	This lesson can be used for Combined Science. The practical becomes required practical 12.
30	4.8.3.1; 4.8.3.6; 4.8.3.7		Not relevant
31	4.8.2.2; 4.8.2.3; 4.8.2.4; 4.8.3.2; 4.8.3.3; 4.8.3.4; 4.8.3.5	5.8.2.1–5.8.2.4	Only the Starter activity can be used in this lesson. The rest is not in the Trilogy specification.
32	4.9.1.1; 4.9.1.2; 4.9.1.3; 4.9.1.4	5.9.1.1; 5.9.1.2; 5.9.1.3; 5.9.1.4	No change
33	4.9.2.1; 4.9.2.2; 4.9.2.3; 4.9.2.4	5.9.2.1; 5.9.2.2; 5.9.2.3; 5.9.2.4	No change
34	4.9.3.1; 4.9.3.2	5.9.3.1; 5.9.3.2	No change
35	4.10.1.1; 4.10.1.2; 4.10.1.3; 4.10.1.4	5.10.1.1; 5.10.1.2; 5.10.1.3; 5.10.1.4	The practical activity will become required practical 13.
36	4.10.2.1; 4.10.2.2	5.10.2.1; 5.10.2.2	No change
37	4.10.3.1; 4.10.3.2; 4.10.3.3		Not relevant
38	4.10.4.1; 4.10.4.2		Not relevant

Needs analysis

For parents and guardians

We have a tutor because...
(Briefly explain why you have employed a tutor.)

Where we are currently...
(Briefly explain the student's current progress. Do you have access to reports and predicted grades?)

For students

Use this space to tell your tutor about yourself.

I am...
Tell your tutor what type of person you think you are. Are you quiet or outgoing? Are you confident about your abilities?

I like...
Explain to your tutor how you like to work. Do you like to work independently or with more guidance? Do you like to write your answers down or talk through them first? Do you like to be creative?

How I feel about Chemistry...
Do you like Chemistry? Try to explain why or why not. What are your favourite and least favourite parts?

Needs analysis

Our goals

Work together to set small, achievable goals for the year ahead. Make them as positive as you can and don't limit your goals to areas of Chemistry – think about personal development too. Together, look back at this list often to see how you are progressing.

Tick off each goal when you've achieved it

In four weeks' time, I will…

☐ _____
☐ _____
☐ _____
☐ _____
☐ _____
☐ _____

In three months' time, I will…

☐ _____
☐ _____
☐ _____
☐ _____
☐ _____
☐ _____

By the time I sit my exam, I will…

☐ _____
☐ _____
☐ _____
☐ _____
☐ _____
☐ _____

Progress report

Fill in the boxes below with help from your tutor.

My strengths are...
Which areas of Chemistry do you think you've done well in recently? List at least three.

My favourite Chemistry topic is...
Which Chemistry topic is your favourite? It doesn't have to be the one you're best at!

because...

The areas of Chemistry I need to work on are...
In which areas of Chemistry do you think you need more practice?

To improve these areas, we are going to...
This space is for your tutor to explain how he/she is going to help you become confident in these areas.

End-of-lesson report

We have looked at last week's homework and my tutor thinks...
This space is for your tutor to give feedback on last week's homework.

Today, we worked on...
This space is for you to list all of the topics and skills that you and your tutor have worked on today.

I feel...
This space is for you to explain how you feel about today's lesson. Did you enjoy it? Do you feel confident?

My tutor thinks...
This space is for your tutor to explain how the lesson went.

At home this week, we can...
This space is for your tutor to explain what your homework is and to give you other ideas for extra revision and practice.

1 Diagnostic lesson

Learning objectives

- To find out where the student envisages their future
- To find out what grade the student wants to achieve
- To assess current understanding of atoms, molecules, elements, compounds and the periodic table
- To assess current mathematical skills and working scientifically skills

Specification links

- Key Stage 3 science specification
- WS: 2.2, 3.1, 3.5
- MS: 4a, 4c

Starter activity

- **The student; 5 minutes; page 18**

  This activity is designed to find out something about the student's aims and motivations and their current knowledge and skills. Work through the activity sheet with the student, adding extra questions as relevant.

Main activities

- **The content; 20 minutes; page 19**

  This activity is based on Key Stage 3 chemistry. You may wish to add more difficult questions, depending on the student's ability and whether they have already completed part or all of a year 10 course at school. It checks basic understanding of atoms, molecules, elements, compounds and the periodic table. You may wish to use this as a discussion activity. It should provide an insight into the student's ability, as well as giving them the confidence to proceed further.

- **Mathematical requirements and working scientifically; 20 minutes; page 20**

  This activity covers some of the mathematical requirements and working scientifically skills that are assessed in GCSE (9–1) chemistry. The sheet is self-explanatory and takes the student through an experimental procedure. The student can complete the activity and then you can discuss their answers together.

Plenary activity

- **The way ahead; 5 minutes**

  Make a verbal assessment of the student's strengths and identify areas that need work. Be as encouraging and positive as possible and describe any necessary catch up work you have identified. Explain to the student how these lessons are structured: how each lesson contains activity sheets and a homework activity, closely orientated towards the AQA GCSE (9–1) Chemistry Higher specification.

Homework activity

- **A new element; 45 minutes; page 21**

  This activity requires the student to use knowledge of the periodic table, group properties, atomic structure (if previously covered) and chemical reactivity to decide where a new element should be placed. If the student finds this task difficult, it could be amended to: 'why do chemists need periodic tables?'

Support ideas

- **The content** The student may need help with time management and methods of study and revision. Parental involvement may be useful here, but the student must be aware that they will need to find out which study skills work best for them.
- **Mathematical requirements and working scientifically** Explain that the graph on this page is a line graph because the variables are continuous.

Extension ideas

- **Mathematical requirements and working scientifically** The student can practise writing and interpreting more difficult chemical formulae involving subscripts and brackets.
- **The content** Ask the student which boxes should be ticked for sodium chloride in question 1.

Progress and observations

CHEMISTRY HIGHER

Starter activity: The student

Learning objectives

- To find out where the student envisages their future
- To assess confidence in chemistry at GCSE (9–1) Higher level
- To find out what the student finds easy and what they find more difficult

Equipment

1. Where do you see yourself in:

a) two years' time?

_____

b) four years' time?

_____

c) ten years' time?

_____

2. What chemistry grade are you aiming for at GCSE?

_____

3. What grade do you think you are at the moment?

_____

4. Look at the chemistry questions in the table. Rate each one from 1 to 5 by putting a tick in the appropriate column.

1 = very confident in this topic

5 = not at all confident, need more information on this

Question	1	2	3	4	5
Can you define an atom, an element and a compound?					
Can you write formulae for molecules?					
Do you understand how the periodic table is arranged?					
Can you list some properties of elements in the same group of the periodic table?					
Do you know which observations might indicate a chemical reaction is occurring?					
Can you describe different types of chemical bond?					
Can you use moles in calculations?					
Can you use chemical reactions to place metals in the correct order in the reactivity series?					

CHEMISTRY HIGHER

Main activity: The content

Time **20** mins

Learning objectives

- To assess current understanding of atoms, molecules, elements and compounds
- To assess ability to write simple chemical formulae
- To assess understanding of the periodic table

Equipment

- copy of the periodic table

1. **The diagrams represent particles. Tick the columns in the table that correctly describe each particle.**

Particle	A single atom	A molecule	An element	A compound
A. (H)(H)				
B. (H)(O)(H)				
C. (Mg)				
D. (O)(C)(O)				
E. (H)(N)(H) (H)				

2. **Write formulae for the particles in the table.**

_____

_____

3. **Oxygen, nitrogen and carbon are in the same period of the periodic table. What does 'period' mean here?**

_____

4. **Name an element in the same group as carbon.**

_____

CHEMISTRY HIGHER

Main activity: Mathematical requirements and working scientifically

Time 20 mins

Learning objectives

- To assess ability to interpret results graphically
- To assess ability to plan a practical procedure
- To assess use of terms associated with a scientific investigation

Equipment

- graph paper
- pencil

Dexter is investigating temperature changes when two substances react together. He placed 25 cm³ dilute hydrochloric acid in a small beaker and added 25 cm³ dilute sodium hydroxide solution. He recorded the temperature every ten seconds. These are his results.

Time (s)	Temperature (°C)
0	16
10	25
20	26
30	25
40	24
50	22
60	21
70	20
80	19

1. On graph paper, draw a suitable graph to show these results.

2. Use your graph to predict how long it will take for the mixture to reach 16 °C again.

_____

3. Dexter is carrying out a second experiment to find out whether dilute hydrochloric acid gives the same temperature change when it reacts with potassium hydroxide solution.

   a) Dexter's experiment must be a fair test. Which variables must Dexter control to make this a fair test?

   _____

   _____

   _____

   b) How can Dexter use the graph you drew in question 2 to record his results?

   _____

   _____

   _____

CHEMISTRY HIGHER

Homework activity: A new element

Time 45 mins

Learning objectives

- To assess writing skills
- To assess understanding of the periodic table and atomic structure

Equipment

- copy of the periodic table

In the eighteenth and nineteenth centuries, new elements were being discovered frequently. The periodic table placed all the known elements in an order. Today, new elements are still being discovered and added to the periodic table. These elements tend to be very unstable and only last for a few milliseconds. They are made artificially in particle accelerators. Elements discovered today are added to the end (or bottom) of the periodic table (based on their properties), whereas the elements discovered a few hundred years ago were added to the first few periods of the periodic table.

1. Imagine you have discovered a new element. You need to place it in the periodic table. Explain in one or two paragraphs below how you will decide where to position the element and which group and period it will belong to. Write a short passage to explain your ideas. Your answer should contain as many points as possible and use scientific language. Try to be logical and place your ideas in order before you start writing.

1 Answers

Starter activity: The student

1. a)–c) These answers may give you an insight into the student's ambitions and motivations.

2–3. The gap between these two grades may be significant if the student is giving an accurate assessment of their abilities.

4. The topics in this table have varying degrees of difficulty; some have been covered at Key Stage 3, others may have been covered in a year 10 course. The answers should give an overall indication of the student's confidence, as well as identifying potential weak and strong areas.

Main activity: The content

1. A: molecule, element
B: molecule, compound
C: single atom, element
D: molecule, compound
E: molecule, compound

2. H_2, H_2O, Mg, CO_2, NH_3

3. Row of the periodic table

4. Silicon, germanium, tin or lead

Main activity: Mathematical requirements and working scientifically

1. This should be a line graph with points joined with a curved line of best fit. The x-axis should be labelled 'time (s)' and the y-axis should be labelled 'temperature (°C)'.

2. About 110 seconds

3. a) Use the same concentration and volume of hydrochloric acid; use the same concentration of potassium hydroxide solution as sodium hydroxide solution; use 25 cm³ potassium hydroxide; use the same sized beaker for the reaction; measure the temperature at the same time intervals

   b) Plot the new temperatures on the same graph and join the points with a second line of best fit. Label the lines. Use different coloured pens/pencils for the two sets of results.

Homework activity: A new element

1. Student's own answers. The level of response will depend on the student's prior experience, particularly whether they have completed part or all of a year 10 course already, or whether they are just starting their year 10 course. A Key Stage 3 response may include: metal/non-metal properties, similar properties in group, with examples (Group 1 and 7), and trends within a group. A student who has completed part of the year 10 course may include atomic number, relative atomic mass, and electronic structure.

CHEMISTRY HIGHER

2 Atoms: Atoms, elements, compounds and mixtures

Learning objectives

- To define the terms atom, element, compound and mixture
- To write chemical formulae
- To write word and symbol equations
- To identify half equations and ionic equations
- To know how physical processes are used to separate mixtures

Specification links

- 4.1.1.1, 4.1.1.2
- WS: 2.2, 2.3

Starter activity

- **Atoms and the periodic table; 5 mins; page 24**

  Remind the student that everything is made of atoms. The student can read the first paragraph on the activity sheet. This should be revision from Key Stage 3. You may need to explain that different versions of the periodic table may show different numbers of elements because new elements are being made synthetically, and these have to be verified before they can be officially added to the periodic table.

Main activities

- **Compounds and formulae; 20 mins; page 25**

  Explain that compounds, formed from elements, can be represented by formulae, which show the number and type of atoms present. Tell the student that, by the end of the course, they should be able to write formulae for all the substances in the specification. The idea of combining powers (question 2) can be used as a tool. Emphasise that the method is not foolproof.

- **Writing equations; 20 minutes; page 26**

  Emphasise the difference in meaning between numbers before formulae in an equation and subscript numbers used within formulae. The student can now answer question 1. Explain that the student will find out how to use and write ionic and half equations in this course. Reassure them that they are a little daunting at this stage, but questions 2 and 3 will act as an introduction.

Plenary activity

- **Mixtures; 5 mins**

  In preparation for the homework activity, remind the student about the work on mixtures and the methods used to separate them at Key Stage 3. Explain the process of crystallisation, which is new. Remind the student that a mixture can contain elements and/or compounds in any proportion.

Homework activity

- **Separating mixtures; 30 mins; page 27**

  The homework activity explores different methods of separating mixtures. Instructions are given on the sheet.

Support ideas

- **Compounds and formulae, Writing equations** The student may need to see more examples if they are finding these difficult.

Extension ideas

- **Writing equations** The student can find formulae that are exceptions to the idea of combining powers (e.g. CO and NO). Tell the student that sodium burns in oxygen to produce sodium oxide. Ask them to write word and symbol equations for the reaction. Ensure that they work out the correct formulae first.
- **Compounds and formulae** The student can try naming compounds from their chemical formulae.

Progress and observations

CHEMISTRY HIGHER

Starter activity: Atoms and the periodic table

Time 5 mins

Learning objectives

- To know that elements contain one type of atom only
- To know that elements have chemical symbols and are shown in the periodic table

Equipment

- copy of the periodic table

There are just over 100 different types of atom and an element contains one type of atom only. Each element has a chemical symbol and these are shown in the periodic table.

1. **Use your periodic table to find the symbols for the following elements:**

   a) chlorine _____

   b) magnesium _____

   c) sodium _____

   d) iron _____

   e) gold _____

2. **Which elements are represented by the following symbols?**

   a) K _____

   b) Al _____

   c) Li _____

   d) Ne _____

   e) Ti _____

3. **The chemical symbol for an element usually contains one or two letters, although some of the newly discovered elements have three letters in their symbols. Identify and circle the correct symbol for calcium.**

   a) ca

   b) CA

   c) cA

   d) Ca

   e) C,a

   Explain your answer.

   _____

   _____

CHEMISTRY HIGHER

Main activity: Compounds and formulae

Learning objectives

- To identify the number and type of elements in a compound
- To write chemical formulae for compounds

Equipment

- copy of the periodic table
- spare paper

1. Look at the formulae for sodium carbonate and calcium hydroxide.

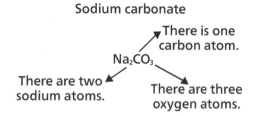

Sodium carbonate

There is one carbon atom.

Na_2CO_3

There are two sodium atoms.

There are three oxygen atoms.

Calcium hydroxide

There is one calcium atom.

$Ca(OH)_2$

The two doubles everything inside the brackets, so there are two oxygen atoms and two hydrogen atoms.

Now complete the table:

Formula	SO_2	H_2SO_4	$Al(OH)_3$	$(NH_4)_2SO_4$
Name				
Type of atom	1. 2.	1. 2. 3.	1. 2. 3.	1. 2. 3. 4.
Number of each type of atom	1. 2.	1. 2. 3.	1. 2. 3.	1. 2. 3. 4.

Elements in the periodic table have the following combining powers:

Group	1	2	3	4	5	6	7	0
Combining power	1	2	3	4	3	2	1	0

These combining powers must balance in a chemical formula. For example, in sodium oxide, the combining power of Na = 1 and the combining power of O = 2, so the formula is Na_2O.

The combining powers of some common ions are as follows:

hydroxide	OH^-	combining power = 1	nitrate	NO_3^-	combining power = 1
ammonium	NH_4^+	combining power = 1	sulfate	SO_4^{2-}	combining power = 2
carbonate	CO_3^{2-}	combining power = 2			

2. Write the formulae for these compounds:

a) potassium bromide _____

b) calcium chloride _____

c) calcium sulfate _____

d) lithium carbonate _____

e) sodium sulfate _____

f) magnesium nitrate _____

g) aluminium chloride _____

h) silicon dioxide _____

i) calcium nitride _____

j) aluminium sulfate _____

CHEMISTRY HIGHER

AQA

Main activity: Writing equations

Time 20 mins

Learning objectives

- To write word and symbol equations
- To identify ionic and half equations

Equipment

- copy of the periodic table

When magnesium burns in oxygen, magnesium oxide is produced.

The word equation is: magnesium + oxygen → magnesium oxide

The symbol equation is: $2Mg + O_2 \rightarrow 2MgO$

1. **Now write word and balanced symbol equations for the following reactions:**

   a) Carbon burns in oxygen to produce carbon dioxide.

   _____

   b) Carbon burns in oxygen to produce carbon monoxide (CO).

   _____

   c) Sodium reacts with water to produce sodium hydroxide and hydrogen.

   _____

   d) Nitrogen reacts with hydrogen to produce ammonia (NH_3).

   _____

When an acid reacts with an alkali, a salt and water are produced.

For example: hydrochloric acid + sodium hydroxide → sodium chloride + water

$$HCl + NaOH \rightarrow NaCl + H_2O$$

An ionic equation shows the essential chemistry of the reaction – that is, water is produced.

The ionic equation is: $H^+ + OH^- \rightarrow H_2O$

2. **Hydrochloric acid reacts with potassium hydroxide to produce potassium chloride and water. For this reaction, write:**

   a) a word equation   _____

   b) a symbol equation   _____

   c) an ionic equation   _____

3. **Half equations show only part of a chemical reaction. For example, when zinc chloride is melted and an electric current passed through it, zinc ions move to the cathode and gain electrons. The half equation is: $Zn^{2+} + 2e^- \rightarrow Zn$ Chloride ions move to the anode and lose electrons. The half equation is: $2Cl^- \rightarrow Cl_2 + 2e^-$**

   a) What would you expect to see at the anode and at the cathode?

   _____

   b) What can you conclude about the charges in each half equation?

   _____

CHEMISTRY HIGHER

Homework activity: Separating mixtures

Learning objective	Equipment
• To know how different mixtures can be separated	• spare paper

1. **Draw lines to connect the correct diagrams and examples to the processes for separating mixtures.**

Process	Apparatus	Example
filtration	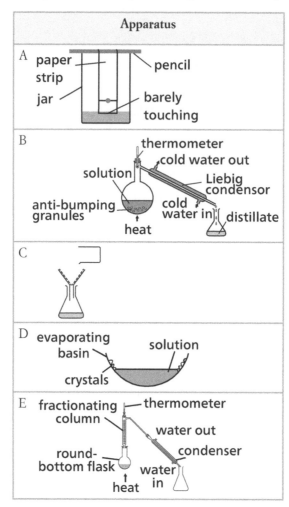 A paper strip, pencil, jar, barely touching	separating two liquids with different boiling points
crystallisation	B thermometer, cold water out, solution, Liebig condensor, anti-bumping granules, cold water in, distillate, heat	separating sand and water
simple distillation	C	separating the coloured pigments in food dyes
fractional distillation	D evaporating basin, solution, crystals	separating water from salt solution
chromatography	E fractionating column, thermometer, water out, condenser, round-bottom flask, water in, heat	producing copper sulfate crystals from copper sulfate solution

2. **Students watched an experiment where a mixture of iron and sulfur was heated. A red glow spread throughout the mixture and a black solid (iron sulfide, FeS) remained in the test tube. On a separate piece of paper:**

   a) Write a word and symbol equation for the reaction.

   b) Identify the elements and compounds in the reaction.

   c) How could you separate the mixture of iron and sulfur?

   d) Would your method in c) have the same result on iron sulfide? Explain your answer.

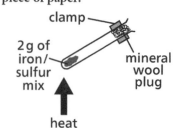

clamp

2g of iron/ sulfur mix

mineral wool plug

heat

3. **On a separate piece of paper, describe which methods can be used to separate each of the following:**

   a) the coloured compounds in black ink

   b) insoluble calcium carbonate from a mixture of calcium carbonate and water

   c) water from red food dye (the food dye contains water and soluble coloured pigments only)

   d) ethanol from a mixture of ethanol and water (water boiling point = 100 °C, ethanol boiling point = 78 °C)

CHEMISTRY HIGHER

2 Answers

Starter activity: Atoms and the periodic table

1. a) Cl
   b) Mg
   c) Na
   d) Fe
   e) Au
2. a) potassium
   b) aluminium
   c) lithium
   d) neon
   e) titanium
3. d) Ca is correct, because the first letter is uppercase and the second lowercase.

Main activity: Compounds and formulae

1.

Formula	SO_2	H_2SO_4	$Al(OH)_3$	$(NH_4)_2SO_4$
Name	sulfur dioxide	sulfuric acid	aluminium hydroxide	ammonium sulfate
Type and number of atoms	1. sulfur, S: 1 2. oxygen, O: 2	1. hydrogen, H: 2 2. sulfur, S: 1 3. oxygen, O: 4	1. aluminium, Al: 1 2. oxygen, O: 3 3. hydrogen, H: 3	1. nitrogen, N: 2 2. hydrogen, H: 8 3. sulfur, S: 1 4. oxygen, O: 4

2. a) KBr
   b) $CaCl_2$
   c) $CaSO_4$
   d) Li_2CO_3
   e) Na_2SO_4
   f) $Mg(NO_3)_2$
   g) $AlCl_3$
   h) SiO_2
   i) Ca_3N_2
   j) $Al_2(SO_4)_3$

Main activity: Writing equations

1. a) carbon + oxygen → carbon dioxide; $C + O_2 → CO_2$
   b) carbon + oxygen → carbon monoxide; $2C + O_2 → 2CO$
   c) sodium + water → sodium hydroxide + hydrogen; $2Na + 2H_2O → 2NaOH + H_2$
   d) nitrogen + hydrogen → ammonia; $N_2 + 3H_2 → 2NH_3$
2. a) hydrochloric acid + potassium hydroxide → potassium chloride + water
   b) $HCl + KOH → KCl + H_2O$
   c) $H^+ + OH^- → H_2O$
3. a) Zinc forms at the cathode; chlorine gas is given off at the anode
   b) The charges balance each other out (same number of positives and negatives)

Homework activity: Separating mixtures

1. Filtration: diagram C, separating sand and water; crystallisation: diagram D, producing copper sulfate crystals from copper sulfate solution; simple distillation: diagram B, separating water from salt solution; fractional distillation: diagram E, separating two liquids with different boiling points; chromatography: diagram A; separating the coloured pigments in food dyes
2. a) iron + sulfur → iron sulfide; $Fe + S → FeS$
   b) Elements are iron and sulfur; compound is iron sulfide
   c) Use a magnet to separate the iron from the sulfur
   d) No, because when the iron is chemically combined with sulfur, its properties change and it can't be separated by physical methods.
3. a) chromatography
   b) filtration
   c) distillation
   d) Fractional distillation

CHEMISTRY HIGHER

3 Atoms: The development of the atomic model and relative electrical charges

Learning objectives

- To describe how new evidence about subatomic particles led to new models of the atom
- To describe the difference between the plum pudding model of the atom and the nuclear model
- To know the relative charges of subatomic particles
- To define atomic number

Specification links

- 4.1.1.3, 4.1.1.4
- WS: 1.1, 1.2

Starter activity

- **Scientific models; 5 minutes; page 30**

  Explain how scientists use models to examine, explain and demonstrate ideas. We use models of atoms because we cannot observe them directly. Tell the student they will find out how new evidence changed ideas about atomic models in this lesson.

Main activities

- **Developing atomic models; 25 minutes; page 31**

  Explain the stages in the development of the atomic model: the early model of atoms as tiny spheres; the discovery of the electron and the plum pudding model; the discovery of the nucleus from the alpha particle scattering experiment; the suggestion of electron shells by Niels Bohr and the discovery of the neutron by James Chadwick. Emphasise the role of the scientific process in developing these models.

- **Relative electrical charges; 15 minutes; page 32**

  Remind the student that the discovery of the electron and the nucleus resulted from the detection of charged particles in atoms. Identify these charges and their links with atomic structure and atomic number.

Plenary activity

- **What next for the atomic model?; 5 minutes**

  Ask the student what future events could change our ideas about the nuclear model of the atom. Discussion points could include the development of more highly powered microscopes and experiments to investigate the composition of electrons, protons and neutrons. Encourage the idea that the nuclear model of the atom is the best we have at the moment, but will probably change as new evidence emerges.

Homework activity

- **Atomic models; 45 minutes; page 33**

  This activity reinforces the lesson content and introduces some exam technique. The student may find it more difficult to answer longer unstructured questions. This activity requires the student to organise their ideas into a logical order. Reassure the student that their technique will improve with practice.

Support ideas

- **Developing atomic models** Key experiments in the development of the atomic model (for example, alpha particle scattering and the use of cathode rays) involve charged particles. The student may need extra help to understand these ideas.

Extension ideas

- **Developing atomic models** The student can find out how John Dalton's work contributed to the atomic model, or why the death of Mosely at Gallipoli in the first world war was a sad loss to science.

Progress and observations

CHEMISTRY HIGHER

Starter activity: Scientific models

Learning objectives

- To understand why we use models in science
- To understand why these models change over time
- To describe the early atomic model

Equipment

Read the following passage, then answer the questions.

People have always wondered what matter is made of. Early scientists thought that everything was made of extremely tiny spheres that could not be divided. They thought that if you cut a substance in half and half again repeatedly, you would eventually end up with a single solid sphere that could not be divided further. These tiny spheres were later called atoms.

Atoms are so small that we have only recently been able to begin to observe them, using the latest microscopes. We use models to describe atoms. We now think that atoms contain smaller subatomic particles called electrons, protons and neutrons. This is called the nuclear model.

The early atomic model

The nuclear model of the atom

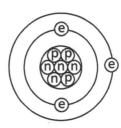

key
ⓟ proton
ⓝ neutron
ⓔ electron

1. Why do we use models to describe atoms?

_____

_____

_____

_____

_____

_____

2. List the events that might change our ideas about atomic models.

_____

_____

_____

_____

_____

TUTORS GUILD CHEMISTRY HIGHER

Main activity: Developing atomic models

Learning objectives

- To understand how the discovery of the electron changed the atomic model
- To understand how new evidence from the scattering experiment led to changes in the atomic model
- To know how the work of James Chadwick and Niels Bohr contributed to the nuclear model of the atom

Equipment

- pencil

Five major stages in the history of atomic models are listed in the table. Complete the table by adding a description and drawing a diagram for each stage.

Stage	Description	Diagram
1. Early atomic model		Sketch the early atomic model.
2. The discovery of the electron Cathode rays are passed through an electric field.	Describe the result.	Sketch the plum pudding model.
3. The discovery of the nucleus and the scattering experiment Positively charged alpha particles are fired at a thin sheet of gold foil. The alpha particles are scattered.	Describe the conclusion.	Sketch the atomic model.
4. Niels Bohr's calculations	Describe the conclusion.	Sketch the atomic model.
5. James Chadwick's work	Describe the discovery.	Sketch the atomic model.

CHEMISTRY HIGHER

Main activity: Relative electrical charges

Time **15** mins

Learning objectives

- To know the relative charges of the proton, electron and neutron
- To explain the link between the number of protons and the number of electrons in an atom
- To define atomic number

Equipment

- copy of the periodic table

1. Complete the table.

Name of particle	Relative charge
proton	
neutron	
electron	

2. What does 'relative' mean?

_____

3. Write a definition for 'atomic number'.

_____

4. If an atom has six protons:

a) how many positive charges does its nucleus contain? _____

b) how many electrons are in the atom? _____

c) what is its atomic number? _____

5. The atomic number of chlorine is 17.

a) How many protons are in a chlorine atom? _____

b) How many electrons are in a chlorine atom? _____

6. The diagrams show the atomic structure of some different atoms. Give the atomic number for each atom.

a) _____   b) _____   c) _____

key
- ⊖ electron
- ⊕ proton
- ◯ neutron

3 protons + 3 neutrons

key
- ⊖ electron
- ⊕ proton
- ◯ neutron

6 protons + 6 neutrons

10 protons + 10 neutrons

key
- ⊖ electron
- ⊕ proton
- ◯ neutron

CHEMISTRY HIGHER

Homework activity: Atomic models

Time **45** mins

Learning objectives

- To reinforce ideas about atomic models
- To understand how detecting charged particles changed atomic models

Equipment

- spare paper for tables

In your GCSE exam, you will have to answer some six mark questions that require you to write an explanation in a logical manner. To gain six marks, your answer must use scientific language, answer the question fully and organise the information in a logical sequence.

Try these six mark questions.

1. **Describe the difference between the plum pudding model of the atom and the nuclear model. You could use a table to make your comparison.**

[6 marks]

_____

_____

_____

_____

_____

_____

_____

_____

_____

_____

_____

2. **You have found out how some ideas about atomic models have changed over time. You have also learned about the relative charges of particles in atoms. Use these ideas to explain how detecting the presence of charged particles in atoms changed ideas about atomic models.**

[6 marks]

_____

_____

_____

_____

_____

_____

_____

_____

_____

_____

3 Answers

Starter activity: Scientific models

1. Atoms are too small to be observed directly; we can use models to explain events.
2. New evidence is provided by experiments/research/observation/calculation. This evidence is repeatable and accepted by the scientific community. New models are suggested.

Main activity: Developing atomic models

Stage	Description	Diagram
1. Early atomic model		Diagram of solid indivisible spheres
2. The discovery of the electron Cathode rays are passed through an electrical field.	The rays are deflected, indicating they contain negatively charged particles. These must have come from the metal atoms in the cathode.	Diagram showing several negatively charged particles in a spherical cloud of positive charge
3. The discovery of the nucleus and the scattering experiment Positively charged alpha particles are fired at a thin sheet of gold foil. The alpha particles are scattered.	The positive charge in an atom is not evenly distributed, but concentrated in a small area – the nucleus.	Diagram showing a central positively charged nucleus surrounded by electrons, randomly arranged
4. Niels Bohr's calculations	Electrons exist in shells or energy levels around the nucleus.	Diagram as in row 3, but showing electrons in shells (energy levels)
5. James Chadwick's work	The neutron	Diagram as in row 4, but also showing neutrons and protons in the nucleus

Main activity: Relative electrical charges

1. proton: +1; neutron: 0; electron: −1
2. Compared to each other (or another specified object)
3. The number of protons in an atom
4. a) 6
   b) 6
   c) 6
5. a) 17
   b) 17
6. a) 3
   b) 6
   c) 10

Homework activity: Atomic models

This is a level of response question. Marks can be awarded as follows:
1. Electrons are randomly distributed in the plum pudding model, but organised in shells in the nuclear model. There is a cloud of positive charge in the plum pudding model, while positive charge is centred in the nucleus in the nuclear model. The plum pudding model does not have neutrons, whereas the nuclear model has neutrons.
   Do not give marks if a comparison is not made. The student may have other valid ways of organising this answer
2. The discovery of negatively charged electrons changed ideas about atoms from atoms as solid spheres to the plum pudding model. The alpha particle scattering experiment detected centres of positive charge in atoms, which suggested a central positive nucleus. Neutrons have no electrical charge and were not discovered until later.

CHEMISTRY HIGHER

AQA

4 Atoms: Atomic mass, relative atomic mass and electronic structure

Learning objectives

- To understand the size of atoms and nuclei
- To calculate the relative atomic mass of an element from the percentage abundance of its isotopes
- To represent the electronic structure of the first 20 elements
- To calculate numbers of protons, neutrons and electrons of atoms and ions from mass numbers

Specification links

- 4.1.1.5, 4.1.1.6, 4.1.1.7
- WS: 1.2, 4.3, 4.4
- MS: 1a, 1b, 1c, 2a, 5b

Starter activity

- **The size of atoms; 5 minutes; page 36**

  Explain that atoms are too small to be measured in metres or millimetres so we use nanometres: $1\,nm = 10^{-9}\,m$.

  The student will need to use a calculator for standard form calculations. You can use this activity to assess their skills.

Main activities

- **The mass of atoms and relative atomic mass; 25 minutes; page 37**

  Explain that we use relative masses to compare the mass of protons, neutrons and electrons. Explain mass number and show the student how we use mass number to calculate numbers of protons, neutrons and electrons in an atom. The student can then answer question 1. Explain the existence of isotopes and show the student how percentage abundances of isotopes are used to calculate relative atomic mass. The student can then complete the rest of the activity.

- **Electronic structure; 15 minutes; page 38**

  Explain how electrons fill the lower energy levels first, and that there is a maximum number in each energy level.

  Note that either of the terms 'electron shell' or 'energy level' can be used.

Plenary activity

- **Atom or element?; 5 minutes**

  Discuss with the student when we should use the terms 'atom' and 'element' when referring to mass number and relative atomic mass.

Homework activity

- **All about strontium; 45 minutes; page 39**

  This activity reinforces ideas covered in the lesson, applying them to the element strontium. Question 3, calculating the relative atomic mass of strontium from percentage abundances, involves four isotopes. The student may need to be told that the procedure is the same as for elements with fewer isotopes.

Support ideas

- **The size of atoms** Standard form calculations are a required maths skill. Extra practice may be needed here.
- **The mass of atoms and relative atomic mass** Confusing mass number and relative atomic mass is a common error and the distinction may need reinforcing, especially since the relative atomic mass on the GCSE periodic table is often the same as the most common mass number for atoms of that element.

Extension ideas

- **The mass of atoms and relative atomic mass** The student could research the isotopes of carbon and their uses.
- **Electronic structure** The student could find out how the electronic structure of scandium breaks the pattern of the first twenty elements.

Progress and observations

TUTORS' GUILD CHEMISTRY HIGHER

Starter activity: The size of atoms

Learning objectives

- To know that we use nanometres to measure the size of atoms
- To relate the size and scale of atoms to physical objects

Equipment

- calculator

We can measure atoms in nanometres (nm).

$1\,\text{nm} = 1 \times 10^{-9}\,\text{m}$

1. Atoms have a radius of about 0.1 nm. What is their radius in metres?

_____

2. The radius of the nucleus of an atom is about $\frac{1}{10\,000}$ the radius of the atom. What is the radius of the nucleus in metres?

_____

3. A size 5 football has a radius of about 0.11 m. How many times bigger is the football than the atom?

_____

4. A tennis ball has a radius of about 0.03 m. How many times bigger is the tennis ball than an atom?

_____

5. Rank these objects in order of size from the largest (1) to the smallest (5):

Object	Size and units	Order of size
a cell	$1 \times 10^{-6}\,\text{m}$	
a hair (diameter)	1 mm	
a molecule	1.0 nm	
an atom	$1 \times 10^{-10}\,\text{m}$	
a microbe	$1 \times 10^{-2}\,\text{mm}$	

CHEMISTRY HIGHER

Main activity: The mass of atoms and relative atomic mass

Learning objectives

- To calculate numbers of protons, neutrons and electrons in an atom or ion from its atomic number and atomic mass
- To understand the term isotope
- To calculate the relative atomic mass of an element from percentage abundance of its isotopes

Equipment

- calculator

1. **Complete the table to show the numbers of protons, neutrons and electrons in the atoms.**

Atomic number	Mass number	Number of protons	Number of neutrons	Number of electrons
15	31			
79	197			
1	1			
29	65			
29	63			

2. **Identify the atoms in the table in the first question and represent them in the form $^{23}_{11}Na$.**

_____

_____

3. **Look at this example.**

   Chlorine has two isotopes, $^{35}_{17}Cl$ and $^{37}_{17}Cl$. Chlorine gas is 75% $^{35}_{17}Cl$ and 25% $^{37}_{17}Cl$.

   The relative atomic mass of chlorine $= \dfrac{(75 \times 35) + (25 \times 37)}{100} = 35.5$

   Now calculate the relative atomic mass of bromine, copper, silver and chromium.

   a) Bromine has two isotopes, $^{79}_{35}Br$ and $^{81}_{35}Br$. Bromine contains 50% of each isotope.

   _____

   b) Copper has two isotopes, $^{63}_{29}Cu$ and $^{65}_{29}Cu$. The percentage abundance is 70% $^{63}_{29}Cu$ and 30% $^{65}_{29}Cu$.

   _____

   c) Silver's isotopes are $^{107}_{47}Ag$ and $^{109}_{47}Ag$. The percentage abundance is 51% $^{107}_{47}Ag$ and 49% $^{109}_{47}Ag$. Calculate the relative atomic mass to the nearest whole number.

   _____

   d) Chromium has four isotopes. The table gives their percentage abundance. Calculate the relative atomic mass of chromium. Give your answer to the nearest whole number.

   _____

   _____

Isotope	Percentage abundance (%)
$^{50}_{24}Cr$	4
$^{52}_{24}Cr$	84
$^{53}_{24}Cr$	10
$^{54}_{24}Cr$	2

CHEMISTRY HIGHER

Main activity: Electronic structure

Learning objective

- To draw the electronic structures for atoms of the first twenty elements

Equipment

1. The grid represents part of the periodic table, showing the first twenty elements. Write the symbol of each element in the top left hand corner of the appropriate box and draw the electronic structure for an atom of the element. Write the numbers for the electronic structure (for example 2,8,1) in the bottom right hand corner.

Homework activity: All about strontium

Learning objectives	Equipment
• To reinforce mass number and atomic number	none
• To understand isotopes	
• To reinforce relative atomic mass calculations	

Strontium is a metal in Group 2. Strontium has four isotopes:

$$^{84}_{38}\text{Sr} \qquad ^{86}_{38}\text{Sr} \qquad ^{87}_{38}\text{Sr} \qquad ^{88}_{38}\text{Sr}$$

1. In the notation $^{84}_{38}$Sr:

a) what is the lower number called?

_____

b) what is the upper number called?

_____

2. Complete the table to show the numbers of protons, neutrons and electrons in atoms of each isotope.

Isotope	Number of protons	Number of neutrons	Number of electrons
$^{84}_{38}$Sr			
$^{86}_{38}$Sr			
$^{87}_{38}$Sr			
$^{88}_{38}$Sr			

3. The table gives the percentage abundance for each isotope.

Isotope	Percentage abundance (%)
$^{84}_{38}$Sr	0.5
$^{86}_{38}$Sr	9.9
$^{87}_{38}$Sr	7.0
$^{88}_{38}$Sr	82.6

Calculate the relative atomic mass of strontium. Give your answer to one decimal place.

_____

4. Explain why the relative atomic mass of many elements is not a whole number.

_____

_____

CHEMISTRY HIGHER

4 Answers

Starter activity: The size of atoms

1. 1×10^{-10} m
2. 1×10^{-14} m
3. 1.1×10^{9} times
4. 3×10^{8} times
5. hair 1; microbe 2; cell 3; molecule 4; atom 5

Main activity: The mass of atoms and relative atomic mass

1.

Atomic number	Mass number	Number of protons	Number of neutrons	Number of electrons
15	31	15	16	15
79	197	79	118	79
1	1	1	0	1
29	65	29	36	29
29	63	29	34	29

2. phosphorus, $^{31}_{15}$P; gold, $^{197}_{79}$Au; hydrogen, $^{1}_{1}$H; copper, $^{65}_{29}$Cu; copper, $^{63}_{29}$Cu

3. a) $\dfrac{(50 \times 79) + (50 \times 81)}{100} = 80$

b) $\dfrac{(70 \times 63) + (30 \times 65)}{100} = 63.6$

c) $\dfrac{(51 \times 107) + (49 \times 109)}{100} = 108$

d) $\dfrac{(4 \times 50) + (84 \times 52) + (10 \times 53) + (2 \times 54)}{100} = 52$

Main activity: Electronic structure

1. Electron shell diagrams should show the following: H 1; He 2; Li 2,1; Be 2,2; B 2,3; C 2,4; N 2,5; O 2,6; F 2,7; Ne 2,8; Na 2,8,1; Mg 2,8,2; Al 2,8,3; Si 2,8,4; P 2,8,5; S 2,8,6; Cl 2,8,7; Ar 2,8,8; K 2,8,8,1; Ca 2,8,8,2

Homework activity: All about strontium

1. a) Atomic number
b) Mass number

2.

Isotope	Number of protons	Number of neutrons	Number of electrons
$^{84}_{38}$Sr	38	46	38
$^{86}_{38}$Sr	38	48	38
$^{87}_{38}$Sr	38	49	38
$^{88}_{38}$Sr	38	50	38

3. $\dfrac{(0.5 \times 84) + (9.9 \times 86) + (7 \times 87) + (82.6 \times 88)}{100} = 87.7$

4. Relative atomic mass is the mean mass of all naturally occurring isotopes of an element, taking abundance into consideration. These calculations do not usually result in a whole number.

5 The periodic table: The periodic table and its development

Learning objectives

- To explain how the position of an element in the periodic table is related to the arrangement of electrons and atomic number
- To know the features of early periodic tables
- To understand how Mendeleev's periodic table solved the problems of early periodic tables

Specification links

- 4.1.2.1, 4.1.2.2
- WS: 1.1, 1.2, 1.6

Starter activity

- **Labelling the periodic table; 5 minutes; page 42**

  Remind or tell the student how the periodic table is organised into groups and periods, and the location of the transition elements. This should be revision from Key Stage 3. The student can then complete the activity sheet.

Main activities

- **Arranging the periodic table; 20 minutes; page 43**

  Remind the student about the electronic structure activity sheet in the previous lesson and ask them to look for patterns. Explain that electrons are rearranged during chemical reactions and the number of electrons in the outer shell is important in determining an element's chemical reactions. The student could make predictions, then complete the activity sheet.

- **The development of the periodic table; 20 minutes; page 44**

  Explain that early periodic tables arranged elements in order of atomic weight (we now use relative atomic mass). Tell the student that Mendeleev left gaps in his periodic table so that elements with similar properties were in the same group. He predicted that these gaps would be filled later, when new elements were discovered.

Plenary activity

- **Periodic table differences; 5 minutes**

  Ask the student to make a list of differences and similarities between early periodic tables and today's modern periodic table.

Homework activity

- **Mendeleev's periodic table; 45 minutes; page 45**

  The activity sheet is self-explanatory and also covers the development of the periodic table.

Support ideas

- **The development of the periodic table** The student may need to revisit lesson 4 if they are struggling to understand why arranging elements in order of relative atomic mass (atomic weight) will give a different order to arranging elements in order of atomic number.
- **Mendeleev's periodic table** The student may need to be told that Mendeleev arranged his periodic table with groups horizontally and periods vertically.

Extension ideas

- **The development of the periodic table** The student could find out where John Newlands' table of octaves was successful and where it produced problems.
- **Arranging the periodic table** The student can use the periodic table to find out which element is named after Mendeleev.

Progress and observations

CHEMISTRY HIGHER

Starter activity: Labelling the periodic table

Learning objectives

- To locate Groups 1 to 0 in the periodic table
- To identify a period and the transition elements in the periodic table

Equipment

1. Label the following on the periodic table below:

Group 1

Group 2

Group 3

Group 4

Group 5

Group 6

Group 7

Group 0

The transition elements

A period

Periodic table of the elements

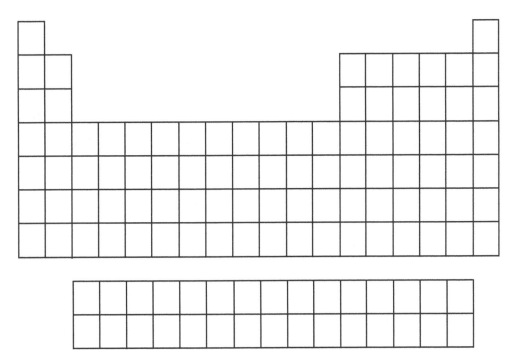

TUTORS GUILD CHEMISTRY HIGHER

Main activity: Arranging the periodic table

Learning objectives

- To know how the elements are arranged in the periodic table
- To explain why elements in the same group have similar chemical properties

Equipment

- copy of the periodic table

1. In what order are the elements arranged in the periodic table?

_____

2. Why is it called the periodic table?

_____

3. Complete the table to show the number of electrons in the outer shell of atoms in each group.

Group	Number of electrons in outer shell
1	
2	
3	
4	
5	
6	
7	
0	

4. Read the following text, then answer the questions.

Elements in Group 1 lose one electron when they react. Elements in Group 2 lose two electrons when they react.

Elements in Group 6 gain two electrons when they react. Elements in Group 7 gain one electron when they react.

Group 0 elements are very unreactive.

a) Explain why the elements in Group 1 have similar chemical reactions.

_____

b) When elements of Groups 1, 2, 6 and 7 react, how many electrons will the new particles have in their outer shells?

_____

c) Why are Group 0 elements unreactive?

_____

5. These are the reactions of three elements with water. Which two are in the same group? _____

A. reacts moderately, gives off a gas, produces an alkaline solution

B. reacts violently, gives off a gas which ignites, produces an alkaline solution

C. dissolves in water to produce an acidic solution

CHEMISTRY HIGHER

Main activity: The development of the periodic table

Time **20** mins

Learning objectives

- To know that early periodic tables arranged elements in order of atomic weight
- To know why Mendeleev left gaps in his periodic table and changed the order based on atomic weight in some places
- To know that elements predicted by Mendeleev were later discovered
- To know how knowledge of isotopes explains why orders based on atomic weight were not always correct

Equipment

- copy of the periodic table

1. How were the elements in early periodic tables arranged?

_____

2. Mendeleev left a gap under silicon in his periodic table. He called the missing element eka-silicon and predicted its properties. Later, germanium was discovered. The table gives the properties and predicted properties of these elements.

	Silicon	Predicted properties of eka-silicon	Germanium
Relative atomic mass	28	72	72.59
Density (g/cm³)	2.3	5.5	5.3
Appearance	grey non-metal	grey metal	grey metal
Formula of oxide	SiO_2	EkO_2	GeO_2

a) Why was Mendeleev able to predict the properties of eka-silicon?

_____

b) Give two reasons why Mendeleev was correct to leave gaps in his periodic table.

_____

c) Mendeleev also left a gap under aluminium for an undiscovered element he called eka-aluminium. What do we call eka-aluminium today?

_____

3. Early periodic tables placed iodine before tellurium. Mendeleev reversed this order, so that iodine was in Group 7 and tellurium in Group 6.

a) Why was iodine placed before tellurium in early periodic tables?

_____

b) Why did Mendeleev change the order?

_____

c) All iodine atoms have mass number 127, but tellurium has several isotopes with mass numbers between 120 and 130. Explain to your tutor why tellurium has a higher relative atomic mass than iodine.

_____

Homework activity: Mendeleev's periodic table

Learning objective

- To compare Mendeleev's periodic table with the modern periodic table

Equipment

- copy of the periodic table

This is a copy of Mendeleev's periodic table. The numbers are atomic weights (relative atomic mass).

1. Give a major difference between Mendeleev's periodic table and the modern periodic table.

   _____

   _____

2. Find the Group 1 elements on Mendeleev's periodic table and on a modern periodic table. Give a difference and a similarity between how these elements are arranged in the two tables.

   _____

   _____

3. Where did Mendeleev place the transition elements?

   _____

   _____

ОПЫТЪ СИСТЕМЫ ЭЛЕМЕНТОВЪ.

ОСНОВАННОЙ НА ИХЪ АТОМНОМЪ ВѢСѢ И ХИМИЧЕСКОМЪ СХОДСТВѢ.

```
                        Ti = 50   Zr = 90    ? = 180.
                        V = 51    Nb = 94    Ta = 182.
                        Cr = 52   Mo = 96    W = 186.
                        Mn = 55   Rh = 104,4  Pt = 197,4.
                        Fe = 56   Ru = 104,4  Ir = 198.
                    Ni = Co = 59  Pl = 106,6  O = 199.
        H = 1                     Cu = 63,4  Ag = 108   Hg = 200.
            Be = 9,4  Mg = 24   Zn = 65,2  Cd = 112
            B = 11    Al = 27,4  ? = 68    Ur = 116   Au = 197?
            C = 12    Si = 28    ? = 70    Sn = 118
            N = 14    P = 31    As = 75    Sb = 122   Bi = 210?
            O = 16    S = 32    Se = 79,4  Te = 128?
            F = 19    Cl = 35,6 Br = 80    I = 127
    Li = 7 Na = 23    K = 39    Rb = 85,4  Cs = 133   Tl = 204.
                      Ca = 40   Sr = 87,6  Ba = 137   Pb = 207.
                      ? = 45    Ce = 92
                    ?Er = 56   La = 94
                    ?Yt = 60   Di = 95
                    ?In = 75,6 Th = 118?
```

Д. Менделѣевъ

4. Why did Mendeleev put question marks in his table?

   _____

5. Why did Mendeleev's table contain fewer elements than the modern periodic table?

   _____

6. Suggest which elements have these atomic weights (relative atomic masses):

   a) 45 _____   b) 68 _____

   c) 70 _____   d) 180 _____

7. Mendeleev's table formed the basis for the periodic table we use today. Write a short paragraph to explain why Mendeleev's table was successful.

   _____

   _____

   _____

   _____

   _____

   _____

   _____

CHEMISTRY HIGHER

5 Answers

Starter activity: Labelling the periodic table

1.

Periodic table of the elements

Group 1 2   3 4 5 6 7 0

transition elements

a period

Main activity: Arranging the periodic table

1. In order of atomic number
2. Elements with similar properties occur at regular periods.
3. 1, 2, 3, 4, 5, 6, 7, 8
4. a) They all have one electron in the outer shell and lose one electron when they react.
   b) They will all have eight.
   c) They already have eight electrons in their outer shell so they do not need to lose or gain electrons to achieve stability.
5. A and B

Main activity: The development of the periodic table

1. In order of atomic weight
2. a) He arranged the elements so that elements in the same group had similar properties.
   b) The gaps kept similar elements in the same group. New elements were being discovered.
   c) gallium
3. a) Tellurium has a higher atomic weight than iodine.
   b) So that elements with similar properties were in the same groups.
   c) Tellurium must contain a high proportion of heavier isotopes, giving it a higher relative atomic mass than iodine.

Homework activity: Mendeleev's periodic table

1. Mendeleev arranged groups horizontally and periods vertically; today's periodic table arranges elements the other way round.
2. Similarity: both contain Li, Na, K, Rb, Cs; difference: thallium is placed in Group 1, not in Group 3
3. In a block at the top of the table
4. For undiscovered elements
5. Fewer elements had been discovered at that time
6. a) scandium
   b) gallium
   c) germanium
   d) tantalum
7. Example answer: Mendeleev put elements with similar properties in the same group. In some cases, he changed the order of increasing atomic weight to keep elements with similar properties in the same group. He left gaps for elements yet to be discovered and predicted their properties. These predictions turned out to be fairly accurate.

6 The periodic table: Groups of elements

Learning objectives

- To know the difference between metals and non-metals
- To explain and predict properties of Group 0 elements
- To know the products of halogen reactions with metals and non-metals
- To describe halogen displacement reactions
- To describe and base predictions upon trends in Groups 0, 1 and 7
- To describe reactions of Group 1 elements with oxygen, chlorine and water

Specification links

- 4.1.2.3, 4.1.2.4, 4.1.2.5, 4.1.2.6
- WS: 1.2

Starter activity

- **Metals and non-metals; 5 minutes; page 48**

  Remind the student of the position of metals and non-metals in the periodic table. Ask the student to work through the activity sheet and reassure them that this activity simply introduces metal ions; they will find out more about them later.

Main activities

- **Group 1; 20 minutes; page 49**

  Remind the student that they have just looked at a Group 1 metal (sodium, in the starter activity). This activity sheet is based on chemical reactions of Group 1 metals and the student may have seen some of these in the laboratory. There are several videos of reactions on the internet which may be useful.

- **Group 7; 20 minutes; page 50**

  Remind the student of the electronic structures of fluorine and chlorine and the number of electrons in their outer shells. Ask why these elements should have similar properties. The student may have completed a similar displacement experiment at school, which they can refer to as they work through the activity sheet.

Plenary activity

- **Trends; 5 minutes**

  Ask the student to compare the reactivity trends in Group 1 and Group 7, with examples. They should conclude that reactivity increases down Group 1 and decreases down Group 7.

Homework activity

- **Group 0; 45 minutes; page 51**

  This is new content, but the processes are similar to those covered in the activity sheets during the lesson.

Support ideas

- **Group 1** The student may need extra help with balancing chemical equations, but you can reassure them that their equation writing skills will improve through the course as it offers plenty of opportunities to practise.
- **Group 7** The graphs on the Group 7 activity sheet should be bar graphs. The student may need extra help to understand that the *x*-axis is not continuous. This activity sheet requires the student to write ionic equations for displacement reactions. These may need more explanation.

Extension ideas

- **Group 0** Element number 117 is newly discovered. The student could suggest why element number 117 should be a halogen.

Progress and observations

CHEMISTRY HIGHER

Starter activity: Metals and non-metals

Learning objective

- To know that metals form positive ions when they react and non-metals do not

Equipment

- pencil

1. Complete this diagram to show the electronic structure of a sodium atom.

2. Sodium is a metal. When a sodium atom reacts, it loses one electron. Complete the diagram to show its new electronic structure.

3. The sodium atom forms a sodium ion when it reacts. Complete the table to show the overall charge on the sodium atom and the sodium ion. Remember that the sodium ion has lost an electron.

Relative charges	Sodium atom	Sodium ion
Number of positive charges		
Number of negative charges		
Overall charge		

4. All metals form positive ions when they react. Non-metals do not.
   How does the overall charge on a non-metal atom change when it reacts to become a non-metal ion?

   _____

   _____

TUTORS GUILD CHEMISTRY HIGHER

Main activity: Group 1

Learning objectives

- To know that the reactivity of Group 1 metals depends on their electronic structure
- To describe the reactions of lithium, sodium and potassium with oxygen, chlorine and water
- To know the reactivity trends in Group 1 and use them to make predictions

Equipment

- spare paper

1. Explain why Group 1 metals have similar chemical reactions.

_____

2. The table shows how group 1 metals react with oxygen. Complete the table by adding the balanced chemical equation for each reaction.

Group 1 metal	Reaction with oxygen	Balanced chemical equation
lithium	burns vigorously with a red flame	
sodium	burns vigorously with a yellow/orange flame	
potassium	burns vigorously with a lilac flame	

3. The diagram shows sodium reacting with chlorine.

a) What would you expect to see on the walls of the gas jar?

_____

b) Write balanced equations for the reactions of lithium, sodium and potassium with chlorine.

_____

_____

_____

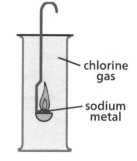

chlorine gas

sodium metal

c) Describe to your tutor how the reactivity of Group 1 metals with chlorine changes down the group.

4. A piece of sodium metal is added to a trough of water containing a few drops of universal indicator. On a separate piece of paper, answer the following questions.

a) What would you expect to see?

b) Write a balanced chemical equation for the reaction.

c) How would the reaction differ if:

   i) lithium was used instead of sodium?

   ii) potassium was used instead of sodium?

d) Write balanced equations for the reactions between lithium and water and between potassium and water.

5. A metal explodes violently with water, producing hydrogen gas and an alkaline solution. Tell your tutor where in Group 1 you would place this metal.

CHEMISTRY HIGHER

Main activity: Group 7

Time **20** mins

Learning objectives

- To explain the reactivity of the halogens in terms of electronic structure
- To know the trends in relative molecular mass, melting point and boiling point in Group 7
- To describe displacement reactions of the halogens and reactivity trends

Equipment

- pencil
- graph paper
- spare paper

1. Why do the halogens have similar chemical reactions?

_____

2. The halogens exist as molecules. What is the formula for a chlorine molecule? _____

3. The table gives some data about halogens.

Halogen	Relative molecular mass	Melting point (°C)	Boiling point (°C)
fluorine		−220	−188
chlorine		−101	−35
bromine		−7	59
iodine		114	184

a) Complete the table and, on a separate piece of graph paper, draw suitable graph(s) to show the data.

b) Describe the trend shown.   _____

c) Use your graphs to predict the melting and boiling points of astatine.
   (relative molecular mass of astatine = 210)

_____

4. A student added halogen solutions to solutions of their salts on a spotting tile. The table below shows whether there was a reaction between each pair of solutions.

On a separate piece of paper, answer the following questions.

Halogen solution	Potassium chloride solution	Potassium bromide solution	Potassium iodide solution
chlorine	✗	✓	✓
bromine	✗	✗	✓
iodine	✗	✗	✗

potassium chloride solution   potassium bromide solution   potassium iodide solution

○○○ chlorine water
○○○ bromine water
○○○ iodine solution

a) Place the halogens in order of reactivity.

b) Write balanced equations for the reactions that took place.

c) Write ionic equations for the reactions.

d) What is this type of reaction called?

TUTORS GUILD CHEMISTRY HIGHER

Homework activity: Group 0

Learning objectives

- To use electronic structures to explain why the noble gases are unreactive
- To know the boiling point trends of the noble gases
- To predict properties from given trends

Equipment

- pencil
- spare paper

1. Draw diagrams to show the electronic structure of:

a) helium

b) neon

c) argon

2. What do the electronic structures of helium, neon and argon have in common and how does this affect their reactivity?

_____

3. Why are there very few compounds of noble gases?

_____

4. The graph shows the boiling points of the noble gases.

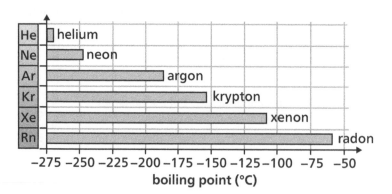

a) What is the boiling point trend in Group 0?

_____

b) Which noble gases are liquid at −200 °C?

_____

c) What is the difference between the boiling point of argon and the boiling point of radon?

_____

6 Answers

Starter activity: Metals and non-metals

1. Diagram should show 2, 8, 1
2. Diagram should show 2, 8
3. Sodium atom: +11, −11, no overall charge; sodium ion: +11, −10, overall charge +1
4. The overall charge changes from zero to negative.

Main activity: Group 1

1. They all have one electron in the outer shell.
2. $4Li + O_2 \rightarrow 2Li_2O$
   $4Na + O_2 \rightarrow 2Na_2O$
   $4K + O_2 \rightarrow 2K_2O$
3. a) A white crystalline solid (salt, NaCl)
   b) $2Li + Cl_2 \rightarrow 2LiCl$
      $2Na + Cl_2 \rightarrow 2NaCl$
      $2K + Cl_2 \rightarrow 2KCl$
   c) Reactivity increases
4. a) Vigorous reaction, fizzes, moves around, universal indicator turns blue
   b) $2Na + 2H_2O \rightarrow 2NaOH + H_2$
   c) i) Less vigorous reaction
      ii) More vigorous reaction
   d) $2Li + 2H_2O \rightarrow 2LiOH + H_2$
      $2K + 2H_2O \rightarrow 2KOH + H_2$
5. Below potassium

Main activity: Group 7

1. They all have seven electrons in their outer shell.
2. Cl_2
3. a) Relative molecular mass: F: 38, Cl: 71, Br: 160, I: 254
      Graph(s) should be bar graphs, with relative molecular mass on the x-axis and temperature (°C) on the y-axis.
      Boiling and melting points can be plotted as two sets of bars on one graph, or individually on two separate graphs.
   b) Melting and boiling points increase down Group 7.
   c) Melting point = 302 °C; boiling point = 337 °C; accept very approximate values
4. a) (Most reactive) Cl, Br, I (least reactive)
   b) $Cl_2 + 2KBr \rightarrow 2KCl + Br_2$
      $Cl_2 + 2KI \rightarrow 2KCl + I_2$
      $Br_2 + 2KI \rightarrow 2KBr + I_2$
   c) $Cl_2 + 2Br^- \rightarrow 2Cl^- + Br_2$
      $Cl_2 + 2I^- \rightarrow 2Cl^- + I_2$
      $Br_2 + 2I^- \rightarrow 2Br^- + I_2$
   d) Displacement reaction

Homework activity: Group 0

1. Electron shell diagrams showing:
   a) 2   b) 2, 8   c) 2, 8, 8
2. All have a complete outer shell of electrons. This makes them stable, so they are unreactive.
3. They are very unreactive and do not form compounds easily.
4. a) Boiling point increases down Group 0.
   b) argon, krypton, xenon, radon
   c) About 120 °C

7 The periodic table: Properties of transition metals

Learning objectives

- To describe the differences between Group 1 metals and transition metals
- To know the typical properties of transition metals

Specification links

- 4.1.3.1, 4.1.3.2
- WS: 3.5

Starter activity

- **Properties of Group 1 metals; 5 minutes; page 54**

  The student may have seen Group 1 metals handled at school. Either remind them or tell them about the physical properties of Group 1 metals such as sodium. There are several videos on the internet that may be useful.

Main activities

- **Group 1 metals and transition metals; 20 minutes; page 55**

  Establish that Group 1 metal properties are not the typical metal properties we normally think of. Ask the student to list a few typical metals and write down how they think their properties compare with those of Group 1 metals. Explain that most metals we use are transition metals. The activity sheet will help the student to compare Group 1 metals with transition metals.

- **Typical properties of transition metals; 20 minutes; page 56**

  Explain that transition metals can form ions with different charges and show the student how these are indicated in the name of the compound formed. The student can then answer questions 1 and 2. Discuss the colour of transition metal compounds with the student and compare with Group 1 compounds. Explain that we use many transition metals as catalysts. The student can then complete the activity sheet.

Plenary activity

- **Summing up metals; 5 minutes**

  The student should produce a spider diagram with the word 'metals' in the centre, summarising the properties of transition metals and Group 1 metals.

Homework activity

- **Which are more useful?; 45 minutes; page 57**

  This is a writing exercise, drawing on the content of this lesson. The student is asked to compare the usefulness of Group 1 metals and transition metals.

Support ideas

- **Group 1 metals and transition metals** The student may need extra input to understand the concept of ions and positive ions. They could refer back to the previous lesson.
- **Typical properties of transition metals** The student may need to refer back to lesson 2 to recap writing formulae.

Extension ideas

- **Group 1 metals and transition metals** The student can research the formulae of the chlorides formed by chromium, manganese, iron, cobalt, nickel and copper. They can use Roman numerals to write their chemical names.
- **Typical properties of transition metals** The student could find out why zinc is not a true transition metal, despite being between Groups 2 and 3.

Progress and observations

Starter activity: Properties of Group 1 metals

Time **5** mins

Learning objectives

- To know that Group 1 metals are grey, shiny, soft and have a low density
- To know how Group 1 metals are stored

Equipment

1. The image shows sodium in a storage jar. Why is sodium stored under oil?

_____

2. What colour is freshly cut sodium metal?

_____

3. When sodium is exposed to air, a white layer forms on its surface. What is this?

_____

4. Sodium metal can be cut with a knife. Why is this unusual?

_____

5. When sodium is added to water, it floats. What does this tell you about the density of sodium?

_____

CHEMISTRY HIGHER

Main activity: Group 1 metals and transition metals

Time **20** mins

Learning objectives

- To describe the difference between melting points, density, strength and hardness of Group 1 metals and transition metals
- To describe how the reactivity of Group 1 metals with oxygen, chlorine and water differs from the reactivity of transition metals

Equipment

- copy of the periodic table
- spare paper

1. Where are transition metals found in the periodic table? _____

2. The table gives some melting points and densities of Group 1 metals and transition metals.

a) Draw two conclusions from this data.

_____

_____

b) Which metals will float in water? (The density of water is 1.0 g/cm³.)

_____

_____

_____

_____

Metal	Melting point (°C)	Density (g/cm³)
chromium	1857	7.20
manganese	1244	7.20
iron	1535	7.86
cobalt	1495	8.90
nickel	1455	8.90
copper	1083	8.92
lithium	181	0.53
sodium	98	0.97
potassium	63	0.86

3. How do the strength and hardness of Group 1 metals compare with transition metals?

_____

4. The table shows the reactions of some metals. Discuss the questions below with your tutor and write your answers on a separate piece of paper.

Metal	Reaction with oxygen	Reaction with chlorine	Reaction with water
sodium	burns easily producing Na_2O	burns to give NaCl	vigorous reaction producing H_2 and NaOH
iron	does not burn; becomes coated with Fe_3O_4	burns when heated to give $FeCl_3$	rusts when water and oxygen are present
copper	does not burn; becomes coated with black CuO	$CuCl_2$ forms on the surface	does not react
gold	no reaction	no reaction	does not react

a) Identify the transition metals.

b) Compare the reactions of the Group 1 metal with oxygen, chlorine and water with the reactions of the transition metals and draw conclusions.

c) What information would you need to increase the validity of your conclusions?

CHEMISTRY HIGHER

Main activity: Typical properties of transition metals

Time **20** mins

Learning objectives

- To know that many transition metals form ions with different charges
- To know that transition metals have coloured compounds
- To know that many transition metals make useful catalysts

Equipment

- copy of the periodic table

When metals react to form compounds, they lose electrons to form positive ions. Sodium metal forms sodium ions in compounds. We can write this as:

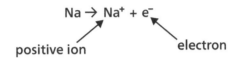

$$Na \rightarrow Na^+ + e^-$$

positive ion   electron

All Group 1 metals form ions with a single positive charge. Transition metals can form ions with different charges.

1. **Complete the table by adding the number of charges on the metal ions in each oxide. The first one has been done for you.**

Transition metal	Formulae of oxides	Positive ions formed
chromium	Cr_2O, CrO, CrO_2	+1
manganese	MnO, Mn_2O_3	
iron	FeO, Fe_2O_3	
copper	Cu_2O, CuO	

2. **We name these compounds using a Roman numeral after the metal to show the number of positive charges. So Cr_2O is chromium(I) oxide. Name the oxides in question 1.**

_____

_____

3. a) What colour are the compounds of Group 1 metals?_____

   b) How is this different to transition metal compounds?

   _____

4. **We use many transition metals as catalysts. Read the following information.**

> 'Millions of tonnes of ammonia (NH_3) are used every year to make fertilisers. These fertilisers help to feed about 50% of the world's population. Ammonia is made in the Haber process from nitrogen and hydrogen gases. In order to get a good yield of ammonia, an iron catalyst is used. This increases the rate of reaction and produces more ammonia in a given time.'

   a) What is a catalyst?

   _____

   _____

   b) Why are catalysts important to industry?

   _____

TUTORS GUILD **CHEMISTRY** HIGHER

Homework activity: Which are more useful?

Time **45** mins

Learning objectives

- To reinforce the properties of transition metals
- To reinforce the comparison between transition metals and Group 1 metals

Equipment

- copy of the periodic table

Transition metals are more useful to us than Group 1 metals.

You may agree or disagree with this statement. You may decide that transition metals are sometimes more useful than Group 1 metals, but not always.

1. **Write about 250 words comparing these two groups of metals, their properties and how we use them.**

   Here are some points you might want to include in your answer:

   - How do we use metals?
   - What properties must they have?
   - Which groups of metals have these properties?
   - How do we use metal compounds?

   Give plenty of examples to illustrate your answer.

_____

_____

_____

_____

_____

_____

_____

_____

_____

_____

_____

_____

_____

_____

_____

_____

_____

_____

_____

_____

_____

_____

7 Answers

Starter activity: Properties of Group 1 metals

1. To prevent sodium reacting with oxygen in the air
2. Grey and shiny
3. sodium oxide
4. Most metals are too hard to be cut with a knife
5. It is less than 1 g/cm³ (the density of water)

Main activity: Group 1 metals and transition metals

1. In a block between Groups 2 and 3
2. a) Transition metals have higher melting points and higher densities than Group 1 metals.
   b) Lithium, sodium and potassium
3. Transition metals are harder and stronger than Group 1 metals.
4. a) Iron, copper and gold
   b) Group 1 metals react readily with oxygen; transition metals are less reactive with oxygen. Group 1 metals react readily with chlorine; the less reactive transition metals react with difficulty, if at all. Group 1 metals react readily with water, iron rusts slowly when water and oxygen are present, and less reactive metals do not react.
   c) Data about reactions with other Group 1 and transition metals

Main activity: Typical properties of transition metals

1. Cr: +1, +2, +4; Mn: +2, +3; Fe: +2, +3; Cu: +1, +2
2. chromium(I) oxide; chromium(II) oxide; chromium(IV) oxide
   manganese(II) oxide; manganese(III) oxide
   iron(II) oxide; iron(III) oxide
   copper(I) oxide; copper(II) oxide
3. a) white
   b) Many transition metals have coloured compounds.
4. a) A substance that increases the rate of a reaction, without being used up in the reaction.
   b) They increase the yield of a product (more profit).

Homework activity: Which are more useful?

Student's own answers. Their answer can agree or disagree with the statement, but should be backed up with evidence and examples. Answers may include:

- Transition metals have higher melting and boiling points than Group 1 metals, so they can be used where the metal needs to be solid at high temperatures.

- Transition metals are more dense, harder and stronger than Group 1 metals, so they can be used where these properties are required (e.g. in car bodies, bridges, buildings).

- Transition metals are less reactive than Group 1 metals and reactions with water and oxygen tend to be slow or non-existent. This makes transition metals more useful where durability is required.

- Group 1 metals require electrolysis to extract them. This process uses large amounts of energy, so it is expensive. Many transition metals can be extracted by reduction with carbon, which uses less energy.

- Some transition metals are used as catalysts, enabling the chemical industry to produce products more quickly and cheaply (e.g. iron is used in the Haber process).

- Group 1 metal compounds have essential uses in the chemical industry. For example, sodium chloride is used to produce sodium hydroxide and sodium carbonate is used in glass making.

AQA

CHEMISTRY HIGHER

8 Chemical bonds: Ionic bonding and compounds

Learning objectives

- To draw dot-and-cross diagrams to show ionic bonding
- To work out the charges on the ions in an ionic compound
- To understand the structure of ionic compounds
- To explain the properties of ionic compounds related to their bonding

Specification links

- 4.2.1.1, 4.2.1.2, 4.2.1.3, 4.2.2.3
- WS: 1.2
- MS: 1a, 1c, 4a, 5b

Starter activity

- **Chemical bonds; 5 minutes; page 60**

  Remind or tell the student that there are three types of strong chemical bond: ionic, covalent and metallic. The student can work through the activity sheet. Encourage them to identify the main features of each type of bond.

Main activities

- **Ionic bonding; 20 minutes; page 61**

  Ask the student to draw the electronic structure of a sodium atom and a chlorine atom. Explain how an electron is transferred when sodium chloride forms and ions are produced. Show the student how this is shown on a dot-and-cross diagram, as on the activity sheet example. The student can complete the sheet. Remind them that more than one electron can be transferred, giving multiple charges on the ion. Link the type of charge to the group.

- **Ionic compounds; 20 minutes; page 62**

  Explain that opposite charges on ions produce strong electrostatic attractions which act in all directions and that these strong electrostatic attractions are ionic bonds. Use question 1 on the activity sheet to discuss different representations of ionic structures with the student. The student could summarise the discussion in a table. Discuss and explain the properties of ionic compounds. Check that the student understands that ionic compounds do not have molecules. The student can complete the activity sheet.

Plenary activity

- **Dot-and-cross diagrams and formulae; 5 minutes**

  Ask the student how dot-and-cross diagrams can be used to determine the (empirical) formula of an ionic compound. Ask the student how group number can be used to work out the (empirical) formula of an ionic compound.

Homework activity

- **Formulae of ionic compounds; 60 minutes; page 63**

  This activity sheet shows the student how to work out the empirical formula of an ionic compound from a diagram. There are two exercises for the student to complete. You may need to talk through this sheet first and reassure the student that this is a difficult homework. They can list any problems they have and bring them to the next lesson.

Support ideas

- **Ionic bonding** Refer back to the electronic structures of Group 1, 2, 6 and 7 elements and numbers of electrons in the outer shell. Explain that electrons are transferred to achieve the structure of a noble gas.
- **Ionic compounds** Explain why we do not use the term 'molecule' when referring to ionic compounds.

Extension ideas

- **Ionic bonding** The student can draw a dot-and-cross diagram to show the arrangement of electrons in aluminium oxide.
- **Ionic compounds** The student can research data to support the statement: ionic compounds have higher melting points than covalent compounds.

Progress and observations

CHEMISTRY HIGHER

Starter activity: Chemical bonds

Time 5 mins

Learning objectives

- To know that strong chemical bonds can be ionic, covalent or metallic
- To know the essential features of each type of bond

Equipment

The diagrams show the three different types of strong chemical bond.

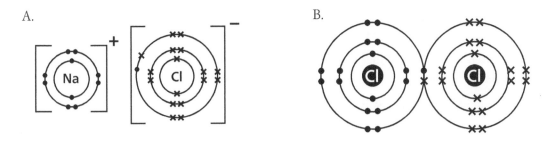

A.

B.

free electrons from outer shells of metal atoms

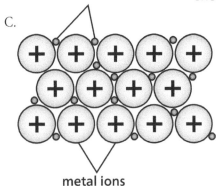

C.

metal ions

A metallic bond is the attraction between positive metal ions and delocalised, or free, electrons.

An ionic bond is the attraction between oppositely charged ions.

A covalent bond is a pair of electrons shared between two atoms.

1. Identify the type of bonding in each of diagram.

A. _____

B. _____

C. _____

2. Name the types of element (metals or non-metals) that form the bonds shown in A, B and C.

A. _____

B. _____

C. _____

CHEMISTRY HIGHER

TUTORS GUILD

Main activity: Ionic bonding

Learning objectives

- To draw dot-and-cross diagrams for the ionic compounds formed between Group 1 and 2 metals and Group 6 and 7 non-metals
- To work out the charges on the ions and know they are related to the group number

Equipment

- copy of the periodic table

These are the rules for dot-and-cross diagrams:

- Show the outer electrons only.
- Use dots for one atom and crosses for the other.
- Use square brackets around ions and write the charge as a superscript.

We show sodium forming an ionic bond with chlorine as follows:

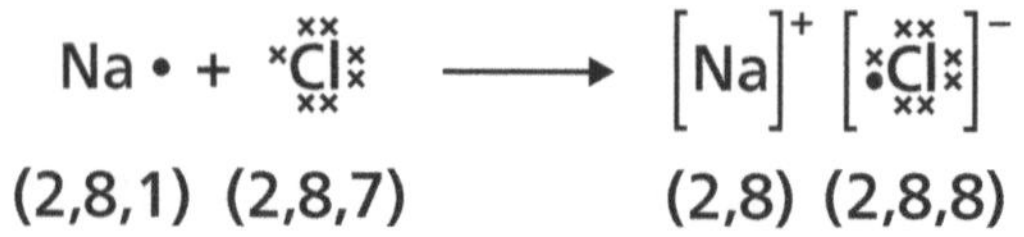

$$\text{Na} \bullet + \ \overset{xx}{\underset{xx}{\times}}\overset{}{\text{Cl}}\overset{}{\times} \longrightarrow \left[\text{Na}\right]^{+} \left[\overset{xx}{\underset{xx}{\bullet}}\text{Cl}\overset{}{\times}\right]^{-}$$

$$(2,8,1) \ (2,8,7) \qquad (2,8) \ (2,8,8)$$

1. **Draw similar dot-and-cross diagrams for the following ionic compounds.**

   a) lithium fluoride

   b) potassium chloride

   c) magnesium oxide

   d) magnesium chloride

   e) sodium oxide

   f) calcium sulfide

   g) lithium sulfide

   h) calcium fluoride

CHEMISTRY HIGHER

Main activity: Ionic compounds

Time **20** mins

Learning objectives

- To know that ionic bonds are strong electrostatic attractions between oppositely charged ions
- To compare dot-and-cross diagrams, ball-and-stick models, close packed models, 2-D and 3-D diagrams as representations of giant ionic structures
- To know and explain the properties of ionic compounds

Equipment

- spare paper

1. What is an ionic bond?

_____

_____

2. These are different ways of showing the structure of a sodium chloride lattice.

A.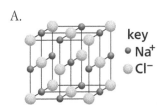

B.

C.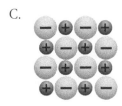

D.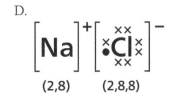

Discuss the pros and cons of these different representations with your tutor. Your tutor may ask you to summarise the key points from the discussion in a table on a separate piece of paper.

3. The table below shows some properties of ionic compounds. Complete the table to explain each property.

Property	Explanation
Ionic compounds have high melting points.	
Ionic compounds have high boiling points.	
Ionic compounds do not conduct electricity when solid.	
Ionic compounds conduct electricity when molten.	
Ionic compounds conduct electricity when dissolved in water.	

CHEMISTRY HIGHER

Homework activity: Formulae of ionic compounds

Time 60 mins

Learning objective

- To work out the empirical formula of an ionic compound from a diagram showing its structure

Equipment

- spare paper

The diagram shows a molecule of water. We can write its formula as H$_2$O, showing the number and type of each particle in one molecule.

An ionic lattice of sodium chloride contains large numbers of sodium ions and chloride ions. We write its formula as NaCl, showing the ratio and type of the ions. In other words, there is one sodium ion to one chloride ion.

This is called an empirical formula. We can work out the empirical formula of a substance from a diagram showing the ions, like the one below.

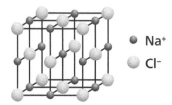

This diagram represents one cube.

You can count the number of sodium ions and chloride ions and count how many cubes each ion shares.

For example, a chloride ion in the centre of a face of this cube shares two cubes – this one and the adjoining one.

Sodium ions	How many cubes do they share?	Total	
1 ion in the centre	1	1/1 = 1	4 sodium
12 ions on the edges	4	12/4 = 3	
Chloride ions	**How many cubes do they share?**	**Total**	
6 in the centre of the faces	2	6/2 = 3	4 chloride
8 at the corners	8	8/8 = 1	

The totals tell us there are four sodium ions to four chloride ions (or one sodium ion to one chloride ion). The empirical formula is NaCl.

1. On a separate piece of paper, draw similar tables to calculate the empirical formulae of these ionic compounds.

a)

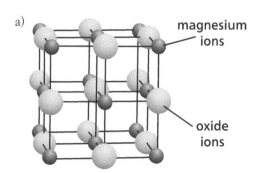

magnesium ions

oxide ions

b)

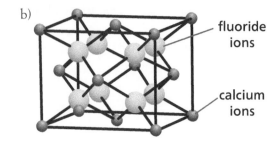

fluoride ions

calcium ions

8 Answers

Starter activity: Chemical bonds

1. A: ionic bond; B: covalent bond; C: metallic bond

2. A: metal and non-metal; B: non-metal and non-metal; C: between metals

Main activity: Ionic bonding

1. a) $\text{Li} \bullet \; + \; _{\times}\overset{\times\times}{\underset{\times\times}{\text{F}}}_{\times} \; \rightarrow \; \left[\text{Li}\right]^{+} \left[:\overset{\times\times}{\underset{\times\times}{\text{F}}}_{\times}\right]^{-}$

b) $\text{K} \bullet \; + \; _{\times}\overset{\times\times}{\underset{\times\times}{\text{Cl}}} \; \rightarrow \; \left[\text{K}\right]^{+} \left[:\overset{\times\times}{\underset{\times\times}{\text{Cl}}}_{\times}\right]^{-}$

c) $\text{Mg} \!\!:\; + \; \overset{\times\times}{\underset{\times\times}{\text{O}}}_{\times} \; \rightarrow \; \left[\text{Mg}\right]^{2+} \left[:\overset{\times\times}{\underset{\times\times}{\text{O}}}_{\times}\right]^{2-}$

d) $\text{Mg} \!\!:\; + 2_{\times}\overset{\times\times}{\underset{\times\times}{\text{Cl}}} \; \rightarrow \; \left[\text{Mg}\right]^{2+} 2\left[:\overset{\times\times}{\underset{\times\times}{\text{Cl}}}_{\times}\right]^{-}$

e) $2\,\text{Na} \bullet \; + \; \overset{\times\times}{\underset{\times\times}{\text{O}}}_{\times} \; \rightarrow \; 2\left[\text{Na}\right]^{-} \left[:\overset{\times\times}{\underset{\times\times}{\text{O}}}_{\times}\right]^{2-}$

f) $\text{Ca} \!\!:\; + \; \overset{\times\times}{\underset{\times\times}{\text{S}}}_{\times} \; \rightarrow \; \left[\text{Ca}\right]^{2+} \left[:\overset{\times\times}{\underset{\times\times}{\text{S}}}_{\times}\right]^{2-}$

g) $2\text{Li} \bullet \; + \; \overset{\times\times}{\underset{\times\times}{\text{S}}}_{\times} \; \rightarrow \; 2\left[\text{Li}\right]^{+} \left[:\overset{\times\times}{\underset{\times\times}{\text{S}}}_{\times}\right]^{2-}$

h) $\text{Ca} \!\!:\; + 2_{\times}\overset{\times\times}{\underset{\times\times}{\text{F}}} \; \rightarrow \; \left[\text{Ca}\right]^{2+} 2\left[:\overset{\times\times}{\underset{\times\times}{\text{F}}}_{\times}\right]^{-}$

Main activity: Ionic compounds

1. A strong electrostatic attraction between oppositely charged ions

2. Discussion points: ball-and-stick model shows arrangement and type of ions, suggests ions are spaced apart and bond is a solid object; close packed model shows arrangement and type of ions, shows that ions are touching; 2-D diagram shows type of ions and partial arrangement, but does not show 3-D structure; dot-and-cross diagram shows how the electrons are rearranged, but not how the ions are arranged

3.

Property	Explanation
Ionic compounds have high melting points.	A lot of energy is needed to break strong ionic bonds (electrostatic attractions), so melting point is high.
Ionic compounds have high boiling points.	A lot of energy is needed to overcome strong electrostatic attractions between ions in the liquid.
Ionic compounds do not conduct electricity when solid.	Ions are not free to move so cannot carry the charge.
Ionic compounds conduct electricity when molten.	Ions are free to move and can carry the charge.
Ionic compounds conduct electricity when dissolved in water.	Ions are free to move and can carry the charge.

Homework activity: Formulae of ionic compounds

1. a)

Mg ions	How many cubes do they share?	Total	
6 on faces	2	3	4 Mg
8 on corners	8	1	

Oxide ions	How many cubes do they share?	Total	
1 in centre	1	1	4 oxide
12 on edges	4	3	

Empirical formula = MgO

b)

Calcium ions	How many cubes do they share?	Total	
8 on corners	8	1	4 Ca
6 on faces	2	3	

Fluoride ions	How many cubes do they share?	Total	
8 in centre	1	8	8 fluoride

Empirical formula = CaF_2

9 Chemical bonds: Covalent bonding and metallic bonding

Learning objectives

- Draw dot-and-cross diagrams to show covalent bonds in small molecules
- Describe limitations of the different methods used to represent covalent bonds
- Deduce the molecular formula from diagrams showing atoms and bonds
- Be able to represent and explain the bonding in metals
- Represent covalent bonds in small molecules, polymers and giant structures using a single line

Specification links

- 4.2.1.4, 4.2.1.5
- WS: 1.2
- MS: 5b

Starter activity

- **Bonding and particles; 5 minutes; page 66**

  Check that the student understands when the term 'molecule' applies and that it should not be used to describe ionic compounds.

Main activities

- **Covalent bonds and dot-and-cross diagrams; 20 minutes; page 67**

  Explain how dot-and-cross diagrams are used to show single, double and triple covalent bonds in small molecules.

- **Covalent bonds and metallic bonds; 20 minutes; page 68**

  Explain that covalent bonding can also result in large molecules, such as polymers, and giant structures. Show the student how poly(ethene) can be represented, using formulae, squared brackets and single lines for bonds. Show the student how giant structures such as diamond and silicon dioxide can be represented. Explain that metals also have giant structures, but metals have metallic bonding. Emphasise that the diagram in the activity can be used to represent all metals and alloys.

Plenary activity

- **Chemical bonds; 5 minutes**

  Ask the student to draw a spider diagram with 'chemical bonds' in the centre of the page and the three different types of strong bond around it. They can then add explanations and examples.

Homework activity

- **Representing molecules and giant structures; 60 minutes; page 69**

  This activity requires the student to identify the limitations of different representations of structures.

Support ideas

- **Covalent bonds and dot-and-cross diagrams** Photographs or diagrams of 3-D structures may help the student to visualise the covalent structures. Encourage the student to check the number of electrons in the outer shells of their dot-and-cross diagrams. They should have a full outer shell (at GCSE); this is a good check for accuracy.

Extension ideas

- **Covalent bonds and dot-and-cross diagrams** The student can draw a dot-and-cross diagram to show the electron arrangement in carbon dioxide.
- **Covalent bonds and metallic bonds** If n in the representation of poly(ethene) is 10 000, what is the molecular formula of a poly(ethene) molecule?

Progress and observations

CHEMISTRY HIGHER

Starter activity: Bonding and particles

Learning objective

- To use the correct terminology when describing substances with different types of bonding

Equipment

1. **The table shows diagrams representing different particles. Complete the table by identifying the types of bonding and whether each particle is a molecule, atom, negative ion or positive ion.**

Particle	Type of bonding	Name of particle
A.		
B.		
C.		
D.		
E.		

TUTORS GUILD CHEMISTRY HIGHER

Main activity: Covalent bonds and dot-and-cross diagrams

Time 20 mins

Learning objectives

- To draw dot-and-cross diagrams to show single covalent bonds in hydrogen, chlorine, hydrogen chloride, water, ammonia and methane
- To draw dot-and-cross diagrams to show double and triple covalent bonds in oxygen and nitrogen

Equipment

- copy of the periodic table
- pencil

We can use dot-and-cross diagrams to show the arrangement of electrons in covalent bonds. This is the dot-and-cross diagram for hydrogen, H_2.

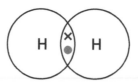

We can also write this as:

H ×• H

1. **Draw dot-and-cross diagrams to show the single covalent bonds in:**

   a) chlorine, Cl_2

   b) hydrogen chloride, HCl

   c) water, H_2O

   d) ammonia, NH_3

   e) methane, CH_4

2. **In a double covalent bond, two pairs of electrons are shared. Draw a dot-and-cross diagram to show the electrons in oxygen, O_2.**

3. **In a triple covalent bond, three pairs of electrons are shared. Draw a dot-and-cross diagram to show the bonding in nitrogen, N_2.**

TUTORS' GUILD CHEMISTRY HIGHER

Main activity: Covalent bonds and metallic bonds

Time **20** mins

Learning objectives

- To recognise and interpret diagrams showing large molecules and giant covalent structures
- To describe metallic bonding

Equipment

1. The diagram shows a polymer called poly(ethene).

a) What does n stand for? _____

b) What do the single lines represent? _____

c) Explain why brackets are used. _____

_____

2. The diagram below shows the structure of diamond. It is a giant covalent structure.

a) What do the black dots represent? _____

b) What do the single lines represent? _____

c) How many bonds does each atom make? _____

3. The diagram below shows the bonding in a metal.

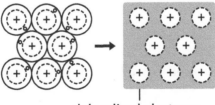

delocalised electrons

a) What does 'delocalised' mean? _____

_____

b) What makes the metallic bond? _____

_____

Homework activity: Representing molecules and giant structures   **Time** **60** mins

Learning objective	Equipment
• To describe the limitations of using dot-and-cross, ball-and-stick, 2-D and 3-D diagrams to represent molecules and giant structures	none

1. These diagrams show different ways of representing the structure of ammonia, NH_3. Identify the strengths and limitations (what it doesn't tell you) of each type of diagram.

   a) **dot-and-cross diagrams**

   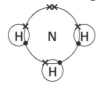

   _____
   _____
   _____
   _____
   _____

   b)   **2-D diagram**

   H—N—H
        |
        H

   _____
   _____
   _____
   _____
   _____

   c) **ball and stick diagram**

   _____
   _____
   _____
   _____
   _____

2. The diagram to the right shows one way of representing polymers, where n is a very large number. This is poly(ethene), commonly called polythene. What are the limitations of this diagram?

   _____
   _____
   _____

3. The diagram to the right shows the structure of diamond. It has a giant covalent structure. What are the limitations of this diagram?

   _____
   _____
   _____

9 Answers

Starter activity: Bonding and particles

1. A: no bonding, atom
   B: covalent bonding, molecule
   C: ionic bonding, negative ion
   D: covalent bonding, molecule
   E: ionic bonding, positive ion

Main activity: Covalent bonds and dot-and-cross diagrams

1. a)
   xx ●●
   ⦂ Cl ⦂ Cl ⦂
   xx ●●

   b)
   xx
   H ⦂ Cl ⦂
   xx

   c)
   xx
   ⦂ O ⦂H
   x●
   H

   d)
   ●●
   H⦂ N ⦂H
   x●
   H

   e)
   H
   ●x
   H⦂ C ⦂H
   x●
   H

2.
   ●● x ⁺⁺
   ● O ⦂ O
   ●● x ⁺⁺

3.
   x
   ⦂ N ⦂ N ⦂

Main activity: Covalent bonds and metallic bonds

1. a) Many/a large number
   b) Single covalent bonds
   c) To show the part of the molecule that is repeated
2. a) Atoms (carbon atoms)
   b) Single covalent bonds
   c) 4
3. a) Free to move throughout the structure/not in a fixed location
   b) The attraction between positive metal ions and delocalised electrons

Homework activity: Representing molecules and giant structures

1. Answers should cover the following points:
   a) Dot-and-cross diagrams show how electrons are arranged but do not show the shape of the molecule.
   b) 2-D diagram shows how atoms are arranged in 2-D but does not show 3-D shape or how electrons are shared.
   c) Ball-and-stick diagram shows how atoms are arranged but does not show how electrons are shared or identify types of atom.
2. It does not show the 3-D shape of the molecule or how electrons are shared.
3. It does not identify the type of atom or show how electrons are shared.

CHEMISTRY HIGHER

10 Chemical bonds: The particle theory and properties of small molecules

Learning objectives

- To use simple models to represent the three states of matter
- To use particle theory to explain changes of state and understand its limitations
- To understand factors affecting melting points and boiling points
- To use state symbols in chemical equations
- To know the properties of small molecules, including the effect of intermolecular forces on melting and boiling points

Specification links

- 4.2.2.1, 4.2.2.2, 4.2.2.4
- WS: 1.2
- MS: 4a, 5b

Starter activity

- **Modelling the three states of matter; 5 minutes; page 72**

  Remind the student of the models we use to describe the arrangement of particles in the three states of matter and the terms used to describe changes of state. This should have been covered at Key Stage 3. Reinforce the idea that liquid particle models should show some particles touching.

Main activities

- **The particle theory; 20 minutes; page 73**

  Explain how the particle theory is used to explain changes of state. Encourage the student to refer to energy transfer in their answers. Explain how the forces of attraction between particles affect melting and boiling points. Extra input may be required with questions 3 and 4 on the limitations of particle theory and properties of bulk materials versus properties of atoms.

- **Properties of small molecules; 20 minutes; page 74**

  Discuss the properties of small molecules (melting point, boiling point and electrical conductivity), explaining the effect of intermolecular forces on melting and boiling points. Explain how the strength of intermolecular forces depends on molecular size.

Plenary activity

- **Models; 5 minutes**

  Ask the student to list the ways in which the models and ideas about the three states of matter they learned at Key Stage 3 are different from the model in this lesson.

Homework activity

- **Bonds and changes of state; 60 minutes; page 75**

  This sheet is self-explanatory and reinforces ideas covered in this lesson and in previous lessons.

Support ideas

- **The particle theory** Discuss how the particle theory considers all particles to be the same, with no forces of attraction between them and inelastic. In reality, particles come in all shapes and sizes, are attracted to other particles and can stick to other particles or to the walls of a container. The student may need extra help to appreciate the relative strength of intermolecular bonds. The strongest intermolecular forces are only one tenth the strength of a covalent bond.

Extension ideas

- **Properties of small molecules** The student could predict the relative melting points of ammonia, poly(ethene) and magnesium oxide. They could research the melting points to check their predictions. Ask the student to explain why the boiling point data in question 2 is a bar graph and not a line graph.

Progress and observations

CHEMISTRY HIGHER

Starter activity: Modelling the three states of matter

Time **5** mins

Learning objectives

- To draw diagrams to represent the arrangement of particles in the three states of matter
- To know how (s), (l), (g) and (aq) are used in chemical equations
- To know the terms used to describe changes of state

Equipment

1. **Complete the boxes by showing how the particles are arranged in solids, liquids and gases. Underneath the boxes, describe the energy of the particles in each of the three states.**

solid

liquid

gas

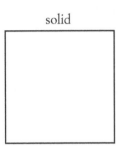 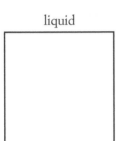 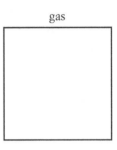

_____

_____

_____

2. **Add these terms to the diagram to show the different changes of state:**

melting   freezing   boiling   condensing

SOLID ⇌————————————→ LIQUID ⇌————————————→ GAS

3. **We use state symbols in chemical equations to show whether a substance is a solid (s), liquid (l), gas (g) or in solution (aq). This is an example:**

$$C(s) + O_2(g) \rightarrow CO_2(g)$$

a) Some students heated magnesium ribbon in air (oxygen). A white powder, magnesium oxide, was produced. Add state symbols to the equation for this reaction.

2Mg _____ + O₂ _____ → 2MgO _____

b) The students then reacted the magnesium oxide with dilute sulfuric acid to produce a solution of magnesium sulfate. Add state symbols to the equation for this reaction.

MgO _____ + H₂SO₄ _____ → MgSO₄ _____ + H₂O _____

CHEMISTRY HIGHER

Main activity: The particle theory

Time 20 mins

Learning objectives

- To understand how the strength of forces between particles affects melting and boiling points
- To understand that bonding and structure affect the nature of the particles
- To recognise that atoms do not have the bulk properties of the substance
- To know the limitations of the particle theory

Equipment

- spare paper

The particle theory says that all matter consists of very small particles which are constantly moving.

The movement of the particles is determined by their energy and their relationships with other particles.

Particle theory can be used to explain changes of state.

Write your answers to the following questions on a separate piece of paper.

1. **Ice is heated until it becomes steam. Use the particle theory to explain the changes from ice (solid) to water (liquid) and from water to steam (gas). You should use ideas about energy transfer in your answer.**

2. **Different substances have different melting and boiling points, depending on the strength of forces between the particles and the amount of energy which needs to be transferred to break them. Look at the table and answer the questions that follow.**

Substance	Melting point (°C)	Boiling point (°C)
water, H_2O	0	100
methane, CH_4	−182	−161
hydrogen, H_2	−260	−253
magnesium oxide, MgO	2852	3600
sodium chloride, NaCl	801	1413

a) Rank the substances in order of the amount of energy which needs to be transferred to overcome the forces between their particles, from the least amount of energy to the highest amount of energy.

b) Explain why magnesium oxide and sodium chloride have the highest melting points in the table.

c) Explain why hydrogen has the lowest melting point in the table.

3. **The particle theory considers all particles to be very small solid spheres with no forces of attraction between them. Explain why the particle theory does not explain the different melting and boiling points of different substances.**

4. **'Atoms do not have the bulk properties of the substance.' Explain to your tutor what this statement means using a gold atom and a lump of gold as an example.**

CHEMISTRY HIGHER

AQA

Main activity: Properties of small molecules

Time 20 mins

Learning objectives

- To know the properties of small molecules
- To know how intermolecular forces affect melting and boiling points
- To know the relationship between intermolecular forces and the size of molecules

Equipment

1. **Complete the table to identify and explain the properties of small molecules.**

Property	Property of small molecules	Explanation
melting point		
boiling point		
electrical conductivity		

The alkanes are a family of hydrocarbons. The more carbon atoms an alkane contains, the longer the molecule.

2. **The bar graph shows the boiling points of different alkanes. Explain why the boiling points of the alkanes increase as the molecules get longer.**

_____

_____

_____

_____

_____

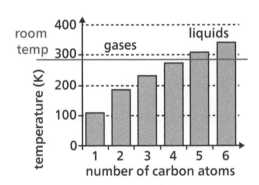

3. **This is an exam question and a student's answer:**

> Question: There are two types of chemical bond in water: covalent bonds and intermolecular forces.
>
> Explain what happens to the bonds when water boils.
>
> [3 marks]

> Answer: As the water molecules gain more energy, the covalent bonds break. The water molecules have enough energy and leave the surface to become a gas.

The student gained zero marks. Explain why, giving the correct answer.

_____

_____

_____

_____

_____

_____

_____

CHEMISTRY HIGHER

Homework activity: Bonds and changes of state

Time **60** mins

Learning objective

- To know the changes to chemical bonds and intermolecular forces that occur during changes of state

Equipment

- spare paper

The diagram shows an ionic compound melting and a covalent substance melting.

ionic compound   covalent substance

melting   melting

solid   liquid   solid   liquid

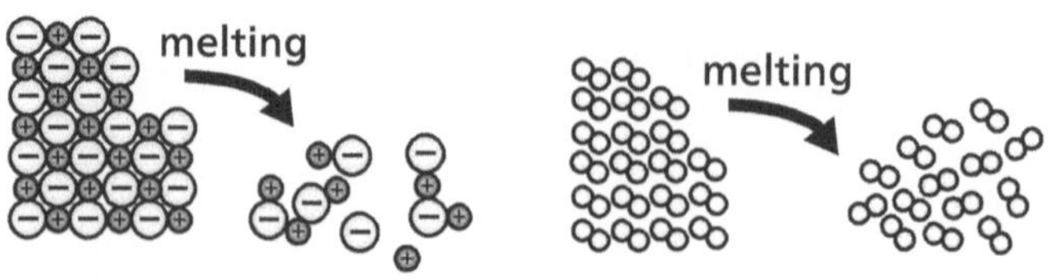

1. What bonds are broken when an ionic compound melts?

   _____

2. Why do ionic compounds have high melting and boiling points?

   _____

3. Which bonds are broken and which are not broken when a covalent substance melts?

   _____

4. What are intermolecular forces?

   _____

5. What types of substance have intermolecular forces?

   _____

6. Name a type of substance that does not have intermolecular forces.

   _____

7. What is the relationship between the strength of the intermolecular force and the size of the molecule?

   _____

8. On a separate piece of paper, answer this exam-style question. Your answer must contain at least six points, use scientific language and be logical.

   Explain, in terms of structure and bonding, why sodium chloride has a much higher melting point than iodine. (Melting point of sodium chloride = 801 °C, melting point of iodine = 114 °C.)

   [6 marks]

10 Answers

Starter activity: Modelling the three states of matter

1.

| solid | liquid | gas |

In a solid, the particles vibrate around a fixed position. In a liquid, the particles move and change position, but do not have enough energy to leave the surface of the liquid. In a gas, the particles have enough energy to move freely in all directions.

2. Solid to liquid = melting; liquid to solid = freezing; liquid to gas = boiling; gas to liquid = condensing
3. a) $2Mg(s) + O_2(g) \rightarrow 2MgO(s)$
   b) $MgO(s) + H_2SO_4(aq) \rightarrow MgSO_4(aq) + H_2O(l)$

Main activity: The particle theory

1. Ice → water: Energy is transferred to the solid (ice) by heating. Once enough energy has been transferred to overcome the intermolecular forces, the particles are free to move and the ice melts.
   Water → steam: Energy is transferred to the liquid (water) by heating. The energy of the particles increases until they overcome the intermolecular forces and escape from the surface of the liquid. The water boils, becoming steam.
2. a) (Least energy) hydrogen, methane, water, sodium chloride, magnesium oxide (most energy)
   b) A lot of energy is required to break the strong ionic bonds in these substances.
   c) Hydrogen has small molecules with weak intermolecular forces. Little energy is needed to overcome the intermolecular forces so melting point is very low.
3. Melting and boiling points are affected by the structures and bonding of different substances, and the forces of attraction between particles. The particle theory does not consider these factors.
4. Gold metal (as a bulk substance) has relatively high density, high melting and boiling points, is hard and strong and is malleable. A single gold atom does not have these properties.

Main activity: Properties of small molecules

1.

Property	Property of small molecules	Explanation
Melting point	Low melting point	Weak intermolecular forces easily broken
Boiling point	Low boiling point	Weak intermolecular forces easily broken
Electrical conductivity	Do not conduct	No charged particles to carry the charge

2. Larger molecules have stronger intermolecular forces.
3. The example answer gains zero marks because the student has confused the strong covalent bonds within molecules and the weak intermolecular forces.
   Answer should be: Energy transferred breaks weak intermolecular forces (1), allowing water molecules to leave the liquid surface (1). Covalent bonds are not broken (1).

Homework activity: Bonds and changes of state

1. Ionic bonds
2. Ionic bonds are strong, so a lot of energy is needed to break them.
3. Intermolecular forces are broken, covalent bonds are not.
4. Weak bonds between molecules
5. Molecular substances
6. An ionic compound/any named ionic compound
7. The larger the molecule, the stronger the intermolecular force.
8. Student's own answers. Marks should be awarded as follows: NaCl has ionic bonds (1); I_2 has covalent bonds (1). Ionic bonds must be broken for NaCl to melt (1); these are strong bonds and require a lot of energy to break (1). Intermolecular forces must be overcome for iodine to melt (1) [no mark if answer states that covalent bonds are broken]; these are weak bonds and require little energy to break (1).

TUTORS' GUILD

CHEMISTRY HIGHER

11 Chemical bonds: Structures and properties

Learning objectives

- To explain the properties of polymers, giant covalent structures, metals and alloys in terms of their structure and bonding
- To know some uses of fullerenes
- To describe the structure and properties of diamond, graphite, graphene and fullerenes

Specification links

- 4.2.2.5, 4.2.2.6, 4.2.2.7, 4.2.2.8, 4.2.3.1, 4.2.3.2, 4.2.3.3
- WS: 1.2, 1.4
- MS: 5b

Starter activity

- **Identifying structures; 5 minutes; page 78**

  This activity reminds the student of work covered in previous lessons. The student can complete the activity by answering verbally. Do not let the student look at the next activity as it leads on from this starter and provides some answers.

Main activities

- **Large molecules and giant structures; 20 minutes; page 79**

  Discuss with the student why polymers are solid at room temperature, and why metals and giant covalent structures have high melting points. Explain why metals are good conductors of heat and electricity. The student should be able to draw on previous knowledge to work this out. Explain why pure metals are soft and the effect of alloying on hardness.

- **The structure and bonding of carbon; 20 minutes; page 80**

  Discuss the structure and bonding of the different forms of carbon, explaining their properties and uses. Ensure the student appreciates the similarity between the bonding in graphite and metallic bonding.

Plenary activity

- **Comparing forms of carbon; 5 minutes**

  Ask the student to list the similarities and differences between the different forms of carbon.

Homework activity

- **Buckminsterfullerene; 60 minutes; page 81**

  This activity is a brief case study of Buckminsterfullerene and includes some working scientifically skills associated with its discovery. The student may need help with some of the terminology.

Support ideas

- **Large molecules and giant structures** Recap which bonds are broken and which are not when different covalently bonded structures are melted. Explain that we design alloys to provide the properties we need for a particular use. The student could find out what solder is and why we use it.

Extension ideas

- **Structure and bonding of carbon** The student can research new uses of fullerenes. Emphasise that this is a fast developing area as new research is being carried out. Ask the student to suggest why C_{60} was not discovered earlier when we now know it exists in ordinary soot.

Progress and observations

CHEMISTRY HIGHER

Starter activity: Identifying structures

Learning objective

- To recall the structure and bonding in polymers, giant covalent structures and metals

Equipment

- none

These diagrams represent three different substances. Each diagram shows a small section of a larger structure.

A.

B.

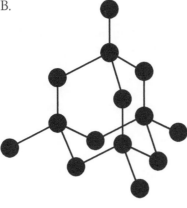

C. free electrons from outer shells of metal atoms

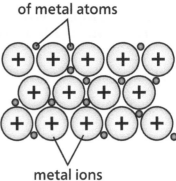

metal ions

1. Identify the types of structure the diagrams represent.

_____

_____

2. Name the type of bonding present in each substance

_____

_____

3. Give an example of each type of substance.

_____

_____

Main activity: Large molecules and giant structures

Time 20 mins

Learning objectives

- To explain why polymers are solid at room temperature
- To explain why giant covalent structures have high melting and boiling points
- To explain why alloys are harder than pure metals
- To explain why metals are good conductors of heat and electricity
- To explain why most metals have high melting and boiling points

Equipment

- pencil
- spare paper

1. **Sam has correctly completed the starter activity. The teacher tells Sam that A is poly(ethene), B is diamond and C is copper. Sam has researched the melting and boiling points of these substances.**

Substance	Melting point (°C)	Boiling point (°C)
poly(ethene)	melts over a range of temperatures from 110 to 145	decomposes before it boils
copper	1085	2562
diamond	3550	4830

a) Why does poly(ethene) not have a sharp melting point?

_____

b) Why is poly(ethene) a solid at room temperature?

_____

c) Why do copper and most other metals have high melting points?

_____

d) Which bonds are broken when diamond melts?

_____

e) Which bonds are broken and not broken when ice melts?

_____

f) Why does diamond have a high melting and boiling point?

_____

2. **The hardness of metals and alloys is measured on a 1 to 10 scale where 1 is soft and 10 is hard. Pure gold has a hardness of 2.5. A gold alloy has a hardness of 4.0. On a separate piece of paper:**

a) Draw annotated diagrams to show the arrangement of particles in pure gold and in the gold alloy.

b) Use your diagrams to explain why pure gold is easier to bend and shape than the gold alloy.

CHEMISTRY HIGHER

Main activity: The structure and bonding of carbon

Learning objectives

- To explain the properties of diamond, graphite, graphene and fullerenes in terms of their structure and bonding
- To know some uses of graphene and fullerenes

Equipment

- pencil

1. **Complete the table using diagrams and/or descriptions.**

Form of carbon	Structure and bonding	Properties explained	Uses
diamond			
graphite			
graphene			
fullerenes			
carbon nanotube (a fullerene)			

CHEMISTRY HIGHER

AQA

Homework activity: Buckminsterfullerene

Time **60** mins

Learning objectives

- To know the structure of Buckminsterfullerene
- To predict the properties of Buckminsterfullerene from its structure and bonding

Equipment

- spare paper

This is a fullerene called Buckminsterfullerene. It was the first fullerene to be discovered, in 1985, and has the molecular formula C_{60}.

1. **Buckminsterfullerene has a regular arrangement of carbon atoms in hexagons and pentagons. How many bonds does each carbon atom make?**

   _____

   _____

2. **Buckminsterfullerene is a black solid at room temperature. How would you expect its melting point to compare with that of diamond? Give reasons for your answer.**

   _____

   _____

   _____

3. **Buckminsterfullerene is considered a small molecule, and not a giant covalent structure. Explain why.**

   _____

   _____

   _____

4. **A group of scientists accidentally discovered a molecule containing 60 carbon atoms in outer space. Read the information about the discovery, then answer the questions below on a separate piece of paper.**

   - **The scientists repeated their investigation several times and obtained the same result.**
   - **They set up a laboratory experiment to provide the same conditions as in outer space.**
   - **They suggested that C_{60} had the same structure as a football.**
   - **They shared their results with other scientists who repeated their work and carried out further investigations.**
   - **They were awarded the Nobel prize for Chemistry in 1996.**

   a) The fullerene was detected in outer space and then in laboratory experiments. What was the controlled variable?

   b) Suggest a hypothesis the scientists could have written when they first detected a molecule containing 60 carbon atoms.

   c) Why did the scientists share their results with other scientists?

   d) Why didn't the scientists simply publish their results in a newspaper?

   e) Before 1985, school textbooks named only two forms of carbon: diamond and graphite. Why were they instantly out of date after 1985?

11 Answers

Starter activity: Identifying structures

1. A: polymer
   B: giant covalent structure
   C: metal
2. A: covalent bonding
   B: covalent bonding
   C: metallic bonding
3. A: poly(ethene)
   B: diamond
   C: copper
   (or other examples)

Main activity: Large molecules and giant structures

1. a) Poly(ethene) molecules contain different numbers of atoms.
   b) Long molecules have stronger intermolecular forces which need a lot of energy to break.
   c) A lot of energy is needed to break strong metallic bonds.
   d) Covalent bonds
   e) Intermolecular forces are broken, covalent bonds are not.
   f) A lot of energy is needed to break strong covalent bonds.
2. a) Diagrams should show a regular arrangement of same sized spheres in the metal and an irregular arrangement of two different sized spheres in the alloy
   b) Layers of particles can slide over each other in pure gold, but not in the alloy.

Main activity: The structure and bonding of carbon

1. Diamond: tetrahedral structure, carbon atoms covalently bonded to four others; hard, high melting and boiling points due to strong bonding; jewellery, cutting tools
   Graphite: carbon atoms bonded covalently to three others in layers of hexagons; layers slide over each other, high melting and boiling points due to strong bonding, electrical conductor due to delocalised electrons; lubricants
   Graphene: a single layer of graphite; high melting and boiling points due to strong bonding, electrical conductor due to delocalised electrons; electronics and composites
   Fullerenes: have hollow structures and some have delocalised electrons; hollow molecules of carbon atoms; drug delivery due to hollow structure, nanotechnology due to shape and reactivity
   Carbon nanotube: tube-shaped fullerene; high length to diameter ratio, electrical conductor due to delocalised electrons, high strength due to strong bonding; electronics, nanotechnology

Homework activity: Buckminsterfullerene

1. three
2. Buckminsterfullerene would have a lower melting point [1]. Only intermolecular forces are broken when C_{60} melts [1]; these are weak bonds and easily broken [1]. Covalent bonds must be broken for diamond to melt [1]; these are strong bonds and more energy is needed to break them [1].
3. It has a molecular formula; large molecules like polymers contain 1000s of atoms
4. a) The same conditions
   b) There are three forms of carbon; C_{60} is another form of carbon
   c) So that their work could be repeated; to increase validity
   d) Newspaper reports are not subject to peer review, and may be inaccurate, oversimplified or biased.
   e) A third form of carbon – Buckminsterfullerene – was discovered in 1985.

12 Chemical bonds: Particle size and nanoparticles

Learning objectives

- To compare nano dimensions to typical dimensions of atoms and molecules
- To understand surface area to volume ratio
- To explain why nanoparticles have different properties to their bulk material
- To know some uses of nanoparticles
- To evaluate the use of nanoparticles
- To know the dimensions of particulate matter (fine and coarse particles)

Specification links

- 4.2.4.1, 4.2.4.2
- WS: 1.2, 1.4, 4.1, 4.2, 4.3, 4.4, 4.5
- MS: 1a, 1b, 2h, 5c

Starter activity

- **The nano scale; 5 minutes; page 84**

  This activity introduces the student to the sizes of atoms and molecules relative to other objects and the measurement scale. The student will need to use standard form. Depending on the student's mathematical skills, this starter may take longer than five minutes.

Main activities

- **Nanoscience; 20 minutes; page 85**

  Explain how particulate matter, such as dust, pollen and particles from diesel emissions, is measured (as PM_{10} for example). Explain that nanoparticles have different properties to their bulk material because of the difference in surface area to volume ratio. The student can then answer questions 3 and 4 to explore these ideas.

- **Properties and uses of nanoparticles; 20 minutes; page 86**

  Emphasise that this is new technology and is changing all the time. Discuss the uses of nanoparticles in medicine, electronics, cosmetics, sunscreen, deodorants and as catalysts, including advantages and possible disadvantages.

Plenary activity

- **The downside of nanoparticles; 5 minutes**

  All the nanoparticles we are using have a common disadvantage. Ask the student to identify it and give examples.

Homework activity

- **Nanoparticles of silver; 60 minutes; page 87**

  The student is asked to write an evaluation of the use of silver nanoparticles. Encourage the student to think beyond the information given on the activity sheet when discussing advantages and disadvantages. They may be able to research additional information.

Support ideas

- **Nanoscience** The use of small cubes, as found in children's toys, or sugar cubes, may help the student to understand these ideas.
- **Properties and uses of nanoparticles** The student will learn later about life cycle assessments, which are useful evaluation tools. At this stage, encourage the student to consider advantages and disadvantages of a product and suggest possible outcomes.

Extension ideas

- **Nanoscience** The student could investigate cubes with other side lengths to see if the surface area to volume ratio always increases by a factor of 10 when the side of the cube decreases by a factor of 10.
- **Properties and uses of nanoparticles** The student could find out why diameters of atoms are often measured in picometres. They could convert some of the measurements in nanometres in this lesson to picometres.

Progress and observations

CHEMISTRY HIGHER

Starter activity: The nano scale

Learning objectives

- To understand units of measurement used to measure atoms and molecules
- To compare sizes of atoms and molecules to other objects

Equipment

- calculator

1. These are the relative sizes of different objects.

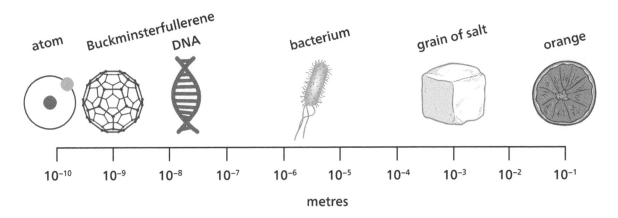

a) What is the size of a typical atom in metres, in decimal form and in standard form?

_____

b) What is the diameter of a molecule of Buckminsterfullerene in metres, in decimal form and in standard form?

_____

2. The table gives some units of length.

Prefix	Decimal number	Standard form
kilo	1000	1×10^3
–	1	1×10^0
centi	0.01	1×10^{-2}
milli	0.001	1×10^{-3}
micro	0.000001	1×10^{-6}
nano	0.000000001	1×10^{-9}

a) 1 nanometre (nm) = 1×10^{-9} m. What is the typical size of an atom in nanometres?

_____

b) What is the diameter of a molecule of Buckminsterfullerene in nanometres?

_____

CHEMISTRY HIGHER

TUTORS GUILD

Main activity: Nanoscience

Time **20** mins

Learning objectives

- To understand the dimensions of fine and coarse particles and nanoparticles
- To understand the relationship between surface area to volume ratio and cube size

Equipment

- pencil
- ruler
- spare paper

1. The atmosphere contains many particles of different sizes. Very small particles can enter the lungs and reach the alveoli, causing severe health problems. These fine particles are classified as $PM_{2.5}$ and are between 1×10^{-7} m and 2.5×10^{-6} m in diameter. Slightly larger particles, PM_{10} (diameter between 2.5×10^{-6} m and 1×10^{-5} m; classified as coarse particles) can also enter the respiratory system and cause breathing problems. On a separate piece of paper:

   a) Draw a measurement scale, as in the starter activity, and annotate your diagram to show fine particles ($PM_{2.5}$) and coarse particles (PM_{10}).

   b) What units of measurement are being used in $PM_{2.5}$?

   _____

   c) Nanoscience refers to particles between 1 and 100 nm. Add this information to your diagram.

2. Why do you think the World Health Organization publishes guidelines for maximum levels of particulate matter in the atmosphere?

   _____

   _____

3. Nanoparticles have different properties to their bulk material because they have a larger surface area to volume ratio than the bulk material. This diagram shows the surface area to volume ratio for different sized cubes.

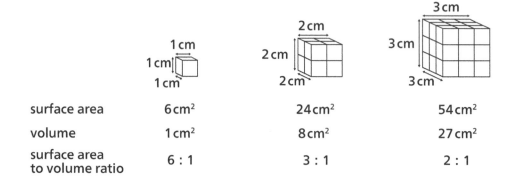

	1 cm cube	2 cm cube	3 cm cube
surface area	6 cm²	24 cm²	54 cm²
volume	1 cm²	8 cm²	27 cm²
surface area to volume ratio	6 : 1	3 : 1	2 : 1

   What happens to the surface area to volume ratio as the cube size gets smaller?

   _____

4. Complete the table below. Explain to your tutor whether or not your answers support the statement: 'As the sides of a cube decrease by a factor of 10, the surface area to volume ratio increases by a factor of 10.'

Length of side of cube (cm)	Surface area (cm²)	Volume (cm³)	Surface area to volume ratio
10			
1			

CHEMISTRY HIGHER

Main activity: Properties and uses of nanoparticles

Time **20** mins

Learning objectives

- To consider the advantages and disadvantages of using nanoparticles
- To know some examples of nanoparticle use

Equipment

1. **The diagram shows a carbon nanotube. Nanotubes are being used more and more in electronics applications.**

   a) Describe the bonding in the nanotube.

   _____

   _____

   b) Explain why carbon nanotubes can conduct electricity.

   _____

   c) Suggest an advantage of using carbon nanotubes in electronics.

   _____

2. **Other fullerenes, such as Buckminsterfullerene, could possibly be used to deliver medicines to the exact place in the body where they are needed.**

   a) What feature of Buckminsterfullerene would enable it to carry a medicine?

   _____

   b) Give an advantage of using fullerenes to deliver drugs.

   _____

   c) Give a possible disadvantage of using fullerenes in medicine.

   _____

3. **Titanium dioxide, TiO_2, has been used for many years in sunscreens. Titanium dioxide is a white unreactive solid, which reflects harmful UV light when used in sunscreen. The disadvantage is that it makes a thick white layer on the skin. Nanoparticles of titanium dioxide also reflect harmful UV light, but do not reflect visible light, so they cannot be seen.**

   a) What is the advantage of using nanoparticles of titanium dioxide in sunscreens?

   _____

   b) Give a possible disadvantage of using nanoparticles of titanium dioxide in sunscreens.

   _____

4. **Nanoparticles are now used in many cosmetics, such as face creams and make up. Some anti-wrinkle creams contain nanoparticles that can penetrate deep into the skin to improve the appearance of the skin. There have been few scientific investigations into the long term effects of using nanoparticles in cosmetics.**

   a) Why are cosmetic manufacturers using nanoparticles?

   _____

   b) What are the possible disadvantages of nanoparticles in cosmetics?

   _____

 **CHEMISTRY** HIGHER

Homework activity: Nanoparticles of silver

Time **60** mins

Learning objective

- To evaluate the use of silver nanoparticles in medicine, deodorants and socks

Equipment

Read this information:

Silver has always been used as a catalyst. A catalyst is a chemical which speeds up a reaction without being used up itself. Reactions happen on the surface of silver particles. Because nanoparticles have a higher surface area to volume ratio than larger particles, nanoparticles of silver are more efficient catalysts; you do not have to use so much.

Large particles of silver do not kill bacteria, but nanoparticles of silver act as a bactericide. Silver nanoparticles can be used in hospitals in wound dressings, surgical instruments, surgical masks, and in cleaning products. They can be added to deodorants to kill the bacteria on the skin that cause body odour. They are even added to yarns used to make socks. Many socks now contain silver nanoparticles to kill the bacteria that cause smelly feet.

All this may come at a cost. We do not know whether nanoparticles will cause damage when absorbed into the skin or inhaled. We also do not know how silver nanoparticles will affect the environment.

1. Write an evaluation of the use of silver nanoparticles. You should include the advantages and disadvantages. Think about the information above and work covered in previous activity sheets. Think about possible effects of nanoparticles on the environment. Remember, silver nanoparticles have only been used for a few years; this is new technology.

_____
_____
_____
_____
_____
_____
_____
_____
_____
_____
_____
_____
_____
_____
_____
_____
_____
_____
_____

12 Answers

Starter activity: The nano scale

1. a) $0.0000000001\,m$, $1 \times 10^{-10}\,m$
   b) $0.000000001\,m$, $1 \times 10^{-9}\,m$
2. a) $0.1\,nm$
   b) $1\,nm$

Main activity: Nanoscience

1. a) Diagram should show $PM_{2.5}$ and PM_{10} marked appropriately
   b) micrometres
   c) Nanoparticles marked between $1\,nm$ and $100\,nm$
2. High levels of particulate matter are damaging to health as they can cause breathing problems.
3. It increases; there is a larger surface area compared to the volume
4.

Length of side of cube (cm)	Surface area (cm²)	Volume (cm³)	Surface area to volume ratio
10	600	1000	6:10; 0.6:1
1	6	1	6:1

It supports the statement since the ratio has increased ten times.

Main activity: Properties and uses of nanoparticles

1. a) A rolled up sheet of graphene/cylindrical fullerene; carbon atoms bonded in hexagons; each carbon atom bonded covalently to three others
   b) Delocalised electrons can carry the charge.
   c) Electronic products using nanotubes can be very small, using less material.
2. a) It is hollow, so a drug can be carried in the 'cage'.
   b) They can target a specific part of the body.
   c) The fullerene remains in the body and may cause problems.
3. a) They do not form a visible white layer on the skin.
   b) They can be absorbed into the skin and may cause health problems.
4. a) To improve the performance of their products
   b) Unknown effects of nanoparticles absorbed into the skin

Homework activity: Nanoparticles of silver

1. Student's own answers. Relevant points include (the student may suggest others):
   Advantages:
   - providing a sterile environment in hospitals and homes
   - providing sterile equipment in hospitals
   - aiding personal hygiene (socks, deodorants)
   - saving money in industry where silver is used as a catalyst as less is required; increasing yield; increasing profit; less waste
   - potentially providing more and different catalysts

   Disadvantages:
   - can be inhaled deep into the lungs (alveoli) – long term effects unknown since silver nanoparticles have only been used for a few years
   - may be absorbed into the body – effects unknown
   - may be absorbed through the skin – effects unknown
   - silver nanoparticles can enter the water system when washed out of socks and other textiles – may interfere with food cycles by killing bacteria
   - may kill 'good' bacteria

13 Quantitative chemistry: Chemical equations and measurements

Learning objectives

- To know that symbol equations are balanced in terms of numbers of atoms of elements on each side
- To know that the sums of the relative formula masses of the reactants and products are equal
- To explain apparent mass gains or losses in reactions in open systems when a reactant or product is a gas
- To understand that all measurements have a degree of uncertainty
- To understand the use of multipliers and subscripts in symbol equations

Specification links

- 4.3.1.1, 4.3.1.2, 4.3.1.3, 4.3.1.4
- WS: 1.2, 3.1, 3.4, 3.5
- MS: 1a, 1c, 4a, 4c

Starter activity

- **Chemical equations; 5 minutes; page 90**

  Explain or recall that numbers of atoms of each element must balance in a symbol equation. Work through an example to recall the use of multipliers before formulae in an equation and the use of subscripts in formulae. The student can then answer the multiple-choice questions on the activity sheet. (The AQA exam papers contain some multiple-choice questions.) Ensure the student realises they cannot balance an equation by changing subscripts.

Main activities

- **Relative formula mass; 20 minutes; page 91**

  Remind the student that relative atomic mass is the average mass of all naturally occurring isotopes of an element, taking abundance into consideration. Show the student how to calculate relative formula mass and the relationship between the sum of the relative formula masses of reactants and products in a balanced equation.

- **Chemical measurements; 20 minutes; page 92**

  Explain that all chemical measurements have a degree of uncertainty. Tell the student how this is shown on apparatus, for example $\pm 0.5 \, \text{cm}^3$. Explain that experimental results also have uncertainty. Show the student how we can represent the distribution of a set of results.

Plenary activity

- **Understanding relative formula mass and chemical measurements; 5 minutes**

  Ask the student to think about relative formula mass and name one thing they definitely understand and one thing they need to know more about. Repeat the activity for chemical measurements and uncertainty. Note areas that need revisiting in future lessons.

Homework activity

- **Range and uncertainty; 45 minutes; page 93**

  The student is asked to explain how the range and distribution of a set of results can be used to estimate uncertainty.

Support ideas

- **Relative formula mass** The student can revisit lesson 4 to revise relative atomic mass.
- **Chemical measurements** The student may need to be reminded how to draw frequency tables and histograms.

Extension ideas

- **Relative formula mass** The student could predict how the mass will change in given reactions in non-enclosed systems involving a gaseous reactant or product.
- **Chemical measurements** The student can identify the origin of uncertainty in a given experiment.

Progress and observations

CHEMISTRY HIGHER

Starter activity: Chemical equations

Learning objectives

- To know the relationship between the mass of the reactants and the mass of the products in a chemical reaction
- To use multipliers in balanced equations and subscripts in formulae

Equipment

1. **If no atoms are gained or lost in a chemical reaction, which of these statements is/are true? Circle the correct answer(s).**

   A. The number of atoms of elements in the reactants equals the number of atoms of elements in the products.

   B. None of the reactants or products is a gas.

   C. The mass of the reactants equals the mass of the products.

   D. The chemical equation is not balanced.

2. **In the reaction $2Mg(s) + O_2(g) \rightarrow 2MgO$, 24 g of magnesium produced 40 g of magnesium oxide. How many grams of oxygen were used? Circle the correct answer.**

   A. 8 g

   B. 24 g

   C. 16 g

   D. 40 g

3. **How many atoms of hydrogen are in one molecule of $(NH_4)_2SO_4$? Circle the correct answer.**

   A. 4

   B. 8

   C. 6

   D. 10

4. **Which is the correct balanced equation for the reaction between ethane (C_2H_6) and oxygen to produce carbon dioxide and water? (All formulae and state symbols are correct.) Circle the correct answer.**

   A. $C_2H_6(g) + O_2(g) \rightarrow H_2O(l) + CO_2(g)$

   B. $C_2H_6(g) + 2O_2(g) \rightarrow 3H_2O(l) + 2CO_2(g)$

   C. $2C_2H_6(g) + 5O_2(g) \rightarrow 6H_2O(l) + 4CO_2(g)$

   D. $2C_2H_6(g) + 7O_2(g) \rightarrow 6H_2O(l) + 4CO_2(g)$

CHEMISTRY HIGHER

Main activity: Relative formula mass

Time 20 mins

Learning objectives

- To define and calculate relative formula mass
- To know the relationship between the sum of the relative formula masses of reactants and products in a balanced chemical equation
- To explain apparent mass losses in non-enclosed systems when a reactant or product is a gas

Equipment

- copy of the periodic table
- calculator

Relative formula mass is the sum of the relative atomic masses of all the atoms shown in a formula.

Here are the relative atomic masses for the elements in this activity:
H = 1; S = 32; O = 16; N = 14; Cl = 35.5; C = 12; Na = 23; Ca = 40

1. Calculate the relative formula mass of:

a) sulfuric acid, H_2SO_4 _____

b) ammonium chloride, NH_4Cl _____

c) ethanol, C_2H_5OH _____

d) glucose, $C_6H_{12}O_6$ _____

e) sodium nitrate, $Na(NO_3)_2$ _____

f) calcium hydrogencarbonate, $Ca(HCO_3)_2$ _____

2. Copper carbonate reacts with hydrochloric acid to produce copper chloride, carbon dioxide and water. The equation is: $CuCO_3(s) + 2HCl(aq) \rightarrow CuCl_2(aq) + CO_2(g) + H_2O(l)$

a) Calculate the sum of the relative formula masses of the reactants and of the products in the equation.

_____

b) What can you conclude from your calculation in a)?

_____

3. Jo used this apparatus to record the total mass of reactants and products during the reaction between magnesium and hydrochloric acid.

Time (s)	Mass (g)
0	90.52
20	90.47
40	90.45
60	90.44
80	90.41

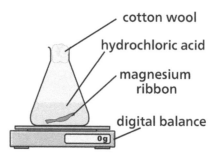

cotton wool

hydrochloric acid

magnesium ribbon

digital balance

0g

Explain the apparent loss in mass in these results.

_____

_____

CHEMISTRY HIGHER

Main activity: Chemical measurements

Learning objectives

- To understand that all measurements have an uncertainty
- To represent the distribution of results

Equipment

- graph paper
- spare paper
- pencil

1. This 100 cm³ measuring cylinder has an uncertainty of ±0.5 cm³. A student uses the measuring cylinder to measure 75 cm³ of liquid. What is the maximum true volume of liquid he could have measured? (The true value is the exact measurement.)

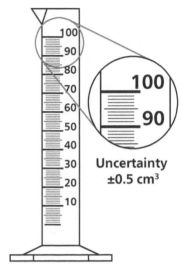

Uncertainty ±0.5 cm³

_____

2. State the maximum and minimum true values for these measurements.

   a) 20 °C ± 0.5 °C   _____

   b) 5.95 cm ± 0.05 cm _____

   c) 27.38 g ± 0.02 g   _____

3. Results from experiments also have uncertainty. Why do experimental results have a degree of uncertainty?

_____

_____

4. Students have all carried out the same experiment and timed how long it takes for a precipitate to form. These are the class results.

   Time (s): 25, 24, 22, 26, 27, 24, 23, 26, 24, 22, 24, 24, 21, 24, 25, 26, 21, 25, 23, 24, 23, 25, 25, 22, 24

   a) On a separate piece of paper, draw a frequency table to show the results.

   b) Use your table to calculate the mean time for the precipitate to form. Give your answer to the nearest second.

   _____

   c) Use your frequency table to draw a histogram of the class results on graph paper.

TUTORS GUILD **CHEMISTRY HIGHER**

AQA

Homework activity: Range and uncertainty

Time **45** mins

Learning objective

- To use the range of a set of measurements about the mean as a measure of uncertainty

Equipment

- graph paper

The range of a set of measurements is the difference between the highest and the lowest values. The closer the measurements are to the mean, the more precise the measurements.

1. **Groups of students in two classes timed how long a reaction took. Each class gathered the results from all the groups and plotted them in a histogram.**

These are class A's results.

These are class B's results.

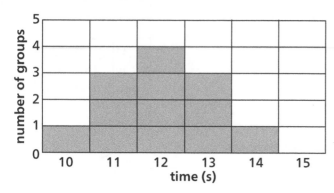

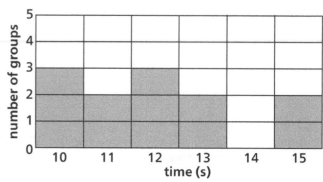

a) What is the range of class A's results? _____

b) What is the mean result for class A? _____

c) What is class B's mean result? _____

d) What is the range of class B's results? _____

e) Which class's results have the larger uncertainty? Explain why.

_____

_____

f) Which class's results are more precise? _____

2. **These are two sets of measurements from two students.**

Jo	2, 7, 13, 9, 14, 11, 5, 12, 16, 9, 10, 14, 8, 9, 16, 5, 12, 11, 12, 7
Sam	10, 11, 13, 12, 9, 11, 13, 9, 12, 10, 11, 11, 13, 9, 12, 10, 11, 12, 11, 10

a) On graph paper, represent these measurements in frequency tables and/or histograms.

b) What is the range of each set of results?

_____

c) Whose results have the larger uncertainty?

_____

13 Answers

Starter activity: Chemical equations

1. A and C
2. C
3. B
4. D

Main activity: Relative formula mass

1. a) 98
   b) 53.5
   c) 46
   d) 180
   e) 147
   f) 162
2. a) 196.5 for both reactants and products: reactants = $(63.5 + 12 + 48) + (2 \times (35.5 + 1))$; products = $(63.5 + 71) +$
   $(12 + 32) + (2 + 16)$
   b) They are equal; overall mass is conserved.
3. Hydrogen gas is a product. This is lost to the atmosphere, so is not included in the balance readings.

Main activity: Chemical measurements

1. 75.5 cm³
2. a) 19.5 °C; 20.5 °C
   b) 5.90 cm; 6.00 cm
   c) 27.36 g; 27.40 g
3. If results have been measured using equipment with a degree of uncertainty, the results will have a degree of uncertainty.
4. a)

Time (s)	21	22	23	24	25	26	27
Frequency	2	3	3	8	5	3	1

   b) $\dfrac{599}{25}$ = 23.96 = 24 s to the nearest second

   c)

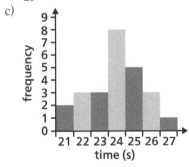

Homework activity: Range and uncertainty

1. a) 4
   b) 12
   c) 12
   d) 5
   e) Class B because the results have a greater spread about the mean
   f) Class A
2. a)

Measurements	2	3	4	5	6	7	8	9	10	11	12	13	14	15	16
Frequency: Jo	1			2		2	1	3	1	2	3	1	2		2
Frequency: Sam								3	4	6	4	3			

   b) Jo: 14, Sam: 4
   c) Jo's

AQA

CHEMISTRY HIGHER

14 Quantitative chemistry: Moles, equations and concentrations

Learning objectives

- To define moles and interpret chemical equations in terms of moles
- To calculate the number of moles in a given mass of substance
- To calculate masses of reactants and products from balanced symbol equations and the given mass of a reactant or product
- To explain the effect of a limiting mass of reactant on the amount of a product in moles or grams
- To know how concentrations are measured in g/dm^3
- To balance equations using moles, from given masses of reactants and products

Specification links

- 4.3.2.1, 4.3.2.2, 4.3.2.3, 4.3.2.4, 4.3.2.5
- WS: 4.1, 4.2, 4.3, 4.4, 4.5, 4.6
- MS: 1a, 1b, 1c, 3a, 3b, 3c

Starter activity

- **Measuring amounts; 5 minutes; page 96**

  Explain why we use moles to measure an amount of a substance, including the Avogadro constant. The calculations on the activity sheet should not take long, but will assess the student's understanding that a mole is an amount and can be applied to different types of particle (atoms, molecules and ions).

Main activities

- **Moles; 20 minutes; page 97**

  Explain that one mole of a substance is the relative formula mass in grams. Show the student how to use relative formula mass to calculate the mass of a mole, and vice versa. The student can then answer questions 1 and 2 on the activity sheet. Explain how to calculate masses of reactants and products from balanced equations and the given mass of a reactant or product. The student can then answer question 3. Remind the student to include units in their answer.

- **Using moles and equations; 20 minutes; page 98**

  Show the student how moles can be used to balance an equation. Explain the effects of a limiting reactant and explain how concentration is measured in g/dm^3.

Plenary activity

- **Mole facts; 5 minutes**

  Ask the student to draw a spider diagram with the word 'moles' at the centre, summarising what they have learned. This can be added to in subsequent lessons and used as a revision tool.

Homework activity

- **Manufacturing calcium chloride; 60 minutes; page 99**

  This activity covers all this lesson's topics and applies them to the manufacture of calcium chloride. You may wish to check the student is using the correct equation (question one), as the rest of the questions follow on from this.

Support ideas

- **Moles** Analogies such as bits and bytes in a computer and other parallel ways of coping with large numbers may help the student to understand the concept of a mole.
- **Using moles and equations** The student may need extra help with calculations, significant figures and use of a calculator.

Extension ideas

- **Using moles and equations** The student can find out how concentration is measured in mol/dm^3 and why industries often make one reactant limiting in chemical reactions.

Progress and observations

CHEMISTRY HIGHER

Starter activity: Measuring amounts

Learning objectives

- To understand the need for a suitable unit to measure an amount of a substance
- To use the Avogadro constant to calculate numbers of particles in moles and vice versa

Equipment

- calculator

Atoms and molecules are too small to count. We use moles to count a number of particles. The symbol for a mole is mol. We say that chemical amounts are measured in moles.

A mole contains 6.02×10^{23} particles. This number is called the Avogadro constant. The particles can be atoms, molecules, ions or electrons.

1. How many particles are in:

a) 1 mol hydrogen atoms, H?

_____

b) 1 mol hydrogen gas, H_2?

_____

c) 0.5 mol carbon atoms, C?

_____

d) 10 mol carbon dioxide, CO_2?

_____

e) 0.1 mol sodium ions, Na^+?

_____

2. How many moles are:

a) 6.02×10^{24} particles?

_____

b) 3.01×10^{23} hydrogen atoms?

_____

c) 3.01×10^{23} hydrogen molecules?

_____

d) 6.02×10^{23} sodium ions?

_____

e) 6.02×10^{22} hydrogen chloride molecules?

_____

CHEMISTRY HIGHER

Main activity: Moles

Time 20 mins

Learning objectives

- To use the relative formula mass of a substance to calculate the number of moles, and vice versa
- To calculate the masses of reactants or products from balanced symbol equations and the given mass of a reactant or product

Equipment

- copy of the periodic table
- calculator
- spare paper

The mass of one mole of a substance in grams is equal to its relative formula mass. For example:

- the relative atomic mass of carbon is 12. One mole of carbon atoms has a mass of 12 g.
- the relative formula mass of carbon dioxide (CO_2) is $12 + (2 \times 16) = 44$. One mole of carbon dioxide has a mass of 44 g.

Answer the following questions on a separate piece of paper.

1. **What is the mass (in g) of:**

   a) 0.1 mol carbon dioxide, CO_2?

   b) 0.5 mol copper sulfate, $CuSO_4$?

   c) 5 mol sodium hydroxide, NaOH?

   d) 0.01 mol ethanol, C_2H_5OH?

   e) 2 mol hydrogen gas, H_2?

2. **How many moles are in:**

   a) 290 g magnesium hydroxide, $Mg(OH)_2$?

   b) 5.6 g potassium hydroxide, KOH?

   c) 0.71 g chlorine gas, Cl_2?

   d) 9.2 g ethanol, C_2H_5OH?

   e) 9.8 g sulfuric acid, H_2SO_4?

3. **Moles also apply to chemical equations.**

   In the reaction $2Mg + O_2 \rightarrow 2MgO$ two moles of magnesium react with one mole of oxygen gas to give two moles of magnesium oxide.

   a) What mass of magnesium oxide can be made from 48 g magnesium?

   b) What mass of magnesium oxide can be made from 2.4 g magnesium?

4. **Methane burns in oxygen to give carbon dioxide and water. The equation is $CH_4 + 2O_2 \rightarrow CO_2 + 2H_2O$**

   a) What mass of carbon dioxide is produced when 0.8 g methane reacts with oxygen?

   b) What mass of oxygen is needed to react with 0.8 g methane?

5. **The equation for the reaction between sodium carbonate and hydrochloric acid is: $Na_2CO_3 + 2HCl \rightarrow 2NaCl + H_2O + CO_2$**

   a) What mass of sodium chloride can be made from 10.6 g sodium carbonate?

   b) What mass of hydrochloric acid is needed to react completely with 10.6 g sodium carbonate?

CHEMISTRY HIGHER

Main activity: Using moles and equations

Time 20 mins

Learning objectives

- To balance equations from given masses of reactants and products
- To understand the effect of a limiting reactant on the mass of a product
- To know that concentration can be measured in g/dm^3
- To calculate the mass of solute in a given volume of a solution

Equipment

- copy of the periodic table
- spare paper

Moles can be used to write balanced equations if you know the masses of reactants and products.

1. 6.0 g ethane (C_2H_6) reacts with 22.4 g oxygen gas to produce 17.6 g carbon dioxide and 10.8 g water. Use these masses of reactants and products to write a balanced equation for the reaction.

_____

2. Hydrazine (N_2H_4) is used as a rocket fuel. When it explodes, it produces ammonia (NH_3) and nitrogen gas (N_2). 4.8 g hydrazine explodes to produce 3.4 g ammonia and 1.4 g nitrogen. Use these masses to write a balanced equation for the reaction.

_____

3. In chemical industries, chemists often use an excess of one reactant to make sure another is used up. In the reaction $Mg + 2HCl \rightarrow MgCl_2 + H_2$ 1.6 g magnesium is added to 7.3 g hydrochloric acid.

a) Which reactant is the limiting reactant? _____

b) What is the maximum mass of magnesium chloride that can be made?

_____

4. In the reaction $MgO + H_2SO_4 \rightarrow MgSO_4 + H_2O$ 4.0 g magnesium oxide is added to 4.9 g sulfuric acid.

a) Which reactant is the limiting reactant? _____

b) What is the maximum mass of magnesium sulfate that can be made?

_____

5. Measuring 4.9 g sulfuric acid is not very convenient. We measure acids and other liquids by volume. The concentration of an acid can be measured in g/dm^3.

a) A solution has a concentration of $10 g/dm^3$. What mass of solute is in $100 cm^3$ of the solution?

_____

b) A solution has a concentration of $2.4 g/dm^3$. What mass of solute is in $10 cm^3$ of the solution?

_____

c) A solution of hydrochloric acid contains $3.65 g/dm^3$. What mass of hydrochloric acid is in $25 cm^3$ of the solution?

_____

CHEMISTRY HIGHER

Homework activity: Manufacturing calcium chloride

Learning objective

- To apply knowledge of moles in equations; reacting masses; limiting reactants; balancing equations from moles and concentration to the manufacture of calcium chloride

Equipment

- copy of the periodic table

Calcium chloride (E509) is a permitted food additive. Calcium chloride can be manufactured by reacting calcium carbonate with hydrochloric acid.

1. **Write a balanced symbol equation for the reaction.**

---

2. **From your equation, how many moles of hydrochloric acid are needed to react with one mole of calcium carbonate?**

---

3. **A manufacturer uses 100 kg of calcium carbonate to make calcium chloride.**

   a) How many kilograms of hydrochloric acid will they need to react with this?

   ---

   b) What is the maximum mass of calcium chloride they can make?

   ---

   c) The manufacturer does not want the calcium chloride contaminated with hydrochloric acid.

      i) Which reactant should they use in excess?

      ---

      ii) Which reactant should be the limiting reactant?

      ---

   d) The manufacturer decides to add 65 kg hydrochloric acid to 100 kg calcium carbonate. What is the maximum mass of calcium chloride they can produce? (Give your answer to three significant figures.)

   ---

   e) There is another method used to make calcium chloride. Calcium carbonate ($CaCO_3$) is reacted with sodium chloride (NaCl) to produce sodium carbonate (Na_2CO_3) and calcium chloride ($CaCl_2$). 10.0 g calcium carbonate reacts with 11.7 g sodium chloride to produce 10.6 g sodium carbonate and 11.1 g calcium chloride. Use moles to write a balanced equation for the reaction.

   ---

   f) Measuring 65 kg of hydrochloric acid is not easy. The concentration of the hydrochloric acid being used is 146 g/dm³. What volume of hydrochloric acid will the manufacturer need to use to provide 65 kg of acid? (Give your answer to three significant figures.)

14 Answers

Starter activity: Measuring amounts

1. a) 6.02×10^{23}
   b) 6.02×10^{23}
   c) 3.01×10^{23}
   d) 6.02×10^{24}
   e) 6.02×10^{22}
2. a) 10 mol
   b) 0.5 mol
   c) 0.5 mol
   d) 1 mol
   e) 0.1 mol

Main activity: Moles

1. a) 4.4 g
   b) 79.75 g
   c) 200 g
   d) 0.46 g
   e) 4 g
2. a) 5 mol
   b) 0.1 mol
   c) 0.01 mol
   d) 0.2 mol
   e) 0.1 mol
3. a) 80 g
   b) 4 g
4. a) 2.2 g
   b) 3.2 g
5. a) 11.7 g
   b) 7.3 g

Main activity: Using moles and equations

1. $2C_2H_6 + 7O_2 \rightarrow 4CO_2 + 6H_2O$
2. $3N_2H_4 \rightarrow 4NH_3 + N_2$
3. a) magnesium
   b) 6.3 g
4. a) sulfuric acid
   b) 6 g
5. a) 1 g
   b) 0.024 g
   c) 0.09125 g

Homework activity: Manufacturing calcium chloride

1. $CaCO_3 + 2HCl \rightarrow CaCl_2 + H_2O + CO_2$
2. 2 mol
3. a) 73 kg
   b) 111 kg
   c) i) calcium carbonate
      ii) hydrochloric acid
   d) 98.8 kg
   e) $CaCO_3 + 2NaCl \rightarrow Na_2CO_3 + CaCl_2$
   f) 445 dm^3

15 Quantitative chemistry: Percentage yield and atom economy

Learning objectives

- To explain why yields are rarely 100%
- To calculate percentage yield from the actual yield of a reaction
- To calculate the atom economy of a reaction to make a product
- To choose a reaction pathway from given data
- To calculate the theoretical mass of a product from the balanced equation and given mass of a reactant

Specification links

- 4.3.3.1, 4.3.3.2
- WS: 3.6, 4.2, 4.6
- MS: 1a, 1c, 3c

Starter activity

- **Experimental losses; 5 minutes; page 102**

  This activity asks the student to suggest where losses of reactants and products occur during an experiment. It could take the form of a discussion, including links to industrial processes and the need to make a profit.

Main activities

- **Percentage yield; 20 minutes; page 103**

  Explain that reversible reactions and side reactions also account for losses of product in some reactions. Explain the term yield and show the student how to calculate the percentage yield given the theoretical yield and the actual yield. You could use the example from the starter activity. Remind the student that theoretical yield can be calculated from the balanced equation.

- **Atom economy; 20 minutes; page 104**

  Explain that 'green' chemistry aims to reduce waste. Show the student how to calculate atom economy and explain what it means. Ensure they realise that 100% atom economy does not mean 100% yield and that they can explain why.

Plenary activity

- **Comparing yield and atom economy; 5 minutes**

  Ask the student to list one difference between percentage yield and atom economy (for example, percentage yield is dependent on reaction conditions, atom economy is not), and one similarity (such as that they are both calculated from balanced chemical equations).

Homework activity

- **Reaction pathways; 60 minutes; page 105**

  This activity requires students to use the skills they have acquired during the lesson to compare the atom economies of different reaction pathways to produce a desired product. Reversible reactions are included; you may wish to explain these before the student attempts the homework.

Support ideas

- **Percentage yield** The student can refer back to the previous lesson to refresh their skills. Explain the idea of an equilibrium being established, in which percentages of reactants and products do not change.

Extension ideas

- **Atom economy** The student could find out how green chemistry principles are affecting industry, or how manufacturers of ibuprofen have changed their methods to improve the atom economy.

Progress and observations

CHEMISTRY HIGHER

AQA

Starter activity: Experimental losses

Time **5** mins

Learning objective

- To identify where reactants and products could be lost during an experimental procedure

Equipment

Students are preparing a sample of copper sulfate from copper oxide and sulfuric acid.
This is their method.

Stage 1: Copper oxide is added to warm sulfuric acid until no more will dissolve.

warmed mixture
of excess
copper oxide
and sulfuric acid

stage 1

Stage 2: The mixture is filtered to remove the excess copper oxide. The filtrate is left to crystallise.

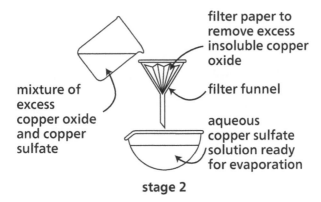

filter paper to
remove excess
insoluble copper
oxide

filter funnel

mixture of
excess
copper oxide
and copper
sulfate

aqueous
copper sulfate
solution ready
for evaporation

stage 2

The students calculate they should make 2.6 g copper sulfate. They actually make 1.4 g copper sulfate.
They conclude some of the reactants and/or products have been lost during the experiment.

1. Where in the experiment could they have lost some of the reactants and/or product?

_____

_____

_____

_____

_____

_____

_____

CHEMISTRY HIGHER

TUTORS GUILD

Main activity: Percentage yield

Learning objectives

- To explain why percentage yields are rarely 100%
- To calculate theoretical yield of a product from the balanced equation
- To calculate percentage yield of a product

Equipment

- copy of the periodic table
- calculator
- spare paper

The percentage yield of a reaction can be calculated using

$$\text{percentage yield} = \frac{\text{mass of product actually made}}{\text{maximum theoretical mass of product}} \times 100$$

1. What do these terms mean?

a) theoretical yield

_____

b) actual yield

_____

2. What do the following percentage yields mean?

a) 0% yield

_____

b) 100% yield

_____

3. Give three reasons why the actual yield is usually less than the theoretical yield.

_____

_____

_____

4. On a separate piece of paper, calculate the percentage yield of the following reactions.

a) The maximum theoretical mass of product is 45 g. The actual yield is 36 g.

b) Chemists calculate they can obtain a maximum of 5200 kg aluminium from a load of aluminium ore. They actually obtain 3900 kg.

c) Students are preparing aspirin. They calculate they should make 2.6 g aspirin. They actually make 1.1 g. Give your answer to two significant figures.

5. Students are preparing magnesium sulfate from copper oxide and sulfuric acid. They use 0.40 g magnesium oxide. The equation is: $MgO + H_2SO_4 \rightarrow MgSO_4 + H_2O$

Answer the questions below on a separate piece of paper.

a) Calculate the theoretical yield of magnesium sulfate.

b) They actually obtain 0.70 g magnesium sulfate. Calculate the percentage yield. Give your answer to two significant figures.

CHEMISTRY HIGHER

Main activity: Atom economy

Learning objectives

- To calculate the atom economy of a reaction to produce a desired product from a balanced equation
- To explain why particular reaction pathways are chosen

Equipment

- copy of the periodic table

A major aim of green chemistry is to reduce waste. This means using as much as possible of the products from reactions used in industry. Atom economy is a measure of the amount of starting material that ends up in useful products.

$$\text{atom economy (\%)} = \frac{\text{relative formula mass of desired product from equation}}{\text{sum of relative formula masses of all reactants from equation}} \times 100$$

1. **What does an atom economy of 100% mean?**

2. **If a reaction to produce a product has 100% atom economy, is the percentage yield 100%? Explain your answer.**

3. **What is the atom economy of the reaction to produce magnesium oxide from magnesium and oxygen?**
   $2Mg + O_2 \rightarrow 2MgO$ (Hint: You should be able to work this out without a calculation.)

4. **Iron is extracted from iron ore by reduction with carbon monoxide.**
   The equation is: $Fe_2O_3 + 3CO \rightarrow 2Fe + 3CO_2$
   Calculate the atom economy of the reaction to produce iron.

5. **Calcium oxide is made by heating calcium carbonate (limestone). The equation is: $CaCO_3 \rightarrow CaO + CO_2$**

   a) Calculate the atom economy of the reaction to produce calcium oxide.

   b) If the carbon dioxide produced is used in industry, what is the new atom economy?

6. **Lithium hydroxide reacts with nitric acid to produce lithium nitrate and water. The equation is:**
   $LiOH + HNO_3 \rightarrow LiNO_3 + H_2O$

   What is the atom economy of the reaction to produce lithium nitrate?

CHEMISTRY HIGHER

AQA

Homework activity: Reaction pathways

Time 60 mins

Learning objectives

- To use atom economy to select a reaction pathway to produce a product
- To use atom economy, rate, yield, equilibrium position and usefulness of by-products to select a reaction pathway

Equipment

- copy of the periodic table

1. **Two methods can be used to produce calcium chloride: calcium carbonate can be reacted with hydrochloric acid, or with sodium chloride.**

   The equations are:

   Method A: $CaCO_3 + 2HCl \rightarrow CaCl_2 + CO_2 + H_2O$ **Method B:** $CaCO_3 + 2NaCl \rightarrow CaCl_2 + Na_2CO_3$

   a) Calculate the theoretical yield of calcium chloride from 1000 g calcium carbonate for each method.

   _____

   b) Calculate the atom economy to produce calcium chloride for each method.

   _____

   c) The sodium carbonate produced in method B is used to make glass. What is the new atom economy for method B?

   _____

   d) Which method of producing calcium chloride is the greener method?

   _____

2. **Several methods are used to produce hydrogen gas in industry. These are the equations for two methods.**

   Method A: $C + 2H_2O \rightarrow CO_2 + 2H_2$ **Method B:** $CH_4 + H_2O \rightarrow 3H_2 + CO$

   a) Calculate the atom economy for each method to produce hydrogen gas.

   _____

   b) Which method is the greener method?

   _____

3. **Ammonia (NH_3) is manufactured in the Haber process. The equation is: $N_2 + 3H_2 \rightleftharpoons 2NH_3$**
   The reaction is reversible (it goes both ways) and is slow.

   a) What is the atom economy for the reaction?   _____

   b) Why will the percentage yield always be less than 100%?

   _____

   _____

   c) Manufacturers recycle the unreacted hydrogen and nitrogen many times. What effect does this have on the percentage yield?

   _____

15 Answers

Starter activity: Experimental losses

1. Not all of the reactants reacted; product is left in the beaker; product is left in the filter paper and in the filter funnel; product is left in the evaporating dish when removed for weighing

Main activity: Percentage yield

1. a) The maximum possible yield of product, calculated from reacting masses and the balanced equation
   b) The mass of product obtained from an experiment
2. a) The reaction has not worked at all.
   b) All the reactants have reacted to produce the required product with no loss.
3. Reactants and products lost during the process; a reversible reaction; side reactions
4. a) 80%
   b) 75%
   c) 42%
5. a) 1.20 g
   b) 58%

Main activity: Atom economy

1. All of the reactants end up in the product.
2. No, because the reaction may be reversible or product may be lost
3. 100%
4. 45.9%
5. a) 56%
   b) 100%
6. 79.1%

Homework activity: Reaction pathways

1. a) 1110 g for both methods
   b) Method A: 64%; method B: 51%
   c) 100%
   d) If the sodium carbonate is used, method B is greener; if not, method A.
2. a) Method A: 8.3%; method B: 17.6%
   b) Method B
3. a) 100%
   b) The reaction is reversible, so ammonia is also reacting to produce hydrogen and nitrogen.
   c) It will increase.

16 Quantitative chemistry: Concentrations and gas volume

Learning objectives	Specification links

Learning objectives

- To explain how concentration in mol/dm³ is related to mass of solute and volume of solution
- To use titration results to calculate the concentration of a solution
- To know the volume occupied by one mole of gas at room temperature and pressure
- To carry out gas volume calculations

Specification links

- 4.3.4, 4.3.5
- WS: 1.2, 2.2, 3.5, 4.1, 4.2, 4.3, 4.5, 4.6
- MS: 1a, 1c, 3b, 3c

Starter activity

- **A titration; 5 minutes; page 108**

  The student may have carried out a titration at school. The procedure is required practical activity 2 and is also covered in lesson 19. Use the activity sheet to discuss the procedure, remind the student of the terminology, and set the context for the calculations. This can be answered verbally.

Main activities

- **Using concentration; 20 minutes; page 109**

  Explain that concentration can be measured in mol/dm³ as well as g/dm³. Show the student how to calculate the amount in moles and mass in grams of solute in a given volume of solution (concentration in mol/dm³). Explain how titration results can be used to determine an unknown concentration. Check that the student does not include the rough titration in the mean titre calculation. Note that titration is revisited in lesson 19.

- **Gas volume; 20 minutes; page 110**

  Explain that it is much easier to measure the volume of a gas than its mass. Tell the student that one mole of gas occupies 24 dm³ at room temperature and pressure and show them how to use gas volumes in calculations involving balanced equations and the mass and relative formula mass of the gas.

Plenary activity

- **Mole facts; 5 minutes**

  The student started a spider diagram in lesson 14 with moles at the centre of the page. They can now add links to gas volume and concentration. The student may find this useful as a revision sheet.

Homework activity

- **Another titration; 45 minutes; page 111**

  This activity requires the student to calculate the concentration of an acid from a set of titration results.

Support ideas

- **Using concentrations** Students who have not yet completed a titration at school will need extra explanation here.
- **Gas volume** To gauge the size of 24 dm³, the student can visualise 24 dm³ of orange juice cartons, or similar.

Extension ideas

- **Using concentrations** Ask the student how a calculation to determine an unknown concentration from a titration of sulfuric acid and sodium hydroxide solution would be different. If a hint is required, focus the student on the balanced equation.
- **Gas volume** Ask the student to predict what will happen to the volume of one mole of gas under different conditions of temperature and pressure. They can do some research to check their answer.

Progress and observations

CHEMISTRY HIGHER

Starter activity: A titration

Time 5 mins

Learning objectives

- To know the terminology used to describe a titration
- To know how a titration is carried out

Equipment

A titration can be used to determine the concentration of an acid or alkali, given the concentration of one of them. A known volume of alkali is reacted with the acid until the solution is neutral. The volume of acid used is measured and the unknown concentration calculated.

1. **This apparatus is used to measure 25 cm³ alkali. Explain how the apparatus is used.**

   _____

   _____

   _____

   _____

   _____

   _____

   _____

   — pipette filler

   — pipette

   — conical flask

2. **This apparatus is used to add the acid until the end point is reached. Explain how this apparatus is used to determine the volume of acid that reacts exactly with 25 cm³ alkali.**

   _____

   _____

   _____

   _____

   _____

   _____

   _____

3. **Name three safety precautions you should take when carrying out a titration.**

   _____

   _____

   _____

CHEMISTRY HIGHER

AQA

Main activity: Using concentrations

Time **20** mins

Learning objectives

- To know that concentrations can be measured in mol/dm³
- To calculate the amount in moles or mass in grams of solute in a given volume of solution (concentration in mol/dm³ or g/dm³)

Equipment

- copy of the periodic table

Concentrations can be measured in g/dm³ or mol/dm³. A solution with a concentration of 0.1 mol/dm³ contains 0.1 mol solute dissolved in 1 dm³ solution.

1. How many moles of solute are in:

a) 100 cm³ of solution with a concentration of 0.5 mol/dm³ _____

b) 25 cm³ of solution with a concentration of 1.0 mol/dm³ _____

c) 50 cm³ of a 0.1 mol/dm³ solution? _____

2. How many grams of solute are in:

a) 25 cm³ of 0.1 mol/dm³ sodium hydroxide solution (NaOH) _____

b) 100 cm³ of 2.0 mol/dm³ sulfuric acid (H_2SO_4) _____

c) 10 cm³ of 0.5 mol/dm³ nitric acid (HNO_3)? _____

3. Students have carried out a titration to find the concentration of a solution of sodium hydroxide. They used 25 cm³ sodium hydroxide solution and titrated it against 0.110 mol/dm³ hydrochloric acid. These are their burette readings.

	Titration			
	Rough	1	2	3
Final burette reading (cm³)	29.0	48.5	21.5	41.5
Initial burette reading (cm³)	7.0	29.0	2.5	21.5
Volume of acid used (cm³) (titre)	22.0	19.5	19.0	20.0

a) What is the mean titre of hydrochloric acid?

_____

b) How many moles of hydrochloric acid were used to neutralise the sodium hydroxide?

_____

c) The equation for the reaction is: NaOH + HCl → NaCl + H_2O
How many moles of sodium hydroxide did the acid react with?

_____

d) What is the concentration of the sodium hydroxide solution in mol/dm³?
Give your answer to three significant figures.

_____

CHEMISTRY HIGHER

Main activity: Gas volume

Time **20** mins

Learning objectives

- To calculate the volume of a gas from its mass and relative formula mass
- To calculate the volume of a gas from a balanced equation and a given volume of a gaseous reactant or product

Equipment

- copy of the periodic table

One mole of any gas occupies $24 \, dm^3$ at room temperature and pressure.

1. **What is the volume of these gases?**

   a) 0.5 mol carbon dioxide, CO_2 _____

   b) 0.1 mol oxygen gas, O_2 _____

   c) 4.4 g carbon dioxide, CO_2 _____

   d) 0.32 g oxygen, O_2 _____

   e) 0.8 g methane, CH_4 _____

In questions 2 to 5, volumes of gases are at room temperature and pressure.

2. **Calcium carbonate produces calcium oxide and carbon dioxide when heated.**

   The equation is: $CaCO_3(s) \rightarrow CaO(s) + CO_2(g)$

   What volume of carbon dioxide is produced when 10 g calcium carbonate are heated?

   _____

3. **Consider this reaction: $CH_4(g) + H_2O(g) \rightarrow 3H_2(g) + CO(g)$**

   What volume of hydrogen gas is produced when $24 \, dm^3$ methane are completely reacted?

   _____

4. **Sulfur dioxide reacts with oxygen to make sulfur trioxide. The equation is: $2SO_2(g) + O_2(g) \rightarrow 2SO_3(g)$**

   a) What volume of oxygen gas is needed to react with $24 \, dm^3$ sulfur dioxide? _____

   b) What volume of sulfur trioxide is produced? _____

5. **Hydrazine is a flammable liquid used in rocket propellants. When it explodes, the reaction is:**

   $3N_2H_4(l) \rightarrow 4NH_3(g) + N_2(g)$

   a) What volume of ammonia (NH_3) is produced when 32 g hydrazine explodes? _____

   b) What volume of nitrogen is produced when 32 g hydrazine explodes? _____

CHEMISTRY HIGHER

Homework activity: Another titration

Learning objectives	Equipment

- To calculate a mean titre from titration results
- To calculate an unknown concentration from an acid–base titration

- calculator

Mo and Olly have carried out a titration to determine the concentration of a solution of nitric acid. They have titrated the nitric acid against 25 cm³ portions of 0.150 mol/dm³ potassium hydroxide solution.

These are their burette readings.

	Titration			
	Rough	**1**	**2**	**3**
Final burette reading (cm³)	18.5	33.4	18.4	37.3
Initial burette reading (cm³)	3.3	18.5	3.4	22.2
Volume of acid used (cm³) (titre)	15.2	14.9	15.0	15.1

1. What is the mean titre of nitric acid?

_____

2. How many moles of potassium hydroxide are in 25 cm³ of a 0.150 mol/dm³ solution?

_____

3. How many moles of nitric acid did this react with?
   (Hint: You will have to write a balanced equation for the reaction first.)

_____

_____

4. What is the concentration of the nitric acid in mol/dm³?

_____

5. What is the concentration of the nitric acid in g/dm³?

_____

16 Answers

Starter activity: A titration

1. The pipette filler is used to draw alkali into the pipette until the level is just above the mark. Alkali is allowed to run out until the bottom of the meniscus is level with the mark. The remaining alkali in the pipette is then run into the flask.
2. The burette is rinsed with acid, then filled with acid using a small funnel. The funnel is removed and some acid is allowed to run out until the acid level is on the scale. The scale is read. Indicator is added to the alkali in the flask. Acid is added, 1 cm³ at a time initially, then drop by drop as the end point is reached. The final volume of acid in the burette is read and the volume needed to neutralise the alkali is calculated.
3. Any three sensible suggestions, such as: place the burette on the floor to fill it; wear safety glasses; mop up spillages immediately

Main activity: Using concentrations

1. a) 0.05 mol
   b) 0.025 mol
   c) 0.005 mol
2. a) 0.1 g
   b) 19.6 g
   c) 0.315 g
3. a) 19.5 cm³
   b) 2.145×10^{-3} mol
   c) 2.145×10^{-3} mol
   d) 0.086 mol/dm³

Main activity: Gas volume

1. a) 12 dm³
   b) 2.4 dm³
   c) 2.4 dm³
   d) 0.24 dm³
   e) 1.2 dm³
2. 2.4 dm³
3. 72 dm³
4. a) 12 dm³
   b) 24 dm³
5. a) 32 dm³
   b) 8 dm³

Homework activity: Another titration

1. 15.0 cm³
2. 3.75×10^{-3} mol
3. 3.75×10^{-3} mol
4. 0.25 mol/dm³
5. 15.75 g/dm³

17 Chemical changes: Metals, oxidation and reduction

Learning objectives

- To explain oxidation and reduction as gain or loss of oxygen
- To use reactions of metals with water and dilute acids to place metals in order of reactivity
- To link the reactivity of metals with the tendency to form positive ions
- To know that metals less reactive than carbon can be extracted from their oxides by reduction with carbon
- To explain oxidation and reduction in terms of electron loss and gain

Specification links

- 4.4.1.1, 4.4.1.2, 4.4.1.3, 4.4.1.4
- WS: 3.5, 4.1

Starter activity

- **Metal oxides; 5 minutes; page 114**

  Ask the student to write a general word equation for the reactions of metals with oxygen. Establish that metal oxides are formed and that these are oxidation reactions, as oxygen is gained. Tell the student that reduction is loss of oxygen.

Main activities

- **The reactivity series; 20 minutes; page 115**

  Establish that positive ions are formed when metals react with oxygen and that more reactive metals have a greater tendency to form positive ions. Explain reactions of metals (K, Na, Li, Ca, Mg, Zn, Fe and Cu) with water and dilute acids. The student can use this information to complete columns 2 and 3 in the activity. Note that only reactions at room temperature are required. Explain why carbon and hydrogen have been included in the table. The student can then complete 4.

- **Oxidation and reduction; 20 minutes; page 116**

  Explain that electrons are lost in oxidation reactions and gained during reduction. You can illustrate this by referring to dot-and-cross diagrams if needed. Show the student how to write ionic equations and half equations. Encourage the student to check that the equations balance, in terms of the number of charges and the numbers and types of atom on either side. Identify the oxidation and reduction reactions.

Plenary activity

- **Ionic and half equations; 5 minutes**

  Ask the student to list some rules for writing ionic and/or half equations.

Homework activity

- **Using experimental results; 60 minutes; page 117**

  This activity requires the student to place metals in order of reactivity from displacement reactions. They need to be able to write ionic and half equations.

Support ideas

- **The reactivity series** The student can revisit lesson 8 to recall that positive ions are formed when metals react.
- **Oxidation and reduction** This activity may need more explanation. There will be plenty of other opportunities to practise ionic and half equations in this course.

Extension ideas

- **The reactivity series** The student could predict where other metals such as gold, silver and caesium should be placed in the reactivity series.
- **Oxidation and reduction** The student can write half equations for reactions between metals and oxygen.

Progress and observations

CHEMISTRY HIGHER

Starter activity: Metal oxides

Time 5 mins

Learning objectives

- To know that metals react with oxygen to form metal oxides
- To know that gaining oxygen is oxidation and losing oxygen is reduction

Equipment

- copy of the periodic table

Metals react with oxygen to produce metal oxides. Gaining oxygen is oxidation. Losing oxygen is reduction.

1. Write balanced symbol equations for these reactions.

a) Sodium reacts with oxygen to form sodium oxide.

_____

b) Calcium reacts with oxygen to form calcium oxide.

_____

c) Aluminium reacts with oxygen to form aluminium oxide.

_____

2. Look at the following equations. Are the metals oxidised or reduced? Write 'oxidised' or 'reduced' next to each equation.

a) $2Mg + O_2 \rightarrow 2MgO$

_____

b) $Fe_2O_3 + 3CO \rightarrow 2Fe + 3CO_2$

_____

c) $2Al_2O_3 \rightarrow 4Al + 3O_2$

_____

d) $2Sr + O_2 \rightarrow 2SrO$

_____

e) $2CuO + C \rightarrow 2Cu + CO_2$

_____

TUTORS GUILD CHEMISTRY HIGHER

Main activity: The reactivity series

Learning objectives

- To relate the reactivity of a metal to its tendency to form positive ions
- To place metals in order of reactivity from their reactions with water and dilute acids
- To know that metals less reactive than carbon can be extracted by reduction with carbon

Equipment

- copy of the periodic table (optional)

1. **Complete the table by briefly describing reactions and products with water and dilute acids and by naming methods used to extract the metals. Then add a labelled arrow showing the tendency to form positive ions.**

Metal	Tendency to form positive ions	Reaction with water	Reaction with dilute acids	Method of extraction
potassium				
sodium				
lithium				
calcium				
magnesium				
carbon				
zinc				
iron				
hydrogen				
copper				

CHEMISTRY HIGHER

Main activity: Oxidation and reduction

Time **20** mins

Learning objectives

- To know that a more reactive metal displaces a less reactive metal from its compound
- To know that oxidation is electron loss and reduction is electron gain
- To write ionic equations
- To write half equations, identifying which species are oxidised and which are reduced

Equipment

- copy of the periodic table

1. **O I L R I G stands for Oxidation Is Loss, Reduction Is Gain, and refers to electrons.**

   a) In the equation: $Mg(s) + Cl_2(g) \rightarrow MgCl_2(s)$ what is losing electrons and what is gaining electrons? (Hint: Think about dot-and-cross diagrams.)

   _____

   b) What is oxidised and what is reduced?

   _____

2. **The diagram shows a strip of zinc placed in copper sulfate solution. The solution turns paler as copper is formed.**

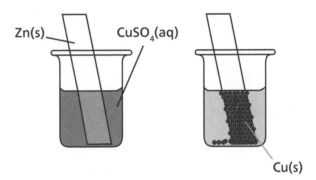

Zn(s)   CuSO$_4$(aq)

Cu(s)

   a) Write a balanced symbol equation for the reaction.

   _____

   b) Write an ionic equation for the reaction.

   _____

   c) Which metal has been oxidised and which metal has been reduced?

   _____

   d) Write half equations to show:

   i) the oxidation reaction   _____

   ii) the reduction reaction   _____

Homework activity: Using experimental results

Time 60 mins

Learning objectives

- To deduce an order of reactivity based on experimental results
- To know that a more reactive metal can displace a less reactive metal from a compound
- To write ionic equations
- To write half equations and identify species oxidised and reduced

Equipment

- copy of the periodic table

Malik investigated displacement reactions of metals. He added strips of metals to metal salt solutions on a spotting tile, as shown in the diagram. His results are shown in the table below. A tick shows there was a reaction, a cross shows there was no reaction.

Solution	Zinc	Magnesium	Copper	Lead
Zinc nitrate	✗	✓	✗	✗
Magnesium nitrate	✗	✗	✗	✗
Copper nitrate	✓	✓	✗	✓
Lead nitrate	✓	✓	✗	✗

spotting tile
zinc nitrate solution
magnesium nitrate solution
copper nitrate solution
lead nitrate solution

zinc magnesium copper lead

1. List the metals in order of reactivity from the most reactive to the least reactive.

_____

2. Which of the metals in the table has the greatest tendency to form positive ions? _____

3. Write a balanced symbol equation for the reaction between magnesium and copper nitrate.

_____

4. This is the ionic equation for the reaction between magnesium and copper nitrate: $Mg + Cu^{2+} \rightarrow Mg^{2+} + Cu$
Write ionic equations for the reactions between:

a) zinc and lead nitrate

_____

b) magnesium and zinc nitrate

_____

5. Write half equations for the reactions between:

a) zinc and lead nitrate

_____

b) magnesium and zinc nitrate

_____

c) Which species are oxidised and which are reduced in the reactions in parts a) and b)?

_____

_____

17 Answers

Starter activity: Metal oxides

1. a) $4Na + O_2 \rightarrow 2Na_2O$
b) $2Ca + O_2 \rightarrow 2CaO$
c) $4Al + 3O_2 \rightarrow 2Al_2O_3$
2. a), d) oxidised
b), c), e) reduced

Main activity: The reactivity series

1.

Metal	Tendency to form positive ions	Reactions with water	Reactions with dilute acids	Method of extraction
potassium	increases	violent	violent	electrolysis
sodium		vigorous	violent	electrolysis
lithium		fast	vigorous	electrolysis
calcium		fast	vigorous	electrolysis
magnesium		slow	fast	electrolysis
carbon				
zinc		no reaction	moderate	reduction with C
iron		rusts when oxygen also present	moderate	reduction with C
hydrogen				
copper		no reaction	very slow	reduction with C or H

Main activity: Oxidation and reduction

1. a) Magnesium loses electrons, chlorine gains electrons
b) Magnesium is oxidised, chlorine is reduced
2. a) $Zn(s) + CuSO_4(aq) \rightarrow ZnSO_4(aq) + Cu(s)$
b) $Zn(s) + Cu^{2+}(aq) \rightarrow Zn^{2+}(aq) + Cu(s)$
c) Zinc is oxidised, copper is reduced
d) i) $Zn \rightarrow Zn^{2+} + 2e^-$
ii) $Cu^{2+} + 2e^- \rightarrow Cu$

Homework activity: Using experimental results

1. magnesium, zinc, lead, copper
2. magnesium
3. $Mg(s) + Cu(NO_3)_2(aq) \rightarrow Mg(NO_3)_2(aq) + Cu(s)$
4. a) $Zn + Pb^{2+} \rightarrow Zn^{2+} + Pb$
b) $Mg + Zn^{2+} \rightarrow Mg^{2+} + Zn$
5. a) $Zn \rightarrow Zn^{2+} + 2e^-$; $Pb^{2+} + 2e^- \rightarrow Pb$
b) $Mg \rightarrow Mg^{2+} + 2e^-$; $Zn^{2+} + 2e^- \rightarrow Zn$
c) Zinc is oxidised, lead is reduced
Magnesium is oxidised, zinc is reduced

18 Chemical changes: Acids and salts

Learning objectives

- To know that acids react with some metals to produce salts and hydrogen
- To identify acid–metal reactions as redox reactions
- To know the neutralisation reactions of acids
- To predict products from neutralisation reactions
- To describe how to make pure dry samples of soluble salts

Specification links

- 4.4.2.1, 4.4.2.2, 4.4.2.3
- WS: 2.2, 2.3, 4.1

Starter activity

- **Name the salt; 5 minutes; page 120**

  The student should have learned about some reactions that produce salts at Key Stage 3. This activity sheet builds on those ideas and requires the student to name salts. Check that the student realises the difference in meaning between 'salt' in everyday use and 'salt' in chemistry.

Main activities

- **Metals and acids; 20 minutes; page 121**

  Describe the reactions between metals and acids and explain why these are redox reactions. Encourage the student to describe oxidation and reduction in terms of electron loss and gain.

- **Neutralisation and salts; 20 minutes; page 122**

  Show the student how to use formulae of ions to write salt formulae. You may find it useful to refer back to lesson 1. Explain that acids are neutralised by alkalis, bases and metal carbonates and discuss the products of each type of reaction.

Plenary activity

- **Main facts; 5 minutes**

  Ask the student to state three facts about acids and three facts about salts from this lesson.

Homework activity

- **Preparing a soluble salt; 60 minutes; page 123**

  In these practice exam questions, the student must describe the preparation of a soluble salt from an insoluble substance and an acid. This is required practical 1, so it is likely that the student will have carried out the procedure at school. Remind them that in order to obtain six marks, they must make as many points as possible, use scientific language and be logical.

Support ideas

- **Metals and acids** Redox reactions may need more explanation. It may be helpful to go back to the basics of dot-and-cross diagrams.
- **Neutralisation and salts** Ammonium ions may need explanation. Ammonium salts are covered later in the course.

Extension ideas

- **Metals and acids** Ask the student to write an ionic equation for the reaction between hydrogen ions and hydroxide ions in acid–alkali reactions.
- **Neutralisation and salts** Ask the student to suggest why insoluble salts are not made from reactions between acids and metals, metal oxides, metal hydroxides or metal carbonates.

Progress and observations

CHEMISTRY HIGHER

Starter activity: Name the salt

Learning objective	Equipment
• To identify the type of product when acids react with metals	none

A salt is made when the hydrogen in an acid is replaced by a metal.

A salt has two parts to its name, for example: sodium chloride, NaCl.

The negative ion comes from an acid. The positive ion comes from a metal, a metal oxide, a metal hydroxide or a metal carbonate.

1. **Complete the table to name the salts which are made when each metal reacts with each acid.**

	Hydrochloric acid	Sulfuric acid	Nitric acid
Magnesium			
Copper oxide			
Sodium hydroxide			
Calcium carbonate			

CHEMISTRY HIGHER

Main activity: Metals and acids

Time **20** mins

Learning objectives

- Identify the type of product formed when acids react with metals
- Explain why acid–metal reactions are redox reactions

Equipment

1. Samples of magnesium, zinc and iron are added to dilute hydrochloric acid.

They all give off hydrogen gas.

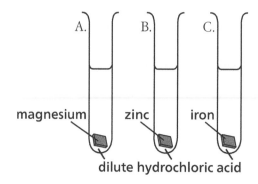

magnesium zinc iron

dilute hydrochloric acid

a) Name the products formed in each test tube.

_____

b) What is oxidised in each test tube? Give a reason for your answer.

_____

c) Oxidation can also be described as loss of electrons. If one substance loses electrons, another substance must gain electrons. Electron gain is reduction. What is reduced in each test tube?

_____

d) These are called redox reactions. Write a definition for the term redox reaction.

_____

2. The experiment is repeated using dilute sulfuric acid instead of dilute hydrochloric acid.

a) What are the new products?

_____

b) Are these redox reactions? Explain your answer.

_____

3. Magnesium oxide reacts with hydrochloric acid to produce magnesium chloride and water. This is not a redox reaction. Explain why.

_____

_____

_____

Main activity: Neutralisation and salts

Time **20** mins

Learning objectives

- To know that acids are neutralised by alkalis and bases to produce a salt and water
- To know that acids are neutralised by metal carbonates to produce a salt, water and carbon dioxide
- To predict products from given reactions
- To use formulae of common ions to write the formulae of salts

Equipment

- copy of the periodic table

1. The table contains the formulae of some common ions.

Ion	Formula	Ion	Formula
hydroxide	OH^-	oxide	O^{2-}
nitrate	NO_3^-	sulfate	SO_4^{2-}
hydrogencarbonate	HCO_3^-	carbonate	CO_3^{2-}
ammonium	NH_4^+		

Write the formulae of:

a) sodium carbonate _____

b) strontium carbonate _____

c) calcium nitrate _____

d) aluminium hydroxide _____

e) magnesium nitrate _____

f) sodium hydrogencarbonate _____

g) ammonium carbonate _____

h) potassium oxide _____

2. Complete these general equations:

a) acid + metal oxide → _____

b) acid + alkali → _____

c) acid + carbonate → _____

3. Complete and balance these equations:

a) __ $HCl(aq)$ + __ $KOH(aq)$ → _____

b) __ $H_2SO_4(aq)$ + __ $MgO(s)$ → _____

c) __ $HNO_3(aq)$ + __ $CuCO_3(s)$ → _____

d) __ $H_2SO_4(aq)$ + __ $NaOH(aq)$ → _____

e) __ $HCl(aq)$ + __ $CuO(s)$ → _____

CHEMISTRY HIGHER

Homework activity: Preparing a soluble salt

Time 60 mins

Learning objectives

- To know that soluble salts can be made by reacting insoluble substances with acids
- To describe how a pure dry sample of a soluble salt is made from an insoluble metal oxide and an acid

Equipment

- copy of the periodic table

Your GCSE exam will include some six mark questions. You will be required to write a paragraph. Your answer must include as many points as possible, use scientific language and be logical. Have a go at this practice question.

1. **You are provided with this apparatus.**

   - **Bunsen burner, tripod, gauze, heatproof mat**
   - **250 cm³ beaker and stirring rod**
   - **filter funnel and filter paper**
   - **evaporating dish**
   - **water bath**

   You have copper oxide powder and dilute sulfuric acid. Describe how you would use this apparatus to prepare a pure, dry sample of copper sulfate crystals.

   [6 marks]

   _____

   _____

   _____

   _____

   _____

   _____

   _____

   _____

2. **Your GCSE exam will also include some questions that need shorter answers, such as the ones below.**

   a) Write a balanced symbol equation for the reaction between copper oxide and sulfuric acid.

   [1 mark]

   _____

   b) Explain why this is a neutralisation reaction and not a redox reaction.

   [2 marks]

   _____

   _____

CHEMISTRY HIGHER

AQA

18 Answers

Starter activity: Name the salt

1.

	Hydrochloric acid	Sulfuric acid	Nitric acid
Magnesium	Magnesium chloride	Magnesium sulfate	Magnesium nitrate
Copper oxide	Copper chloride	Copper sulfate	Copper nitrate
Sodium hydroxide	Sodium chloride	Sodium sulfate	Sodium nitrate
Calcium carbonate	Calcium chloride	Calcium sulfate	Calcium nitrate

Main activity: Metals and acids

1. a) A: magnesium chloride and hydrogen; B: zinc chloride and hydrogen; C: iron chloride and hydrogen
   b) The metals (metal atoms are oxidised as they lose electrons to form metal ions)
   c) The hydrogen ions in hydrochloric acid are reduced to form hydrogen gas.
   d) A reaction in which one substance is oxidised and another is reduced
2. a) A: magnesium sulfate; B: zinc sulfate; C: iron sulfate
   b) Yes; metals lose electrons to form positive ions (oxidation), while hydrogen ions in acid gain electrons (reduction)
3. There are Mg^{2+} ions in magnesium oxide and in magnesium chloride: the charge on the ions does not change from the reactant to the products

Main activity: Neutralisation and salts

1. a) Na_2CO_3
   b) $SrCO_3$
   c) $Ca(NO_3)_2$
   d) $Al(OH)_3$
   e) $Mg(NO_3)_2$
   f) $NaHCO_3$
   g) $(NH_4)_2CO_3$
   h) K_2O
2. a) acid + metal oxide → salt + water
   b) acid + alkali → salt + water
   c) acid + carbonate → salt + water + carbon dioxide
3. a) $HCl(aq) + KOH(aq) \rightarrow KCl(aq) + H_2O(l)$
   b) $H_2SO_4(aq) + MgO(s) \rightarrow MgSO_4(aq) + H_2O(l)$
   c) $2HNO_3(aq) + CuCO_3(s) \rightarrow Cu(NO_3)_2(aq) + H_2O(l) + CO_2(g)$
   d) $H_2SO_4(aq) + 2NaOH(aq) \rightarrow Na_2SO_4(aq) + 2H_2O(l)$
   e) $2HCl(aq) + CuO(s) \rightarrow CuCl_2(aq) + H_2O(l)$

Homework activity: Preparing a soluble salt

1. Student's own answers. You can assess this as a level of response question. Award 5–6 marks for a detailed, logical answer, including full instructions; award 3–4 marks for an answer including some coherent points and understanding; award 1–2 marks for an answer containing simple statements only and describing a method that would fail to produce a soluble salt.
2. a) $CuO(s) + H_2SO_4(aq) \rightarrow CuSO_4(aq) + H_2O(l)$
   b) The charges on the ions do not change from the reactants to the products

19 Chemical changes: Acids and pH

Learning objectives

- To use the pH scale to identify acids and alkalis
- To represent acid–alkali reactions with an ionic equation
- To calculate the chemical quantities in titrations
- To use and explain the terms strong and weak acid
- To use and explain the terms dilute and concentrated acid
- To describe the relationship between pH and hydrogen ion concentration
- To describe how to carry out titrations between strong acids and strong alkalis

Specification links

- 4.4.2.4, 4.4.2.5, 4.4.2.6
- WS: 3.5, 3.7, 4.1, 4.3, 4.6
- MS: 1a, 1b, 1c, 2a, 2h, 3b, 4a

Starter activity

- **The pH scale; 5 minutes; page 126**

  Ask the student to write down the formulae of some acids and alkalis. Establish that the acids all contain hydrogen ions and the alkalis all contain hydroxide ions. Link this to the pH scale and work covered at Key Stage 3 on pH.

Main activities

- **Titrations; 20 minutes; page 127**

  This procedure is required practical activity 2 and is also covered in lesson 16. Discuss what happens to the hydrogen ion and hydroxide ion concentrations as the titration proceeds. Explain the equation: $H^+ + OH^- \rightarrow H_2O$. The student can then answer question 1. Remind the student of the titration calculations in lesson 16. They can then answer question 2.

- **Strong and weak acids; 20 minutes; page 128**

  Ask the student what the difference is between a strong and a weak acid and a dilute and a concentrated acid. Build on their ideas to explain these terms. Explain the link between the numerical value of pH and the hydrogen ion concentration. You might find the table in question 2 useful.

Plenary activity

- **Strong, weak, dilute and concentrated; 5 minutes**

  Ask the student to identify the most important fact about each of these descriptions of an acid: strong, weak, dilute and concentrated.

Homework activity

- **pH and strong and weak acids; 60 minutes; page 129**

  This activity reinforces ideas about strong and weak acids and concentrated and dilute acids, and links them with the pH scale. Question 4 is a good indicator of the student's understanding.

Support ideas

- **Titrations** The student may need to practise these calculations. They can refer back to lesson 16 where the calculations are laid out as structured questions.
- **Strong and weak acids** The student may need extra help understanding orders of magnitude.

Extension ideas

- **Strong and weak acids** The student can find out how the pH scale is related to logarithms.
- **pH and strong and weak acids** Ask the student to plan an investigation to find out how the pH of weak and strong acids varies with the concentration.

Progress and observations

CHEMISTRY HIGHER

Starter activity: The pH scale

Learning objectives

- To know that the pH scale is a measure of acidity and alkalinity
- To know that acids produce hydrogen ions and alkalis contain hydroxide ions in aqueous solution

Equipment

1. This is the pH scale:

1	2	3	4	5	6	7	8	9	10	11	12	13	14

Add labels to the scale to show the pH of:

a) a neutral solution

b) an acidic solution

c) an alkaline solution

d) a solution with a high concentration of hydrogen ions

e) a solution with a low concentration of hydrogen ions

f) a solution with a high concentration of hydroxide ions

g) a solution with a low concentration of hydroxide ions.

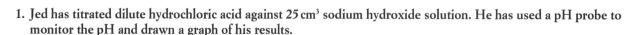

CHEMISTRY HIGHER

AQA

Main activity: Titrations

Time 20 mins

Learning objectives

- To understand pH changes when a strong acid neutralises a strong alkali
- To know the procedure for carrying out a strong acid/strong alkali titration
- To calculate the chemical quantities in titrations involving concentrations in mol/dm³ and g/dm³

Equipment

- copy of the periodic table

1. **Jed has titrated dilute hydrochloric acid against 25 cm³ sodium hydroxide solution. He has used a pH probe to monitor the pH and drawn a graph of his results.**

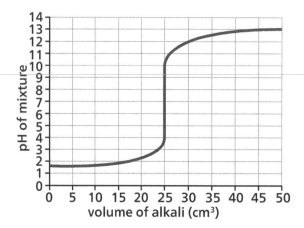

a) On the graph, label: i) where hydrogen ions are in excess

ii) where hydroxide ions are in excess

iii) where the number of hydrogen ions equals the number of hydroxide ions.

b) What other information does Jed need to find the concentration of the dilute hydrochloric acid?

_____

2. **Maya has titrated dilute sulfuric acid against 25 cm³ portions of 0.120 mol/dm³ potassium hydroxide solution. These are her titration results.**

Titration	Rough	1	2	3
Final volume (cm³)	16.5	31.8	47.0	41.8
Initial volume (cm³)	0.5	16.5	31.8	26.7
Volume of acid added (cm³)	16.0	15.3	15.2	15.1

a) What is the mean titre of sulfuric acid?

_____

b) Calculate the concentration of the sulfuric acid to three significant figures in:

i) mol/dm³ _____

ii) g/dm³ _____

CHEMISTRY HIGHER

Main activity: Strong and weak acids

Learning objectives

- To know the difference between a strong and a weak acid
- To know the difference between a dilute and a concentrated acid
- To describe how pH is related to the hydrogen ion concentration

Equipment

1. Look at the diagram of acids.

a) Use the diagram to explain the difference between a strong and a weak acid.

_____

_____

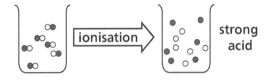

b) Name three strong acids and one weak acid.

_____

_____

c) A strong acid and a weak acid both have concentrations of $2\,mol/dm^3$. Explain why the strong acid has a pH of 1 and the weak acid has a pH of 3.

_____

_____

2. The table shows the hydrogen concentrations of solutions with different pH values.

pH	Hydrogen ion concentration (mol/dm³) (standard form)	Hydrogen ion concentration (mol/dm³) (decimal number)
1	1×10^{-1}	0.1
2	1×10^{-2}	
3	1×10^{-3}	
4	1×10^{-4}	
5	1×10^{-5}	
6	1×10^{-6}	
7	1×10^{-7}	

a) Complete the table.

b) What happens to the hydrogen ion concentration when the pH decreases by 1?

_____

c) What is the hydroxide ion concentration of a solution with a pH of 7?

_____

d) How many times greater is the hydrogen ion concentration of a solution with pH 3 than the hydrogen ion concentration of a solution with pH 5?

_____

CHEMISTRY HIGHER

AQA

Homework activity: pH and strong and weak acids

Time **60** mins

Learning objectives

- To know that strong acids are fully ionised and weak acids are partially ionised in solution
- To relate pH to hydrogen ion concentration
- To distinguish between concentrated and dilute acids, and strong and weak acids

Equipment

1. Jack has used a pH probe to measure the pH of four acids, A, B, C and D. They all have the same concentration of $1.0 \, mol/dm^3$.

His results are:

Acid	pH
A	1
B	5
C	3
D	1

a) Which two acids are strong acids?

_____

b) Which acid could be sulfuric acid?

_____

c) If the hydrogen ion concentration of acid A is $1 \times 10^{-1} \, mol/dm^3$:

   i) what is the hydrogen ion concentration of acid C?

   _____

   ii) what is the hydrogen ion concentration of acid B?

   _____

d) Jack thinks he can change acid A into a weak acid by diluting it. He dilutes it to give a concentration of $0.001 \, mol/dm^3$. The diluted acid has a pH of 3. Jack concludes he can change a strong acid to a weak one by diluting it. Explain why Jack's conclusion is not valid.

_____

_____

_____

2. Complete the table by ticking the properties of each acid.

Acid	Strong	Weak	Concentrated	Dilute
$0.0001 \, mol/dm^3$ nitric acid				
$14 \, mol/dm^3$ ethanoic acid				
$12 \, mol/dm^3$ hydrochloric acid				

19 Answers

Starter activity: The pH scale

1. a) 7
   b) 1–6
   c) 8–14
   d) 1–2
   e) 5–6
   f) 13–14
   g) 8–9

Main activity: Titrations

1. a) i) $< 25\,cm^3$ acid added
      ii) $> 25\,cm^3$ acid added
      iii) Exactly $25\,cm^3$ acid added
   b) The concentration of the sodium hydroxide solution
2. a) $15.2\,cm^3$
   b) i) $0.099\,mol/dm^3$
      ii) $9.70\,g/dm^3$

Main activity: Strong and weak acids

1. a) Strong acid is completely ionised, weak acid is partially ionised
   b) Accept any valid examples, such as: strong acids: hydrochloric acid, sulfuric acid, nitric acid; weak acids: ethanoic acid, citric acid, carbonic acid
   c) A strong acid has a higher concentration of hydrogen ions than a weak acid.
2. a) Missing numbers: 0.01, 0.001, 0.0001, 0.00001, 0.000001, 0.0000001
   b) Increases ten times
   c) $1 \times 10^{-7}\,mol/dm^3$
   d) 100 times

Homework activity: pH and strong and weak acids

1. a) A and D
   b) A or D
   c) i) $1 \times 10^{-3}\,mol/dm^3$
      ii) $1 \times 10^{-5}\,mol/dm^3$
   d) Acid A is still a strong acid. Jack has added water, so there is less acid present and the hydrogen ion concentration is lower. pH is a measure of hydrogen ion concentration, but acid A is still fully ionised.

2.

Acid	Strong	Weak	Concentrated	Dilute
$0.0001\,mol/dm^3$ nitric acid	✓			✓
$14\,mol/dm^3$ ethanoic acid		✓	✓	
$12\,mol/dm^3$ hydrochloric acid	✓		✓	

20 Chemical changes: Electrolysis

Learning objectives

- To understand the process of electrolysis
- To predict the products of electrolysis of molten binary compounds
- To explain how electrolysis is used to extract metals
- To predict the products of electrolysis of aqueous solutions of a single compound
- To use half equations to represent reactions at the electrodes

Specification links

- 4.4.3.1, 4.4.3.2, 4.4.3.3, 4.4.3.4, 4.4.3.5
- WS: 2.1, 4.1

Starter activity

- **Electrolysis language; 5 minutes; page 132**

  Ask the student to recall the properties of ionic compounds in conducting electricity (lesson 8). This activity covers the language used to describe electrolysis.

Main activities

- **Electrolysis and extracting metals; 20 minutes; page 133**

  Explain the electrolysis of molten lead bromide and the products at the electrodes. Remind the student how to write half equations for these reactions, identifying the oxidation and reduction reactions. Note that electrolysis of zinc chloride is the preferred and safer option in schools, but lead bromide is in the specification. Remind the student that metals below carbon in the reactivity series can be extracted by reduction with carbon. Explain that metals above carbon are extracted by electrolysis, using aluminium as the example.

- **Electrolysis of aqueous solutions; 20 minutes; page 134**

  Discuss the electrolysis of aqueous solutions such as sodium chloride solution, and factors determining the products at the electrodes.

Plenary activity

- **Electrolysis summary; 5 minutes**

  Ask the student to state three important electrolysis facts they are sure of and one thing they need more help with. Use this feedback to inform future work.

Homework activity

- **Predicting products; 60 minutes; page 135**

  This activity draws on the lesson content and requires the student to predict products from the electrolysis of aqueous solutions of ionic compounds, and to write half equations for the reactions at the electrodes. This relates to required practical 3 in the specification.

Support ideas

- **Electrolysis and extracting metals** Half equations may need more explanation and practice. The student can refer back to lesson 17 to check the order of metals in the reactivity series.

Extension ideas

- **Electrolysis and extracting metals** The student can find out how electrolysis is used to purify copper after it has been extracted from its ore.
- **Electrolysis of aqueous solutions** The student can suggest how the electrolysis of dilute sulfuric acid can be used to confirm the formula of water.

Progress and observations

CHEMISTRY HIGHER

Starter activity: Electrolysis language

Time 5 mins

Learning objectives

- To use the terms electrolyte, electrolysis, electrode, cathode and anode to describe the process of electrolysis
- To recall the conditions needed for ionic compounds to conduct electricity

Equipment

1. The diagram shows a typical apparatus used in electrolysis experiments.

   Add the following labels to the diagram:

   electrolyte   electrodes   cathode   anode   power supply   ammeter   beaker

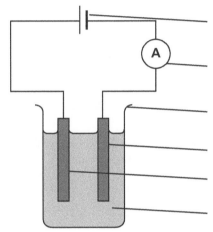

2. Solid sodium chloride does not conduct electricity. What conditions are needed for sodium chloride to conduct electricity?

   _____

   _____

3. What happens to the positively charged ions and the negatively charged ions during electrolysis?

   _____

   _____

CHEMISTRY HIGHER

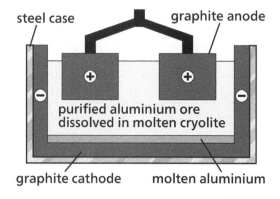

Main activity: Electrolysis and extracting metals

Time 20 mins

Learning objectives

- To predict the products of the electrolysis of a molten binary ionic compound
- To write half equations to represent the reactions at the cathode and anode
- To describe the extraction of aluminium by electrolysis

Equipment

1. **Students are watching a demonstration of the electrolysis of lead bromide. The apparatus is shown in the diagram.**

   a) What will they observe at the anode and at the cathode?

   _____

   _____

   b) Write half equations to represent the reactions at the anode and cathode.

   _____

   _____

   molten
   lead (II)
   bromide

2. **The students watch a second demonstration, the electrolysis of zinc chloride. Name the products formed at the anode and cathode and write half equations to show the reactions.**

   _____

   _____

3. **Why is electrolysis used to extract some metals?**

   _____

4. **This process is used to extract aluminium from aluminium oxide.**

   a) Explain why aluminium oxide is dissolved in molten cryolite.

   _____

   _____

   b) Explain why the anodes have to be replaced regularly.

   _____

   _____

   _____

   steel case   graphite anode

   purified aluminium ore
   dissolved in molten cryolite

   graphite cathode   molten aluminium

   c) Write half equations for the reactions occurring at the anode and cathode.

   _____

   _____

   d) Which equation in c) is an oxidation reaction and which is a reduction reaction?

   _____

CHEMISTRY HIGHER

Main activity: Electrolysis of aqueous solutions

Time **20** mins

Learning objectives	Equipment
• To know the factors that determine which ions react at the anode and cathode • To predict the products of the electrolysis of aqueous solutions	none

1. This apparatus is used to pass electricity through sodium chloride solution.

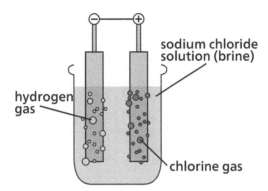

a) List all the ions present in the sodium chloride solution.

_____

b) Explain why hydrogen gas is produced at the cathode and not sodium metal.

_____

c) Chlorine gas is produced at the anode. What is left in the solution?

_____

d) How would the products at the electrodes change if molten sodium chloride were used instead of sodium chloride solution?

_____

2. Complete the table to give the products at the anode and cathode for the electrolysis of different aqueous solutions.

Aqueous solution	Product at anode	Product at cathode
magnesium sulfate		
sodium bromide		
silver nitrate		
copper chloride		

CHEMISTRY HIGHER

Homework activity: Predicting products

Time **60** mins

Learning objectives	Equipment
• To predict the products of electrolysis of aqueous solutions	none
• To use half equations to represent reactions at electrodes	

Harry is investigating the products of electrolysis of aqueous solutions. He is using the solutions in the table and graphite electrodes. This is his apparatus.

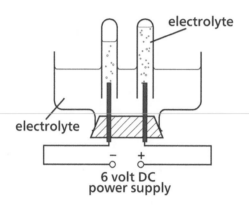

electrolyte

electrolyte

6 volt DC
power supply

1. Complete the table by predicting the products formed at each electrode.

Aqueous solution	Product at cathode	Product at anode
potassium bromide		
sodium iodide		
zinc chloride		
calcium nitrate		
copper sulfate		

2. Which ions are present in potassium bromide solution? _____

3. Explain your predicted products for the electrolysis of potassium bromide solution.

   _____

   _____

4. Write half equations to show the reactions at the anode and cathode for the electrolysis of potassium bromide solution.

   _____

   _____

5. Write half equations to show the reactions at the anode and cathode for the electrolysis of copper sulfate solution.

   _____

   _____

20 Answers

Starter activity: Electrolysis language

1. (Reading downwards) power supply, ammeter, beaker, cathode, anode, electrolyte; a label also needs to be added showing that the cathode and anode are electrodes
2. It must be molten or in solution, so the ions are free to move and carry the charge.
3. Positively charged ions move to the cathode and negatively charged ions move to the anode.

Main activity: Electrolysis and extracting metals

1. a) Anode: red/brown fumes; cathode: grey metal deposited
   b) Anode: $2Br^- \rightarrow Br_2 + 2e^-$; cathode: $Pb^{2+} + 2e^- \rightarrow Pb$
2. Anode: $2Cl^- \rightarrow Cl_2 + 2e^-$; product = chlorine gas. Cathode: $Zn^{2+} + 2e^- \rightarrow Zn$; product = zinc.
3. The metals are more reactive than carbon, or react with carbon.
4. a) Aluminium oxide dissolved in cryolite has a lower melting point than aluminium oxide.
   b) Oxygen forms at the carbon anode and reacts with it at the high extraction temperature to produce carbon dioxide.
   c) Anode: $2O^{2-} \rightarrow O_2 + 4e^-$; cathode: $Al^{3+} + 3e^- \rightarrow Al$
   d) Anode = oxidation; cathode = reduction

Main activity: Electrolysis of aqueous solutions

1. a) Na^+, Cl^-, H^+, OH^-
   b) Sodium is more reactive than hydrogen
   c) Sodium hydroxide, NaOH(aq)
   d) Sodium would form at the cathode rather than hydrogen. The product at the anode (chlorine) would be unchanged.

2.
Aqueous solution	Product at anode	Product at cathode
magnesium sulfate	oxygen	hydrogen
sodium bromide	bromine	hydrogen
silver nitrate	oxygen	silver
copper chloride	chlorine	copper

Homework activity: Predicting products

1.
Aqueous solution	Product at cathode	Product at anode
potassium bromide	hydrogen	bromine
sodium iodide	hydrogen	iodine
zinc chloride	zinc	chlorine
calcium nitrate	hydrogen	oxygen
copper sulfate	copper	oxygen

2. K^+, Br^-, H^+, OH^-
3. Potassium is above hydrogen in the reactivity series so hydrogen is produced at the cathode. Potassium bromide contains a halogen, so bromine is produced and not oxygen.
4. Cathode: $2H^+ + 2e^- \rightarrow H_2$; anode: $2Br^- \rightarrow Br_2 + 2e^-$
5. Cathode: $Cu^{2+} + 2e^- \rightarrow Cu$; anode: $4OH^- \rightarrow 2H_2O + O_2 + 4e^-$

CHEMISTRY HIGHER

21 Energy changes: Exothermic and endothermic reactions

<table>
<tr><td>

Learning objectives

- To understand that energy is conserved in chemical reactions
- To define and give examples of exothermic and endothermic reactions
- To use reaction profiles
- To use bond energies to calculate the energy transferred in chemical reactions

</td><td>

Specification links

- 4.5.1.1, 4.5.1.2, 4.5.1.3
- WS: 2.2, 3.1, 3.3, 4.1
- MS: 1a, 4a, 4c

</td></tr>
</table>

Starter activity

- **Hand warmers and sports injury packs; 5 minutes; page 138**

  Explain that energy is conserved in chemical reactions and discuss energy transfers in terms of exothermic and endothermic reactions and temperature changes in the surroundings. Encourage the student to use the term 'energy transfer' rather than heat given out or taken in.

Main activities

- **Reaction profiles; 15 minutes; page 139**

  Explain how we use reaction profiles (energy level diagrams) to track the energy changes in exothermic and endothermic reactions, including activation energy. You could use question 2 to explain this.

- **Bond energies; 25 minutes; page 140**

  Explain that chemical reactions involve breaking old bonds and making new bonds. Tell the student that bond breaking is endothermic and bond making is exothermic. The student can suggest how the energy changes in bond breaking and bond making compare in exothermic and endothermic reactions. Explain bond energies and how we use them to calculate energy changes. The student can then work through the activity sheet. The first question is structured to guide the student through the calculation.

Plenary activity

- **Hand warmers and sports injury packs explained; 5 minutes**

  Ask the student to draw reaction profiles for the reactions in hand warmers and in sports injury packs. Since both products are activated when the reactants mix, you could discuss the relative activation energy.

Homework activity

- **Investigating energy transfers; 60 minutes; page 141**

  This activity requires the student to interpret the results from an investigation into the effect of the amount of magnesium on the temperature change when magnesium reacts with an acid. Investigating the variables that affect temperature changes in reacting solutions is required practical 4.

Support ideas

- **Reaction profiles** Examples such as lighting a gas burner or fire may help the student understand activation energy.
- **Bond energies** The student may need extra practice calculating energy changes and may need some more examples, such as $H_2 + Br_2 \rightarrow 2HBr$

Extension ideas

- **Bond energies** The student can find out why some dissolving reactions are exothermic and others are endothermic. The student can calculate the overall energy change when ethane reacts with oxygen (bond energy for C–C bond is 348 kJ/mol)

Progress and observations

CHEMISTRY HIGHER

Starter activity: Hand warmers and sports injury packs

Learning objectives	Equipment
• To know that energy is conserved in chemical reactions	none
• To understand the energy transfers in exothermic and endothermic reactions	
• To know some uses of exothermic and endothermic reactions	

1. **The diagram shows a hand warmer. When it is activated, chemical reactions inside the sachet transfer heat energy to the surroundings, the hand.**

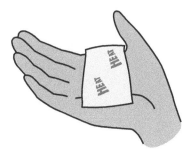

a) What type of chemical reaction takes place inside the hand warmer?

_____

b) How does the total energy of the product particles in the pack compare with the total energy of the reactants?

_____

_____

c) What happens to the temperature of the surroundings during this reaction?

_____

2. **The diagram shows a sports injury pack. When the cold pack is activated, chemical reactions inside the sachet take in energy from the surroundings, the ankle.**

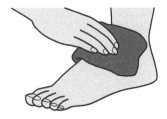

a) What type of chemical reaction happens inside the sports injury pack?

_____

b) How does the total energy of the product molecules compare with the total energy of the reactants in the sports injury pack?

_____

c) What happens to the temperature of the surroundings during the reaction?

_____

TUTORS GUILD CHEMISTRY HIGHER

Main activity: Reaction profiles

Learning objectives

- To draw reaction profiles for exothermic and endothermic reactions, including activation energy
- To explain activation energy

Equipment

- pencil

1. What must particles do before a chemical reaction can happen?

_____

2. The diagram shows a reaction profile for an exothermic reaction.

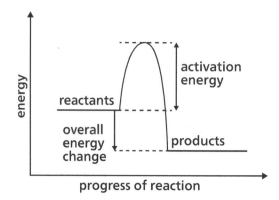

a) Why is this an exothermic reaction?

_____

b) What is activation energy?

_____

3. Complete the diagram to show a reaction profile for an endothermic reaction. Label your diagram to show the reactants and products, the activation energy, and the overall energy change.

CHEMISTRY HIGHER

Main activity: Bond energies

Learning objectives

- To know that energy must be supplied to break bonds in reactants and is released when products form
- To describe the overall energy change of a reaction as the difference between the energy needed to break bonds and the energy released when new bonds are made
- To use bond energies to calculate the energy transferred in reactions

Equipment

- calculator

1. The equation and table give information about bond energies and the reaction of methane with oxygen.

$$\text{H-C-H (with H above and below) } + 2\ O=O \rightarrow O=C=O\ +2\ H-O-H$$

Bond	Bond energy (kJ/mol)
C – H	413
O = O	498
O – H	463
C = O	803 (in carbon dioxide)

Use bond energies to complete the table below and calculate the overall energy change when methane reacts with oxygen.

Bonds broken	Energy needed to break bonds (kJ/mol)	Bonds made	Energy released when bonds are made (kJ/mol)
4 × (C – H)		4 × (O – H)	
2 × (O = O)		2 × (C = O)	
Total energy to break bonds		Total energy released	
Overall energy change			

2. Hydrogen and chlorine react to give hydrogen chloride. The equation is: $H_2 + Cl_2 \rightarrow 2HCl$

Use the bond energies in the table to calculate the overall energy change for the reaction.

Bond	Bond energy (kJ/mol)
H – H	436
Cl – Cl	243
H – Cl	432

_____

_____

_____

_____

140

CHEMISTRY HIGHER

Homework activity: Investigating energy transfers

Time **60** mins

Learning objectives

- To distinguish between exothermic and endothermic reactions on the basis of temperature change of the surroundings.
- To interpret investigations into the variables that affect temperature change in reacting solutions

Equipment

- graph paper
- pencil
- spare paper

Livi has investigated the temperature changes that take place in the reaction between $2 \, mol/dm^3$ hydrochloric acid and magnesium ribbon. The diagram shows Livi's apparatus.

This is Livi's method:

- Place $25 \, cm^3$ hydrochloric acid in the insulated cup and record the temperature.
- Add a 1 cm length of magnesium ribbon, replace the lid and stir the reaction mixture with the thermometer.
- Record the highest temperature reached.
- Immediately add a second 1 cm length of magnesium ribbon and repeat the process, recording the highest temperature reached.
- Continue adding 1 cm lengths of magnesium ribbon until there is no further reaction.

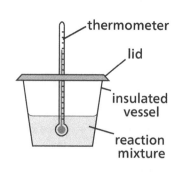

thermometer

lid

insulated vessel

reaction mixture

These are Livi's results:

Length of magnesium ribbon added (cm)	0	1	2	3	4	5	6	7	8
Temperature of mixture (°C)	18	22	26	29	31	33	33	32	29

1. Write a balanced equation for the reaction.

_____

2. What is the:

a) independent variable _____

b) dependent variable? _____

3. Name three controlled variables.

_____

_____

4. On a separate piece of paper, draw a suitable graph of the results.

5. Explain the shape of your graph.

_____

_____

_____

_____

21 Answers

Starter activity: Hand warmers and sports injury packs

1. a) exothermic
   b) The total energy of the product particles is less than the total energy of the reactant particles.
   c) Temperature increases
2. a) endothermic
   b) The total energy of the product molecules is greater than the total energy of the reactant molecules.
   c) Temperature decreases

Main activity: Reaction profiles

1. Collide with sufficient energy to break bonds
2. a) Products have less energy than reactants; energy is transferred to the surroundings/released
   b) The energy needed to start a reaction
3.
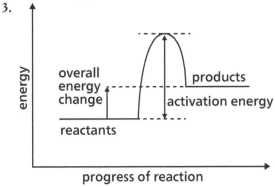

Main activity: Bond energies

1.

Bonds broken	Energy needed to break bonds (kJ/mol)	Bonds made	Energy released when bonds are made (kJ/mol)
4 × (C – H)	1652	4 × (O – H)	1852
2 × (O = O)	996	2 × (C = O)	1606
Total energy to break bonds	2648	Total energy released	3458
Overall energy change	810		

2. –185 kJ/mol

Homework activity: Investigating energy transfers

1. $Mg(s) + 2HCl(aq) \rightarrow MgCl_2(aq) + H_2(g)$
2. a) The length of magnesium ribbon
   b) The temperature change
3. Three of the following: concentration of acid; volume of acid; same polystyrene cup; same procedure; same stirring
4. x-axis labelled 'length of magnesium ribbon (cm)'; y-axis labelled 'temperature (°C)'; all points plotted correctly; points joined with a line of best fit
5. Increasing the amount of magnesium gives more reactant particles so more heat energy is transferred to the surroundings. After 5 cm of magnesium have been added, the acid has all reacted/is now the limiting factor. The temperature falls as the mixture cools.

CHEMISTRY HIGHER

AQA

22 Energy changes: Cells, batteries and fuel cells

Learning objectives

- To describe simple cells and batteries
- To interpret data for the relative reactivity of different metals in cells
- To explain rechargeable and non-rechargeable batteries
- To describe hydrogen fuel cells and evaluate their use
- To write half equations for electrode reactions in hydrogen fuel cells

Specification links

- 4.5.2.1, 4.5.2.2
- WS: 1.4, 3.5, 4.1
- MS: 1a

Starter activity

- **Electricity from chemicals; 5 minutes; page 144**

  Make sure the student is familiar with the essential features of a simple cell. Explain how the voltage produced by the cell is dependent on the type of metal used to make the electrodes, and on the type of electrolyte.

Main activities

- **Simple cells and batteries; 20 minutes; page 145**

  Remind the student that the reactivity of a metal depends on how easily it forms positive ions. You could explain the electron flow in a simple cell with positive and negative electrodes. This isn't strictly required by the specification, but may help the student to understand why different cells give different voltages. Explain how relative reactivity data can be used to predict the voltage of a cell. You could use the table in question 1. Tell the student how cells are used to make batteries and explain non-rechargeable and rechargeable batteries.

- **Hydrogen fuel cells; 20 minutes; page 146**

  Explain how a hydrogen fuel cell works. You could use the diagram in the activity sheet as an aid. Discuss the reactions at the electrodes and their half equations.

Plenary activity

- **Quick facts; 5 minutes**

  Ask the student to list the three most important facts about simple cells and the three most important facts about hydrogen fuel cells.

Homework activity

- **Hydrogen fuel cells or batteries?; 60 minutes; page 147**

  The student must analyse and evaluate information to make judgements and conclusions about the use of fuel cells versus batteries. This is an AO3 skill and can be marked as a level of response question. Encourage the student to use the information in the question as a basis for their reasoning, as well as drawing on information not provided, such as the availability of hydrogen fuel.

Support ideas

- **Hydrogen fuel cells or batteries?** Encourage the student to use and evaluate the information given in the question, as well as drawing on other knowledge (for example polluting effects) to make judgements and conclusions.

Extension ideas

- **Simple cells and batteries** The student can suggest which metal has a positive charge and which has a negative charge in a simple cell by comparing the reactivity of each metal and how easily they can push electrons around the circuit. The student can write half equations for the reactions in question 1. They can assume that dilute sulfuric acid is used as the electrolyte.

Progress and observations

CHEMISTRY HIGHER

AQA

Starter activity: Electricity from chemicals

Time **5** mins

Learning objectives

- To know that chemical reactions can be used to produce electricity in a simple cell
- To know that a simple cell consists of two different metals, connected in a circuit, in an electrolyte
- To know that the voltage of a cell is dependent on several factors

Equipment

- pencil

1. **The diagram shows a simple cell. The more reactive metal loses electrons to form metal ions.**

   The electrons are pushed through the circuit to produce a voltage.

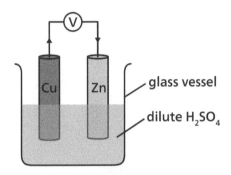

   a) What happens when the copper and zinc strips are connected with a voltmeter in the circuit?

   _____

   b) The essentials for a simple cell are:

   - two different metal strips
   - an electrolyte
   - wires connecting the metal strips.

   Draw a diagram of a different simple cell.

   c) Your simple cell will probably have a different voltage to the cell in the first question. Suggest why.

   _____

   _____

CHEMISTRY HIGHER

Main activity: Simple cells and batteries

Learning objectives	Equipment

- To know that the voltage of a cell is dependent on several factors
- To interpret data for relative reactivity of different metals in cells
- To know that a battery consists of two or more cells connected in series
- To explain why non-rechargeable batteries eventually stop working and rechargeable batteries can be recharged

1. The table shows the voltages produced by cells with a metal as one electrode and hydrogen as the other (this is possible).

Electrode	Voltage (V)
magnesium	−2.35
zinc	−0.76
iron	−0.45
tin	−0.15
hydrogen	−0.00
copper	+0.34
silver	+0.80

You can use the table to predict the voltage of a simple cell:

voltage = the more positive voltage – the less positive voltage

Predict the voltages of simple cells with these metals:

a) copper and magnesium

_____

b) iron and silver

_____

c) magnesium and zinc

_____

d) zinc and copper

_____

2. A battery consists of two or more cells connected together in series. The voltage of the battery is the sum of the voltages of the cells. What is the voltage of a battery consisting of two cells, each with a zinc and a copper metal strip as the electrodes?

_____

3. Why do non-rechargeable batteries eventually stop working?

_____

4. What happens inside a rechargeable battery when it is recharged?

_____

CHEMISTRY HIGHER

Main activity: Hydrogen fuel cells

Time **20** mins

Learning objectives

- To know that the overall reaction in a hydrogen fuel cell is the oxidation of hydrogen to produce water
- To write half equations for the reactions at the electrodes

Equipment

The diagram shows a hydrogen fuel cell.

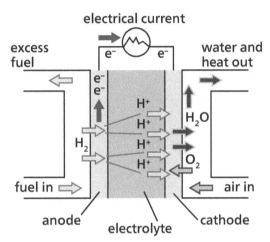

1. **Use the diagram to explain how the fuel cell works.**

_____
_____
_____
_____
_____
_____
_____

2. **Write a balanced equation to show the overall reaction in a hydrogen fuel cell.**

_____

3. **Use the diagram to answer the following questions about the reaction at the anode.**

   a) Write a half equation to show the reaction of the hydrogen fuel at the anode.

   _____

   b) What type of reaction is this? _____

   c) What happens to the electrons released at the anode?

   _____

   _____

4. **Now use the diagram to answer the following questions about the reaction at the cathode.**

   a) Write a half equation to show the reaction at the cathode. _____

   b) What type of reaction is this? _____

CHEMISTRY HIGHER

Homework activity: Hydrogen fuel cells or batteries?

Time 60 mins

Learning objectives

- To know that hydrogen fuel cells offer an alternative to rechargeable batteries
- To evaluate the use of hydrogen fuel cells in comparison with rechargeable batteries

Equipment

- spare paper

Electric cars can run on rechargeable batteries or on hydrogen fuel cells. The table gives some benefits and disadvantages of using hydrogen fuel cells compared to rechargeable batteries.

Hydrogen fuel cells	Rechargeable batteries
They do not need recharging as long as the hydrogen and oxygen are continually supplied.	They need regular recharging, which uses electricity.
They work continually as long as hydrogen and oxygen are supplied.	They do not work continually due to the need to recharge.
They last longer than rechargeable batteries.	They can only be recharged a limited number of times, and then need replacing.
The fuel cells produce water; there is no pollution.	Rechargeable batteries contain harmful substances such as cadmium, nickel and lithium which have to be disposed of safely. The lithium ion battery is the most common type used in cars.
Hydrogen fuel is an explosive gas that needs careful storage.	
Hydrogen is usually produced from fossil fuels, such as petroleum.	
If hydrogen is made from water or from methane from landfill sites, it can be renewable.	

1. On a separate piece of paper, write a passage comparing the use of hydrogen fuel cells with rechargeable batteries. This can be limited to uses in vehicles, or include other uses such as space craft and generating electricity. You need to make judgements and draw conclusions.

   The table gives you some information, but not the whole story.

   Also think about:

   - the problems of using a gaseous explosive fuel
   - recycling issues
   - day to day convenience.

   [6 marks]

22 Answers

Starter activity: Electricity from chemicals

1. a) A current flows in the circuit.

b) The diagram should be similar to that in the worksheet, but with different metals and a different electrolyte.

c) Different metals and different electrolytes give different voltages; the larger the gap between the reactivity of the metals, the larger the voltage.

Main activity: Simple cells and batteries

1. a) 2.69 V

b) 1.25 V

c) 1.59 V

d) 1.10 V

2. 2.20 V

3. Chemicals are used up.

4. The reactions are reversed.

Main activity: Hydrogen fuel cells

1. Hydrogen fuel reacts at the anode to give hydrogen ions and electrons. The hydrogen ions are attracted across the electrolyte to the cathode. The electrons move round the circuit and electrical energy is produced. The hydrogen ions react with oxygen at the cathode to produce water.

2. $2H_2 + O_2 \rightarrow 2H_2O$

3. a) $H_2 \rightarrow 2H^+ + 2e^-$

b) oxidation

c) The electrons released at the anode travel around the circuit and react at the cathode with the H^+ ions to form H_2 gas.

4. a) $4H^+ + O_2 + 4e^- \rightarrow 2H_2O$

b) reduction

Homework activity: Hydrogen fuel cells or batteries?

1. Student's own answers. This can be marked as a 6 mark level of response question, awarding marks as follows:

5–6 marks: A detailed and coherent answer, showing broad knowledge and understanding of scientific facts, making logical links with examples and using information not given in the question.

3–4 marks: Reasonable knowledge is shown, comparisons are made, but the answer is not fully articulated and relies mostly on information from the table.

1–2 marks: Simple statements are made, but the answer fails to make a comparison or draw conclusions.

23 Rate of reaction: Rates of reaction

Learning objectives

- To calculate rates of reaction
- To know how concentration of solutions, pressure of gases, temperature, size of particles and a catalyst affect rates of reaction
- To know how catalysts increase a rate of reaction by providing a different reaction pathway with a lower activation energy
- To predict and explain using collision theory how changes in conditions affect a rate of reaction

Specification links

- 4.6.1.1, 4.6.1.2, 4.6.1.3, 4.6.1.4
- WS: 2.2, 2.3, 3.1
- MS: 1a, 1c, 3c, 4a, 4c, 4e

Starter activity

- **Tracking a reaction; 5 minutes; page 150**

  Ask the student what is meant by the rate of reaction. Discuss how a reaction can be followed by measuring the mass or volume of a product or reactant over time.

Main activities

- **Calculating rates of reaction; 20 minutes; page 151**

  Discuss how mean rates of reaction are calculated, ensuring that the student realises the units must be appropriate to the example (g/s, cm³/s or mol/s). Show the student how to construct tangents to the curve at specific points to calculate rates of reaction. Check that the correct units are used.

- **Factors affecting the rate of a reaction; 20 minutes; page 152**

  Discuss how concentration of solutions, pressure of gases, temperature, particle size and the use of a catalyst affect the rate of a reaction. Use the collision theory to explain these effects. Check the student appreciates that when describing more successful collisions in an answer, they need to relate this to time and refer to more frequent, successful, collisions. The student can then complete the activity sheet; questions 4 and 5 can be answered verbally.

Plenary activity

- **A rates summary; 5 minutes**

  Ask the student to produce a spider diagram with the words 'rates of reaction' at the centre of the page and use it to summarise what they have learned in this lesson. This may be useful as a revision tool.

Homework activity

- **Investigating the rate of a reaction; 60 minutes; page 153**

  This activity is based on the effects of concentration on the reaction between sodium thiosulfate and dilute hydrochloric acid. The student may have carried out this experiment at school, as this is required practical 5. Encourage the student to refer to the different variables when answering question 3.

Support ideas

- **Calculating rates of reaction** The student may need more support with calculating rates from tangents. Their maths textbook may help.
- **Factors affecting the rate of a reaction** The student can refer back to lesson 21 to revise activation energy.

Extension ideas

- **Factors affecting the rate of reaction** Ask the student to describe an experiment to determine the catalytic effect of different metal oxides on the decomposition of hydrogen peroxide.
- **Investigating the rate of a reaction** The student can plot a graph of concentration against 1/t for the experiment on the homework activity sheet. They can interpret their graph.

Progress and observations

CHEMISTRY HIGHER

Starter activity: Tracking a reaction

Learning objectives	Equipment
• To describe how a reaction can be followed • To match the graph of results with the apparatus	none

Diagrams A and B show apparatus that can be used to follow a reaction, such as magnesium ribbon reacting with hydrochloric acid.

A.

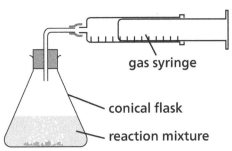

B.

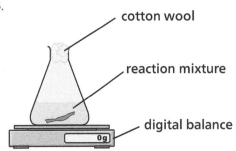

Diagrams C and D are two graphs of results.

C.

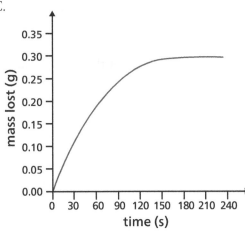

D.

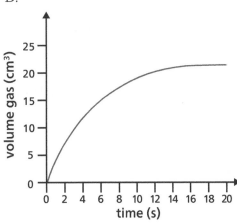

1. **Draw two lines to match each graph with the correct set of apparatus.**

2. **What do the two graphs have in common?**

_____

_____

_____

CHEMISTRY HIGHER

AQA

Main activity: Calculating rates of reaction

Time **20** mins

Learning objectives

- To calculate the rate of a reaction in g/s, cm³/s and mol/s
- To draw and interpret graphs of quantity of product formed or reactant used up against time
- To calculate the gradient of a tangent to a curve as a measure of the rate of reaction at a specific time

Equipment

- calculator
- pencil

This equation can be used to calculate the mean rate of reaction:

$$\text{mean rate of reaction} = \frac{\text{quantity of reactant used or product formed}}{\text{time}}$$

1. **What is the mean rate of reaction when:**

   a) 25 cm³ hydrogen gas is produced in 35 seconds

   _____

   b) 2.8 g calcium carbonate reacts completely in 42 seconds

   _____

   c) 2.0 mol hydrogen gas explodes completely in 0.20 seconds?

   _____

2. **The graph follows the reaction between magnesium and hydrochloric acid.**

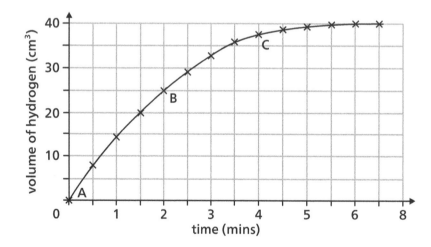

   a) What is the mean rate of reaction between the start and finish of the reaction?

   _____

   b) Draw tangents to the curve at A, B and C. Use the tangents to calculate the rate of reaction at each point.

   Calculate the rates of reaction below.

   _____

   _____

   _____

CHEMISTRY HIGHER

Main activity: Factors affecting the rate of a reaction

Time **20** mins

Learning objectives	Equipment
• To know how changes in concentration of solutions, pressure of gases, temperature, particle size and the use of a catalyst affect the rate of reaction • To use the collision theory to explain these effects	none

1. Name the factors that affect the rate of a reaction.

_____

_____

2. Ed is reacting marble chips (calcium carbonate) with 2 mol/dm³ hydrochloric acid at room temperature. What effect will the following changes have on the rate of reaction?

a) replacing the 2 mol/dm³ hydrochloric acid with 1 mol/dm³ hydrochloric acid

_____

b) carrying out the reaction at 0 °C

_____

c) using calcium carbonate powder instead of marble chips

_____

3. This is the equation for the reaction between hydrogen and chlorine: $H_2(g) + Cl_2(g) \rightarrow 2HCl(g)$

What must happen to the hydrogen and chlorine molecules before they can react?

_____

_____

4. Use collision theory to explain the following to your tutor:

a) Increasing the concentration of a solution increases the rate of reaction.

b) Increasing the temperature of the reactants increases the rate of reaction.

c) Using smaller particles of a solid reactant increases the rate of reaction.

5. Use this graph to explain to your tutor how a catalyst increases the rate of reaction.

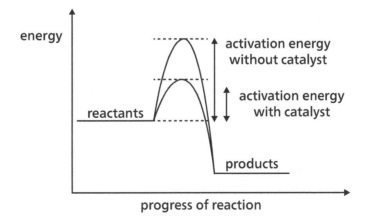

CHEMISTRY HIGHER

Homework activity: Investigating the rate of a reaction

Time **60** mins

Learning objectives

- To investigate the effect of changing concentration on the reaction between sodium thiosulfate solution and dilute hydrochloric acid
- To adapt the experiment to investigate the effect of changing temperature

Equipment

- graph paper
- pencil

Maddie and Isaac are reacting sodium thiosulfate with dilute hydrochloric acid. They are using different concentrations of sodium thiosulfate solution to investigate the effects of changing concentration.

This is their method:

- Place 50 cm³ sodium thiosulfate solution in the flask and place the flask on a piece of paper with a cross drawn on it.
- Measure 5 cm³ dilute hydrochloric acid.
- Add the acid to the sodium thiosulfate solution, swirl the flask and immediately start the clock.
- Stop the clock when you can no longer see the cross from above.
- Repeat the procedure using the amounts in the table.

Volume of sodium thiosulfate solution (cm³)	Volume of water (cm³)	Concentration of sodium thiosulfate solution (g/dm³)	Time taken for cross to disappear (s)
50	0	50	12
40	10		24
30	20		37
20	30		56
10	40		124

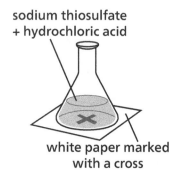

sodium thiosulfate + hydrochloric acid

white paper marked with a cross

1. Complete the table then draw a graph of these results. You need to plot concentration (g/dm³) on the *x*-axis and time (s) on the *y*-axis.

2. Use your graph to predict the time taken using sodium thiosulfate solution with a concentration of 25 g/dm³.

_____

3. Describe how you could adapt this experiment to investigate the effect of temperature on the reaction between sodium thiosulfate and dilute hydrochloric acid.

_____

_____

_____

_____

_____

23 Answers

Starter activity: Tracking a reaction

1. Apparatus B and graph C; apparatus A and graph D
2. Both are steepest/have highest gradient/show fastest rate of reaction at the beginning; both become less steep/gradient decreases/reaction rate slows as reaction proceeds; both level out when reaction is complete

Main activity: Calculating rates of reaction

1. a) $0.71 \, cm^3/s$
   b) $0.067 \, g/s$
   c) $10 \, mol/s$
2. a) $\dfrac{40 \, cm^3}{300 \, seconds} = 0.13 \, cm^3/s$
   b) A: $0.27 \, cm^3/s$; B: $0.16 \, cm^3/s$; C: $0.05 \, cm^3/s$

Main activity: Factors affecting the rate of a reaction

1. Concentration of solutions, pressure of gases, temperature, size of particles, presence of catalyst
2. a) Decreases the rate of reaction
   b) Decreases the rate of reaction
   c) Increases the rate of reaction
3. Molecules must collide with sufficient energy to overcome the activation energy.
4. a) More reactants and more frequent successful collisions increase the rate of reaction.
   b) More energy so more frequent collisions and more energetic collisions increase the rate of reaction.
   c) A greater surface area means more frequent collisions, increasing the rate of reaction.
5. The catalyst provides a reaction pathway with a lower activation energy.

Homework activity: Investigating the rate of a reaction

1. Concentrations are 40, 30, 20, 10 g/dm³; the graph should be a line graph with a line of best fit
2. 44 to 46 seconds
3. Use the same concentration of sodium thiosulfate and dilute acid for all experiments (controlled variables). Carry out the experiment at different temperatures by heating the reactants in a water bath or similar (independent variable). Record the time taken at each temperature (dependent variable).

CHEMISTRY HIGHER

24 Rate of reaction: Reversible reactions and equilibrium

Learning objectives

- To describe a reversible reaction
- To know that the same amount of energy is transferred in each direction of a reversible reaction
- To know that the forward and reverse reactions occur at the same rate
- To know that changing conditions can change the direction of a reversible reaction

Specification links

- 4.6.2.1, 4.6.2.2, 4.6.2.3
- WS: 1.2, 1.4
- MS: 1a, 4a

Starter activity

- **Rechargeable batteries; 5 minutes; page 156**

  Remind the student of the work covered in lesson 22.

Main activities

- **Reversible reactions; 20 minutes; page 157**

  Discuss the nature of the reversible reaction in the starter and the effect of changing conditions. Explain that many chemical reactions are reversible and show the student how the reversible reaction sign is used in equations, by referring to the general equation $A + B \rightleftharpoons C + D$. Explain that the same amount of energy is transferred in both the forward and backward directions of a reversible reaction. A reaction that is endothermic in one direction will be exothermic in the opposite direction.

- **Equilibrium; 20 minutes; page 158**

  Explain that the reversible reactions covered so far have gone (almost) completely in one direction with the right conditions, but some reactions go in both directions with the same conditions and an equilibrium is established. Models of reactions are useful to demonstrate how equilibria are established. Explain the properties of a system at equilibrium.

Plenary activity

- **Summarising reversible reactions and equilibrium; 5 minutes**

  Ask the student to state the three most important facts from this lesson about reversible reactions and equilibria.

Homework activity

- **Investigating copper sulfate; 60 minutes; page 159**

  This is a synoptic question using skills from lessons 14 and 21 as well as this lesson. Full instructions are provided on the activity sheet.

Support ideas

- **Reversible reactions** The student can refer to lesson 21 to recap exothermic and endothermic reactions. The student can refer back to lesson 14 to recap how to balance equations.

Extension ideas

- **Reversible reactions** The student can find out about the reversible reaction $NO_2 \rightleftharpoons N_2O_4$.
- **Equilibrium** The student could find out how the position of the equilibrium can vary in preparation for the next lesson.

Progress and observations

Starter activity: Rechargeable batteries

Learning objective	Equipment
• To recall that rechargeable batteries are recharged when the chemical reactions inside them are reversed	none

The diagram shows a lithium ion battery like the ones used in cameras and laptops.

It is rechargeable. The cathode inside the battery contains lithium. When the battery is in use, lithium atoms produce lithium ions and electrons. The electrons provide the electric current.

The reaction is: $Li \rightarrow Li^+ + e^-$

When the battery is being recharged, the direction of the current is reversed. Electrons from the electricity supply react with the lithium ions to make lithium atoms. These are deposited back on the cathode.

1. Write a half equation to show the reverse reaction when the battery is being recharged.

_____

CHEMISTRY HIGHER

Main activity: Reversible reactions

Learning objectives

- To know that the direction of a reversible reaction can be changed by changing the conditions
- To know that the same amount of energy is transferred in the forward and reverse reactions

Equipment

1. **The diagram shows ammonium chloride, NH_4Cl, being heated.**

   a) How does the diagram show that the reaction is reversible?

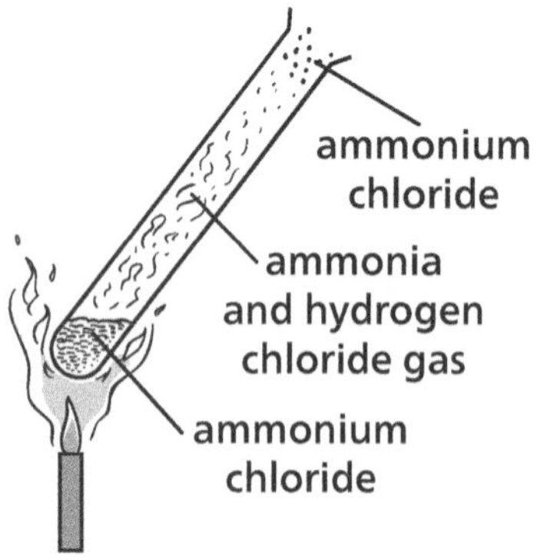

   _____

   _____

   _____

ammonium chloride

ammonia and hydrogen chloride gas

ammonium chloride

   b) Write an equation for this reaction, including the reversible reaction sign. The formula for ammonia is NH_3.

   _____

   c) Which is the forward reaction and which is the reverse reaction?

   _____

   _____

   d) What conditions determine the direction of the reaction?

   _____

   _____

2. **Hydrated copper sulfate crystals are blue and contain water of crystallisation. When they are heated, the water of crystallisation is given off and white anhydrous copper sulfate is left. If water is added to white anhydrous copper sulfate, blue hydrated copper sulfate is produced and heat energy is released.**

   a) Write a word equation showing that this is a reversible reaction.

   _____

   b) Which reaction is exothermic and which is endothermic?

   _____

   c) If 5 kJ of heat energy are needed to convert a sample of hydrated copper sulfate to anhydrous copper sulfate, how many kJ of heat energy are released when water is added to the sample of anhydrous copper sulfate?

   _____

CHEMISTRY HIGHER

Main activity: Equilibrium

Time 20 mins

Learning objectives	Equipment
• To know that the forward and reverse reactions occur at the same rate when an equilibrium is established • To know that the apparatus must prevent reactants and products escaping to establish an equilibrium	none

Students are observing bromine. Bromine is a dark red/brown liquid at room temperature. Its boiling point is 59 °C. A few cm³ of bromine are poured into a beaker in a fume cupboard and the beaker is sealed with a lid.

The space above the liquid bromine gradually turns red/brown as bromine fumes are given off. After a few minutes, the colour of the bromine fumes does not change.

1. Write an equation to show liquid bromine turning to gaseous bromine. Remember, this is a reversible reaction.

_____

2. Use these diagrams to explain what is happening:

a) initially _____

_____

b) when equilibrium is reached. _____

_____

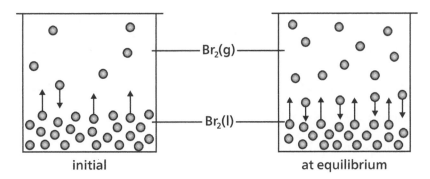

initial   at equilibrium

3. How does the rate of the forward reaction compare with the rate of the reverse reaction:

a) initially _____

_____

b) at equilibrium? _____

_____

4. How is the amount of bromine gas changing:

a) initially _____

b) at equilibrium? _____

5. What will happen to the equilibrium if the lid is removed?

_____

_____

CHEMISTRY HIGHER

AQA

Homework activity: Investigating copper sulfate

Time **60** mins

Learning objectives

- To know that the same amount of energy is transferred in the forward and reverse reactions of reversible reactions
- To draw reaction profiles
- To balance equations given the masses of reactants and products

Equipment

- copy of the periodic table
- calculator
- spare paper
- pencil

Max has heated blue hydrated copper sulfate to produce anhydrous copper sulfate. This is his method.

- Weigh an empty crucible.
- Add hydrated copper sulfate to the crucible and weigh the crucible and hydrated copper sulfate.
- Heat the hydrated copper sulfate as in the diagram, until it turns white.
- Weigh the crucible and contents.

These are his results:

	Mass (g)
mass of crucible	16.00
mass of crucible + hydrated copper sulfate	22.25
mass of crucible + anhydrous copper sulfate	20.00

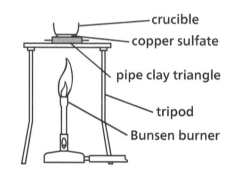

crucible
copper sulfate
pipe clay triangle
tripod
Bunsen burner

1. **On a separate piece of paper draw a reaction profile for the reaction to produce anhydrous copper sulfate from hydrated copper sulfate.**

2. **Max adds drops of water to the anhydrous copper sulfate. It turns blue and gets hot. Draw a reaction profile for the reaction between water and anhydrous copper sulfate to produce hydrated copper sulfate. Draw your profile alongside the profile from question 1 so the amounts of energy transferred can be compared.**

3. **Hydrated copper sulfate has the formula $CuSO_4.xH_2O$ where x is the number of water molecules.**

   Use Max's results to calculate the value of x. Calculate the reacting masses first.

   (Hint: You need the equation: $CuSO_4.xH_2O \rightleftharpoons CuSO_4 + xH_2O$)

_____

_____

_____

_____

24 Answers

Starter activity: Rechargeable batteries

1. $Li^+ + e^- \rightarrow Li$

Main activity: Reversible reactions

1. a) Ammonium chloride decomposes to ammonia and hydrogen chloride gas, and ammonia and hydrogen chloride react to give ammonium chloride.
  b) $NH_4Cl \rightleftharpoons NH_3 + HCl$
  c) Forward reaction: $NH_4Cl \rightarrow NH_3 + HCl$
  Reverse reaction: $NH_3 + HCl \rightarrow NH_4Cl$
  d) The temperature, pressure and concentration of the reactants.
2. a) hydrated copper sulfate $\rightleftharpoons$ anhydrous copper sulfate + water
  b) The reverse reaction is exothermic, the forward reaction is endothermic.
  c) $5\,kJ$

Main activity: Equilibrium

1. $Br_2(l) \rightleftharpoons Br_2(g)$
2. a) Many bromine molecules changing from liquid to gas, a few changing from gas to liquid
  b) Bromine molecules changing from liquid to gas and from gas to liquid, at the same rate
3. a) The rate of the forward reaction is greater than the rate of the reverse reaction.
  b) The rate of the forward reaction is equal to the rate of the reverse reaction.
4. a) increasing
  b) not changing
5. It will no longer exist as bromine gas will escape and more bromine will evaporate.

Homework activity: Investigating copper sulfate

1. The reaction profile should show an endothermic reaction.
2. The reaction profile should show an exothermic reaction. The total amount of energy transferred should be the same as in the diagram drawn for question 1.
3. 6.25 g hydrated copper sulfate $\rightarrow$ 4.00 g anhydrous copper sulfate + 2.25 g water; 0.025 mol anhydrous copper sulfate combines with 0.125 mol water; 1 mol anhydrous copper sulfate combines with 5 mol water. $x = 5$

25 Rate of reaction: Changing conditions

Learning objectives

- To use Le Chatelier's principle to predict the effects of changing conditions on equilibrium
- To predict the effects of changing concentration, temperature and pressure on equilibrium

Specification links

- 4.6.2.4, 4.6.2.5, 4.6.2.6, 4.6.2.7
- WS: 1.2
- MS: 3a

Starter activity

- **Equilibrium position; 5 minutes; page 162**

  Discuss what is meant by 'the position of equilibrium'. Check the student realises that this does not usually lie in the centre.

Main activities

- **Le Chatelier's principle and concentration; 20 minutes; page 163**

  Explain Le Chatelier's principle and the conditions that can be changed when a system is at equilibrium. Discuss the effects of changing concentrations of reactants and products on systems at equilibrium, and why these effects are adjustments until a new equilibrium is established. Models may be useful to illustrate the effects of concentration changes.

- **Changing temperature and pressure; 20 minutes; page 164**

  Explain the effects of changing temperature on a system at equilibrium and the relevance of the direction of the exothermic and endothermic reactions. Discuss the effects of pressure changes on systems at equilibrium involving gaseous reactants and products. The activity sheet involves predicting the effects of changing conditions on reactions at equilibrium used in the chemical industry.

Plenary activity

- **Managing a chemical industry; 5 minutes**

  Ask the student to imagine they are the manager of a chemical industry. Allow them two minutes to prepare a short talk on why reversible reactions can be a problem in their industry and how to overcome them.

Homework activity

- **Ammonia; 60 minutes; page 165**

  This activity sheet applies Le Chatelier's principle to the manufacture of ammonia. Details of the plant are covered in lesson 38. The activity also includes rate of reaction and you may wish to differentiate between rate and equilibrium before the student completes the sheet.

Support ideas

- **Changing temperature and pressure** Diagrams, models and video sequences may help the student to understand why changing conditions affect an equilibrium.
- **Ammonia** The student can read about this in their textbook and the process is covered in lesson 38.

Extension ideas

- **Le Chatelier's principle and concentration** The student can explain why the carbon dioxide in a sealed bottle of sparkling mineral water is in equilibrium with the carbon dioxide in the space above the water, and how this changes when the cap is removed.
- **Changing temperature and pressure** The student could research the equilibrium constant and find out what values <1, 1 and >1 mean.

Progress and observations

CHEMISTRY HIGHER

Starter activity: Equilibrium position

Learning objective

- To understand terminology used to describe the position of the equilibrium

Equipment

We can represent a chemical reaction using letters for the substances.

$$A + B \rightleftharpoons C + D$$

1. The table shows some percentages of reactants and products at equilibrium. For each row, put a tick in the correct column to show where the position of equilibrium lies.

	Percentage of reactants (A and B)	Percentage of products (C and D)	Position of equilibrium lies to the left	Position of equilibrium is in the centre	Position of equilibrium lies to the right
a)	90	10			
b)	50	50			
c)	20	80			
d)	65	35			

2. A chemical industry manufactures substances C and D. If the position of equilibrium lies to the left, what problem does this cause for the manufacturer?

_____

_____

TUTORS GUILD CHEMISTRY HIGHER

Main activity: Le Chatelier's principle and concentration

Learning objectives

- To know Le Chatelier's principle
- To make qualitative predictions about the effects of changes on systems at equilibrium
- To predict the effects of changes in the concentration of reactants and products on systems at equilibrium
- To predict the effects of changes in pressure of gaseous reactants on systems at equilibrium

Equipment

Le Chatelier's principle states that:

If a system is at equilibrium and a change is made to any of the conditions, the system will respond to counteract the change.

1. Name three conditions that affect the position of an equilibrium.

_____

2. The diagram shows a lime kiln. Calcium carbonate is heated to produce calcium oxide.

The reaction is: $CaCO_3 \rightleftharpoons CaO + CO_2$.

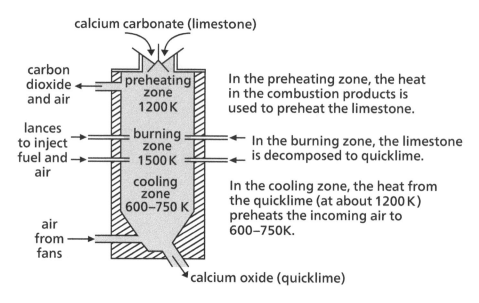

calcium carbonate (limestone)

carbon dioxide and air ← preheating zone 1200 K — In the preheating zone, the heat in the combustion products is used to preheat the limestone.

lances to inject fuel and air → burning zone 1500 K ← In the burning zone, the limestone is decomposed to quicklime.

cooling zone 600–750 K — In the cooling zone, the heat from the quicklime (at about 1200 K) preheats the incoming air to 600–750K.

air from fans →

calcium oxide (quicklime)

a) If calcium carbonate is heated in a closed container, an equilibrium is established. Name the substances present in the container at equilibrium.

_____

b) In the industrial process, the manufacturers obtain a yield of almost 100% calcium oxide. Use Le Chatelier's principle to explain why.

_____

_____

3. Predict the effect of these changes on a reaction at equilibrium.

a) The concentration of a reactant is increased. _____

b) The concentration of a product is decreased. _____

CHEMISTRY HIGHER

Main activity: Changing temperature and pressure

Time 20 mins

Learning objectives

- To predict the effects of increasing or decreasing the temperature on systems at equilibrium
- To predict the effects of increasing or decreasing the pressure of gaseous reactions at equilibrium

Equipment

These questions are about reactions used in industry to manufacture chemicals. Use Le Chatelier's principle to answer the questions.

1. **Sulfur trioxide is used to make sulfuric acid. Sulfur trioxide is manufactured from sulfur dioxide and oxygen in a reversible reaction.**

   The reaction is: $2SO_2(g) + O_2(g) \rightleftharpoons 2SO_3$ The forward reaction to produce sulfur trioxide is exothermic.

   a) Would a high temperature or a low temperature give a higher yield of sulfur trioxide? Explain your answer.

   _____

   _____

   b) Would high or low pressure give a higher yield of sulfur trioxide? Explain your answer.

   _____

   _____

2. **This reaction is used to produce hydrogen gas from methane. Methane is a product of petroleum.**

   $CH_4(g) + H_2O(g) \rightleftharpoons CO(g) + 3H_2(g)$ The reaction to produce hydrogen is endothermic.

   a) Would high or low temperature give a higher yield of hydrogen? Explain your answer.

   _____

   _____

   b) Would high or low pressure give a higher yield of hydrogen? Explain your answer.

   _____

   _____

3. **This reaction can be used to produce ethanol (an alcohol).**

   $C_2H_4(g) + H_2O(g) \rightleftharpoons C_2H_5OH(g)$ The reaction to produce ethanol is exothermic.

   a) Would high or low temperature give a higher yield of ethanol? Explain your answer.

   _____

   _____

   b) Would high or low pressure give a higher yield of ethanol? Explain your answer.

   _____

   _____

CHEMISTRY HIGHER

Homework activity: Ammonia

Time 60 mins

Learning objective	Equipment
• To apply Le Chatelier's principle to the manufacture of ammonia	none

Ammonia, NH_3, is manufactured from hydrogen and nitrogen gas. The reaction is: $N_2(g) + 3H_2(g) \rightleftharpoons 2NH_3$
The reaction to produce ammonia is exothermic.

The graph shows how changes in pressure and temperature affect the yield of ammonia.

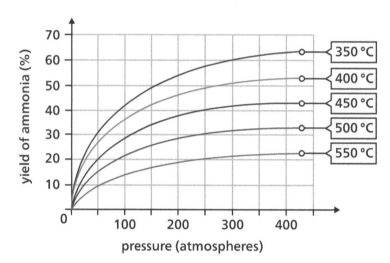

1. **What is the percentage yield of ammonia at:**

   a) 450 °C and 300 atmospheres? _____

   b) 500 °C and 100 atmospheres? _____

2. **How does temperature affect the yield of ammonia? Explain your answer using Le Chatelier's principle.**

   _____

   _____

3. **How does pressure affect the yield of ammonia? Use Le Chatelier's principle to explain your answer.**

   _____

   _____

4. **Maintaining high pressures is difficult and expensive. A high temperature is best for a high rate of reaction. This affects the time taken for the reaction to reach equilibrium. Suggest why manufacturers usually use a pressure of about 200 atmospheres and a temperature of 450 °C.**

   _____

   _____

   _____

5. **The manufacturers use an iron catalyst in the production ammonia. What effect does this have on:**

   a) the rate of reaction? _____

   b) the equilibrium? _____

25 Answers

Starter activity: Equilibrium position

1. a) left
   b) centre
   c) right
   d) left
2. Potentially, a low yield of product

Main activity: Le Chatelier's principle and concentration

1. Temperature, concentration and pressure of gaseous systems
2. a) Calcium carbonate, calcium oxide, carbon dioxide
   b) Carbon dioxide (a product) is removed, so the concentration of carbon dioxide decreases; more calcium carbonate reacts to restore equilibrium, which is never reached
3. a) More product is produced
   b) More reactants react

Main activity: Changing temperature and pressure

1. a) Low temperature; amount of product increases at equilibrium for exothermic reaction
   b) High pressure; 3 moles → 2 moles; increased pressure moves equilibrium to side with fewer moles
2. a) High temperature; amount of product increases at equilibrium for endothermic reaction
   b) Low pressure; 2 moles → 4 moles; decreased pressure moves equilibrium to side with more moles
3. a) Low temperature; amount of product increases at equilibrium for exothermic reaction
   b) High pressure; 2 moles → 1 mole; increased pressure moves equilibrium to side with fewer moles

Homework activity: Ammonia

1. a) 40%
   b) 20%
2. A low temperature favours a high yield of ammonia; a decrease in temperature shifts the equilibrium in the exothermic direction
3. 4 moles → 2 moles; high pressure favours a higher yield of ammonia because equilibrium shifts to the side with fewer moles
4. 200 atmospheres is a compromise pressure, since higher pressures are expensive and difficult to maintain. A low temperature is better for yield, but the rate of reaction would be very slow; 450 °C is a compromise temperature. Ammonia is produced little and often.
5. a) Increases it
   b) No effect

26 Organic chemistry: Crude oil and alkanes

Learning objectives	Specification links

Learning objectives

- To name and draw displayed formulae for the first four alkanes
- To know that crude oil is a source of alkanes
- To describe the fractional distillation of crude oil
- To explain hydrocarbon properties of flammability, viscosity and boiling point

Specification links

- 4.7.1.1, 4.7.1.2, 4.7.1.3
- WS: 1.2, 3.1, 3.5
- MS: 4c

Starter activity

- **Crude oil; 5 minutes; page 168**

  Discuss the formation of crude oil and establish that it is a mixture of many compounds. Note that crude oil is also called petroleum, not to be confused with petrol.

Main activities

- **Fractional distillation and alkanes; 15 minutes; page 169**

  Explain that crude oil is a mixture of many compounds, mostly hydrocarbons (compounds containing hydrogen and carbon only), that need to be separated before they can be used. Discuss the structure of alkanes and their general formula, C_nH_{2n+2}. The student may already have used molecular models to make 3-D models. Explain the process of fractional distillation.

- **Properties of hydrocarbons; 25 minutes; page 170**

  Remind the student about intermolecular forces between molecules and ask them to predict how these will affect the boiling points of alkanes. You can link this to fractional distillation. Explain the meaning of the term viscosity and the effects of intermolecular forces on viscosity and hence flammability.

Plenary activity

- **Summarising carbon chemistry; 5 minutes**

  The student can start a spider diagram to summarise carbon chemistry with 'carbon chemistry' at the centre of the page, and add the main points from this lesson.

Homework activity

- **Investigating fractional distillation; 60 minutes; page 171**

  This activity sheet applies the lesson's content to the laboratory fractional distillation of crude oil substitute. You might remind the student that alkane boiling points are given in 'properties of hydrocarbons'.

Support ideas

- **Properties of hydrocarbons** The student can use the electronic structure of a carbon atom and covalent bonding to understand how carbon atoms can form long chains and many compounds. The student can refer back to lesson 10.

Extension ideas

- **Fractional distillation and alkanes** The student can compare the information given by displayed formulae of alkanes with images of 3-D models.
- **Investigating fractional distillation** The student can draw dot-and-cross diagrams to show the electron arrangement in ethane and propane.

Progress and observations

CHEMISTRY HIGHER

Starter activity: Crude oil

Learning objectives

- To know that crude oil is the remains of ancient biomass
- To describe the formation of crude oil

Equipment

Look at the diagram. It shows a deposit of crude oil and gas in rock layers.

Circle the correct sentence endings to describe the formation of crude oil.

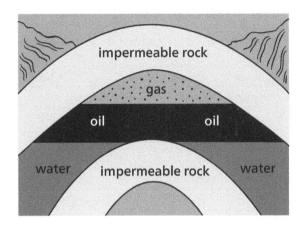

1. **Millions of years ago, plankton in the sea died and…**

   A. … slowly decayed over millions of years.

   B. … collected on the surface of the water.

   C. … were eaten by larger predators.

   D. … were deposited on the sea bed and covered in mud.

2. **Layers of sediment were deposited on top of the biomass which…**

   A. …prevented decay by excluding oxygen.

   B. …increased the rate of decay.

   C. …changed the biomass into sedimentary rock.

   D. …prevented decay by excluding water.

3. **Over millions of years, chemical reactions…**

   A. …increased the pressure on the biomass.

   B. …increased the rate of decay.

   C. …converted the remains of the biomass into crude oil.

   D. …became more frequent.

4. **Crude oil collected in pockets where…**

   A. …it could dissolve in the ground water.

   B. …layers of impermeable rock and the rock structure prevented its escape.

   C. …layers of permeable rock trapped the oil.

   D. …gas could escape.

CHEMISTRY HIGHER

Main activity: Fractional distillation and alkanes

Time 15 mins

Learning objectives

- To draw the displayed formulae for the first four alkanes
- To know how fractional distillation is used to separate crude oil into fractions
- To know some uses of some fractions

Equipment

- spare paper

1. **Complete the table by adding the formulae of the alkanes.**

Alkane	Chemical formula	Displayed formula
methane		
ethane		
propane		
butane		

2. **The diagram shows a fractionating column used to separate crude oil into fractions.**

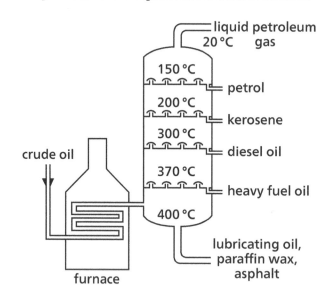

a) i) Add labels to the diagram to show how the fractions are used.

   ii) Add an arrow to show the direction in which the number of carbon atoms in the hydrocarbons increases.

b) On a separate piece of paper, explain how fractional distillation works. Include the words 'evaporation' and 'condensation' in your answer.

CHEMISTRY HIGHER

Main activity: Properties of hydrocarbons

Time 25 mins

Learning objectives

- To understand how intermolecular forces in alkanes affect their boiling points
- To explain viscosity and flammability in terms of the size of alkane molecules
- To write balanced equations for the complete combustion of hydrocarbons

Equipment

- pencil
- graph paper
- ruler

The table gives the boiling points of the first six alkanes.

Alkane	Chemical formula	Boiling point (°C)
methane	CH_4	−162
ethane	C_2H_6	−89
propane	C_3H_8	−42
butane	C_4H_{10}	0.5
pentane	C_5H_{12}	36
hexane	C_6H_{14}	69

1. On graph paper, plot a suitable graph of the number of carbon atoms in an alkane against boiling point.

2. Explain the trend in boiling points. Your answer should refer to intermolecular forces.

_____

_____

_____

3. As the alkane chains get longer, the alkanes become more viscous (thick and sticky). Explain why.

_____

_____

_____

4. A good fuel must ignite easily. Before a liquid fuel can burn, it has to evaporate. Explain why alkanes with shorter carbon chains make better fuels than alkanes with longer carbon chains.

_____

_____

_____

5. When alkanes burn completely, carbon dioxide and water are produced. Write balanced symbol equations for the complete combustion of:

a) methane _____

b) propane _____

TUTORS GUILD

CHEMISTRY HIGHER

AQA

Homework activity: Investigating fractional distillation

Time **60** mins

Learning objectives

- Apply knowledge of fractional distillation to experimental results
- Compare the properties of fractions from crude oil

Students watched a demonstration to fractionally distil crude oil substitute. This is the apparatus. Four fractions were collected.

Equipment

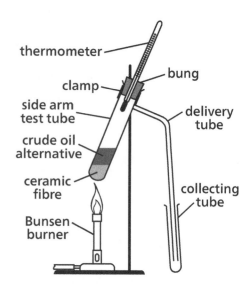

Fraction	Temperature range (°C)	Viscosity	Flammability
A	room temperature –100		
B	100 – 150		
C	150 – 200		
D	200 – 250		

1. Complete the table by predicting the properties of the fractions. Rank each fraction from 1 to 4, with 1 indicating the highest viscosity or flammability and 4 the lowest.

2. Give reasons for your predictions in question 1.

_____

_____

_____

_____

3. Why do the compounds in fraction D have the highest boiling points?

_____

_____

4. Which fraction will make the best fuel? Give reasons for your answer.

_____

_____

5. Name an alkane in fraction A and write a balanced equation for its complete combustion.

_____

_____

26 Answers

Starter activity: Crude oil

1. D
2. A
3. C
4. B

Main activity: Fractional distillation and alkanes

1.

Alkane	Chemical formula	Displayed formula
methane	CH_4	H | H—C—H | H
ethane	C_2H_6	H H | | H—C—C—H | | H H
propane	C_3H_8	H H H | | | H—C—C—C—H | | | H H H
butane	C_4H_{10}	H H H H | | | | H—C—C—C—C—H | | | | H H H H

2. a) i) LPG: heating and cooking; petrol: fuel for vehicles; kerosene: fuel for aircraft; diesel: fuel for vehicles; heavy fuel oil: fuel for ships
   ii) Arrow should point downwards to indicate increase in number of carbon atoms
b) Crude oil is evaporated and passes up the fractionating column. The temperature of the fractionating column decreases as you go up. Alkanes condense when they reach their boiling point and are collected at that point.

Main activity: Properties of hydrocarbons

1. Graph should be a bar graph, with number of carbon atoms on the x-axis and boiling point (°C) on the y-axis
2. Longer alkanes have stronger intermolecular forces. More energy is needed to break these forces so their boiling point is higher.
3. Longer alkanes have stronger intermolecular forces, and longer carbon chains become more tangled.
4. Shorter alkanes have lower boiling points and can evaporate more easily , and therefore ignite more easily.
5. a) $CH_4(g) + 2O_2(g) \rightarrow CO_2(g) + 2H_2O$
   b) $C_3H_8(g) + 5O_2(g) \rightarrow 3CO_2(g) + 4H_2O$

Homework activity: Investigating fractional distillation

1. Viscosity: A = 4, B = 3, C = 2, D = 1; flammability: A = 1, B = 2, C = 3, D = 4
2. Viscosity increases as molecules increase in length, because intermolecular forces increase and molecules become more tangled. Flammability decreases because boiling points increase and fractions evaporate less easily.
3. Fraction D has the longest molecules so the intermolecular forces are stronger and more energy is needed to break them.
4. Fraction A evaporates most easily, flows easily and therefore ignites easily.
5. For example, pentane ($C_5H_{12} + 8O_2 \rightarrow 5CO_2 + 6H_2O$) or hexane ($2C_6H_{14} + 19O_2 \rightarrow 12CO_2 + 14H_2O$)

CHEMISTRY HIGHER

27 Organic chemistry: Alkenes, alcohols and carboxylic acids

Learning objectives

- To know the uses and products of cracking reactions
- To describe the structure of the first four alkenes, alcohols and carboxylic acids
- To know the properties of alkenes, alcohols and carboxylic acids

Specification links

- 4.7.1.4, 4.7.2.1, 4.7.2.2, 4.7.2.3, 4.7.2.4
- WS: 1.2, 2.2
- MS: 4a

Starter activity

- **Supply and demand; 5 minutes; page 174**

  Remind the student of the fractional distillation of crude oil (lesson 26). Discuss the usefulness of cracking and how the chemical industry uses the products of cracking to produce a wide range of materials we depend on.

Main activities

- **Cracking and ethene; 15 minutes; page 175**

  Explain the cracking of hydrocarbons, the products and the nature of alkenes. Include the general formula of alkenes, C_nH_{2n}, and explain that they are described as unsaturated. Discuss the difference between catalytic cracking and steam cracking. Check that the student realises there are no hard and fast rules for the products formed during cracking reactions.

- **Structure and properties; 25 minutes; page 176**

  Explain the prefixes and suffixes used to name alkenes, alcohols and carboxylic acids. Only the first four of each series are required. Discuss their molecular and displayed formulae and their properties as the student works through the worksheet. Explain the main uses of alcohols: in alcoholic drinks and as a solvent in industry. Note that equations are not required for reactions of alcohols and carboxylic acids, and ethyl ethanoate is the only ester required. Remind the student that carboxylic acids are weak acids (refer back to lesson 19 if necessary). Emphasise that the functional group determines the reactions and all compounds with the same functional group have similar reactions. Encourage the student to develop study skills to help them remember the chemical reactions involved.

Plenary activity

- **More homologous series; 5 minutes**

  The student can add alkenes, alcohols and carboxylic acids to the spider diagram started in the last lesson.

Homework activity

- **Fermentation and ethanol; 60 minutes; page 177**

  This activity is partly synoptic, including methods covered in lesson 1. The activity sheet is self-explanatory.

Support ideas

- **Structure and properties** The student can draw the displayed formula of an alkene, alcohol or carboxylic acid given its name. The concepts of saturated and unsaturated may need extra explanation.

Extension ideas

- **Cracking and ethene** The student can find the difference between but-1-ene and but-2-ene and draw their displayed formulae.
- **Structure and properties** The student could draw displayed formulae for any alternative structures (isomers) of the compounds covered in this lesson.

Progress and observations

CHEMISTRY HIGHER

Starter activity: Supply and demand

Learning objective	Equipment
• To understand the need for cracking	none

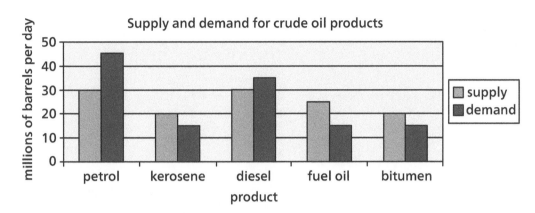

1. **Look at the graph. Crude oil is measured in barrels. 1 barrel = 159 dm³**

   a) Which fractions from the fractional distillation of crude oil are in short supply?

   _____

   b) What do these fractions have in common?

   _____

   c) Which fractions do we have more of than we need?

   _____

   d) How does cracking solve this problem?

   _____

   _____

CHEMISTRY HIGHER

Main activity: Cracking and ethene

Time 15 mins

Learning objectives

- To know the products of cracking
- To write balanced equations for cracking reactions
- To describe reactions and observations of alkanes and alkenes with bromine water
- To describe incomplete combustion

Equipment

Students are observing this experiment to crack a hydrocarbon. Two test tubes of gas are collected.

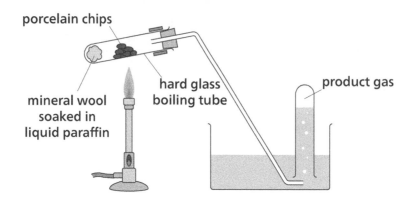

1. **A few cm³ of yellow bromine water are added to the first test tube.**

   a) What do you expect to observe?

   _____

   b) If the gas is ethene, write the displayed formula of the product formed.

   c) How would the result differ if bromine water was added to ethane? Explain why.

   _____

   _____

2. **The second test tube of gas is ignited. It burns with a smoky flame producing carbon and water.**

   a) What type of combustion is this? _____

   b) Write a balanced symbol equation for the combustion reaction. _____

3. **During the experiment, longer hydrocarbon molecules have been broken into smaller more useful molecules. How is ethene useful?**

   _____

4. **Complete these equations showing cracking reactions.**

   a) $C_{14}H_{30} \rightarrow$ _____ $+ C_2H_4$

   b) $C_{14}H_{30} \rightarrow C_7H_{16} +$ _____ $+ 2C_2H_4$

   c) _____ $\rightarrow C_8H_{18} + C_3H_6 + 2C_2H_4$

CHEMISTRY HIGHER

Main activity: Structure and properties

Learning objectives

- To know the molecular and displayed formulae for the first four alkenes, alcohols and carboxylic acids
- To know the reactions of alkenes, alcohols and carboxylic acids
- To know the functional groups of alkenes, alcohols and carboxylic acids

Equipment

- A3 sheet of paper

1. Copy the table onto a piece of A3 paper and complete it.

Homologous series	a) Functional group	b) Name, molecular formulae and displayed formulae	c) Reactions
1. alkenes		ethene propene butene pentene	*Draw the displayed formulae for the products of the reaction of ethene with each of the following, and add the conditions required for each reaction to take place.* bromine water hydrogen water
2. alcohols		methanol ethanol propanol butanol	*Describe what happens when alcohols react with each of the following.* with sodium with oxygen (combustion) with water with an oxidising agent
3. carboxylic acids		methanoic acid ethanoic acid propanoic acid butanoic acid	*Describe what happens when carboxylic acids react with each of the following.* with carbonates with water with alcohols

CHEMISTRY HIGHER

Homework activity: Fermentation and ethanol

Time **60** mins

Learning objectives

- To know that ethanol is produced during fermentation reactions
- To know the conditions required for the fermentation of sugar solution using yeast

Equipment

1. You are planning an experiment to investigate the conditions required for the fermentation of sugar to produce ethanol.

   Write your plan. It must include a hypothesis and full details of your experiment, including identification of controlled variables.

   _____

   _____

   _____

   _____

   _____

   _____

   _____

   _____

   _____

   _____

   _____

   _____

2. Your experiment should produce an aqueous solution of ethanol.

   a) What technique could you use to produce a pure sample of ethanol from its aqueous solution?

   _____

   b) How will you know if the ethanol sample is pure?

   _____

CHEMISTRY HIGHER

27 Answers

Starter activity: Supply and demand

1. a) Petrol and diesel   b) Both are used as vehicle fuels   c) Kerosene, fuel oil and bitumen
   d) Converts longer chained alkanes into shorter, more useful molecules

Main activity: Cracking and ethene

1. a) Bromine water is decolourised.

b)
```
H  H
 \ /
  C=C
 / \
H  H
```

c) Bromine water is not decolourised. Ethane does not have a double bond, so cannot react with bromine water.

2. a) Incomplete combustion
   b) $C_2H_4 + O_2 \rightarrow 2C + 2H_2O$

3. Used to make polymers and other chemicals

4. a) $C_{14}H_{30} \rightarrow C_{12}H_{26} + C_2H_4$
   b) $C_{14}H_{30} \rightarrow C_7H_{16} + C_3H_6 + 2C_2H_4$
   c) $C_{15}H_{32} \rightarrow C_8H_{18} + C_3H_6 + 2C_2H_4$

Main activity: Structure and properties

1. a) Alkenes: C = C
   b) C_2H_4, C_3H_6, C_4H_8, C_5H_{10} (see diagrams on the right)
   c) With bromine water: bromine water is decolourised; reaction occurs at room temperature with hydrogen: reaction occurs at 150 °C with a nickel catalyst; with water: reaction occurs with steam at 300 °C, 60–70 atm and phosphoric acid catalyst (see diagrams on the right)

2. a) Alcohols: –O–H
   b) CH_3OH, C_2H_5OH, C_3H_7OH C_4H_9OH (see diagrams on the right)
   c) With sodium: sodium ethanoate formed; reaction happens at room temperature; with oxygen: combustion (complete) reaction occurs when alcohol is heated in a plentiful supply of air/oxygen; the temperature required supplies the activation energy for the reaction; the reaction is exothermic and proceeds with no further heat source with water: alcohol dissolves at room temperature; with an oxidising agent: oxidised to carboxylic acid; reaction occurs when alcohol is warmed with a sulfuric acid catalyst

3. a) Carboxylic acids: –COOH
   b) HCOOH, CH_3COOH, C_2H_5COOH, C_3H_7COOH (see diagrams on the right)
   c) With carbonates: gives carbon dioxide, water and a salt; reaction happens at room temperature; with water: carboxylic acids dissolve at room temperature with an alcohol: produces an ester
   (ethanol + ethanoic acid → ethyl ethanoate + water); reaction happens when warmed with a sulfuric acid catalyst

1 b) ethene   propene   butene   pentene

```
ethene
H  H
 \ /
  C=C
 / \
H  H

propene
H  H  H
|  |  |
H-C-C=C
|     |
H     H

butene
H  H  H  H
|  |  |  |
H-C-C-C=C
|  |     |
H  H     H

pentene
H  H  H  H  H
|  |  |  |  |
H-C-C-C-C=C
|  |  |  |  |
H  H  H  H  H
```

c) bromine water   hydrogen   water

```
bromine water
     H  H
     |  |
Br – C – C – Br
     |  |
     H  H

hydrogen
    H  H
    |  |
H – C – C – H
    |  |
    H  H

water
    H  H
    |  |
H – C – C – O – H
    |  |
    H  H
```

2 b) methanol   ethanol   propanol   butanol

```
methanol
    H
    |
H – C – OH
    |
    H

ethanol
    H  H
    |  |
H – C – C – OH
    |  |
    H  H

propanol
    H  H  H
    |  |  |
H – C – C – C – OH
    |  |  |
    H  H  H

butanol
    H  H  H  H
    |  |  |  |
H – C – C – C – C – OH
    |  |  |  |
    H  H  H  H
```

3 b) methanoic acid   ethanoic acid   propanoic acid   butanoic acid

```
methanoic acid
      O
      ‖
H – C
      \
       OH

ethanoic acid
    H  O
    |  ‖
H – C – C
    |   \
    H    OH

propanoic acid
    H  H  O
    |  |  ‖
H – C – C – C
    |  |   \
    H  H    OH

butanoic acid
    H  H  H  O
    |  |  |  ‖
H – C – C – C – C
    |  |  |   \
    H  H  H    OH
```

Homework activity: Fermentation and ethanol

1. Student's own answers. You can mark this as a level of response question, awarding marks as follows: 5-6 marks: A logical plan that will produce valid results, uses scientific language and demonstrates relevant knowledge; 3-4 marks: A plan that will produce some results, probably lacks precision and correct use of scientific terms; 1-2 marks: A plan that will not produce valid results, but includes some relevant facts.

2. a) Fractional distillation
   b) The boiling point of ethanol is 78 °C; if this is the exact boiling point of the ethanol fraction collected, then the sample is pure.

28 Organic chemistry: Polymers

Learning objectives

- To describe addition polymerisation and condensation polymerisation
- To describe condensation reactions of amino acids to produce polypeptides
- To name the monomers from which naturally occurring polymers such as DNA are made

Specification links

- 4.7.3.1, 4.7.3.2, 4.7.3.3, 4.6.3.4
- WS: 1.2
- MS: 5b

Starter activities

- **Introducing polymerisation; 5 minutes; page 180**

  Remind the student of the structure of ethene and ask them what is produced if the double bonds in ethene molecules break and many ethene molecules join up in a long line. Use the photo of a section of a poly(ethene) chain to illustrate the answer. Check that the student can relate the photo of the 3-D model to its displayed formula.

Main activities

- **Addition and condensation polymerisation; 20 minutes; page 181**

  Explain that poly(ethene) is an addition polymer, introduce the term 'monomer' and show the student how to write repeating units. Discuss structures of monomers and polymers of other addition polymers, including poly(propene). Discuss the essential features of condensation polymerisation and how it differs from addition polymerisation. You can use the example on the activity sheet.

- **Amino acids and naturally occurring polymers; 20 minutes; page 182**

  Explain that protein molecules are polymers made from amino acid monomers. Discuss how twenty or so monomers can produce a large variety of proteins. Discuss other natural polymers and their monomers, such as DNA, starch and cellulose.

Plenary activity

- **Five sentences; 5 minutes**

  Ask the student to summarise today's lesson in five sentences. This can be a verbal exercise. The student can also add polymerisation to the spider diagram started in lesson 26.

Homework activity

- **The O2 arena; 45 minutes; page 183**

  In this activity, the student must apply the content from this lesson to the material used to construct the roof of the O2 arena and the Eden Project domes. Reassure the student that, although the context may not be familiar, the content has been covered in this lesson and they should be able to answer everything.

Support ideas

- **Addition and condensation polymerisation** The student may need more practice at drawing repeating units for condensation polymers.
- **Amino acids and naturally occurring polymers** The role of DNA in living things may need more explanation, depending on the work the student has covered in biology.

Extension ideas

- **Addition and condensation polymerisation** The student can draw the displayed formula of nylon (a condensation polymer), if they are given the monomers.
- **Amino acids and naturally occurring polymers** The student can find out why starch and cellulose are different even though they are made from the same monomer.

Progress and observations

CHEMISTRY HIGHER

AQA

Starter activity: Introducing polymerisation

Time 5 mins

Learning objectives

- To know the essential features of a polymer
- To relate an image of a 3-D structure to its displayed formula

Equipment

- pencil

This is an image of a section of a polymer called poly(ethene). The carbon atoms are black and the hydrogen atoms are white.

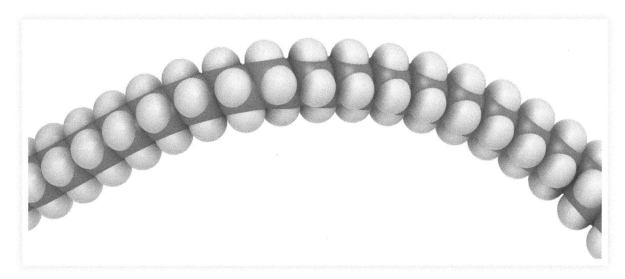

1. Draw the displayed formula of a section of poly(ethene) chain six carbon atoms long.

2. Poly(ethene) is made from ethene. Ethene molecules contain a double covalent bond. Explain why poly(ethene) molecules contain only single covalent bonds.

_____

_____

3. A student suggests that poly(ethene) can be made from ethane. Explain why they are wrong.

_____

_____

_____

Main activity: Addition and condensation polymerisation

Learning objectives

- To identify the monomer of a given addition polymer
- To draw diagrams to show the polymer formed by a given monomer
- To use repeating units
- To know the principles of condensation polymerisation

Equipment

- pencil

The table shows the monomers and polymers of some addition polymers.

Polymer	Displayed formula of monomer	Repeating unit of polymer
poly(ethene)	H H C=C H H	
poly(propene)		$\left(\begin{array}{c}\text{H} \ \text{H} \\ -\text{C}-\text{C}- \\ \text{H} \ \text{CH}_3\end{array}\right)_n$
poly(chloroethene)		$\left(\begin{array}{c}\text{H} \ \text{Cl} \\ -\text{C}-\text{C}- \\ \text{H} \ \text{H}\end{array}\right)_n$
poly(tetrafluoroethene)	F F C=C F F	

1. Complete the table.

2. The two monomers ethane diol and hexanedioic acid react to form a polyester.

   Ethane diol: $HO – CH_2 – CH_2 – OH$ can be shown as: HO –☐– OH

   Hexanedioic acid: $HOOC – CH_2 – CH_2 – CH_2 – CH_2 – COOH$ can be shown as: HOOC –☐– COOH

   a) Draw the repeating unit of the polyester formed. (Use the 'box' notation.)

   b) Why is this process called condensation polymerisation?

   _____

3. State two differences between the monomers of addition polymers and the monomers of condensation polymers.

   _____

   _____

   _____

Main activity: Amino acids and naturally occurring polymers

 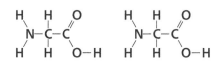
Learning objectives

- To know that proteins are polymers made from amino acid monomers
- To describe how glycine polymerises to produce a polypeptide
- To describe the monomers that make the polymer chains in DNA
- To know that starch and cellulose are naturally occurring polymers

Equipment

- pencil

1. The diagram shows two molecules of glycine.

a) Name the functional groups in glycine.

_____

_____

b) Add dotted lines to the displayed formulae to show the atoms that are lost in the condensation reaction to produce a polypeptide. (A polypeptide is part of a protein molecule.)

c) What is the repeating unit of the glycine polypeptide? _____

2. This is a section of a DNA molecule.

a) What term is used to describe the shape of the DNA molecule?

_____

b) Label the two polymer chains in the molecule.

_____

c) The polymer chains are made from four different monomers. What is the general name for these monomers?

_____

d) How does the structure of the polymer chains in DNA encode genetic instructions?

_____

3. Starch and cellulose are two other naturally occurring polymers. Name their monomers.

_____

CHEMISTRY HIGHER

Homework activity: The O2 arena

Learning objective

- To apply knowledge of monomers, addition polymerisation and polymers to an unfamiliar context

Equipment

- pencil

1. **This is a photo of the O2 arena in London.**

   The roof is made from a polymer known as ETFE. ETFE is made from two monomers, ethene and tetrafluoroethene (C_2F_4).

   a) Draw the displayed formulae of the two monomers.

   b) Ethene molecules have two shared pairs of electrons between their carbon atoms. How does this change when ethene polymerises?

   _____

   _____

When the two monomers polymerise, they join up alternately: an ethene joins with a tetrafluoroethene, then an ethene, then another tetrafluoroethene and so on.

   c) Draw the displayed formula of a section of the polymer eight carbon atoms long.

   d) What is the repeating unit?_____

   e) What type of polymerisation is this? Give a reason for your answer.

   _____

   _____

CHEMISTRY HIGHER

28 Answers

Starter activity: Introducing polymerisation

1.

H H H H H H
| | | | | |
–C–C–C–C–C–C–
| | | | | |
H H H H H H

2. The double bonds break open to make the links.

3. There are no double bonds in ethane to break open to form the links.

Main activity: Addition and condensation polymerisation

1.

| repeating unit of poly(ethene) | monomer of poly(propene) | monomer of poly(chloroethene) | repeating unit of poly(tetrafluoroethene) |

2. a) $(-\boxed{} - OOC - \boxed{} - COO -)_n$

   b) A small molecule, often water, is eliminated.

3. The monomers of addition polymers have double bonds, but the monomers of condensation polymers do not. The monomers of condensation polymers have two functional groups, but the monomers of addition polymers do not.

Main activity: Amino acids and naturally occurring polymers

1. a) Amine, NH_2, and carboxyl, $C(=O)OH$

   b) Dotted line should enclose OH at the bottom right of the left-hand molecule, and the H at the bottom left of the right-hand molecule

   c) $(-HNCH_2C(=O)-)$

2. a) A double helix

   b) The outer spiral chains are the polymer chains

   c) nucleotides

   d) The order of the different nucleotides varies to provide genetic code.

3. Glucose is the monomer for both.

Homework activity: The O2 arena

1. a)

ethene   tetrafluoroethene

   b) In the polymer, there is one shared pair of electrons between the carbon atoms

   c)

H H F F H H F F
| | | | | | | |
–C–C–C–C– C–C–C–C–
| | | | | | | |
H H F F H H F F

   d) $(- CH_2- CH_2 - CF_2 - CF_2-)_n$

   e) Addition polymerisation; the monomers contain double bonds (which break open) and no small molecules are eliminated.

29 Chemical analysis: Purity, formulations and chromatography

Learning objectives

- To use melting point and boiling point data to distinguish between pure and impure substances
- To know the characteristics of a formulation
- To explain how chromatography separates mixtures
- To calculate R_f values

Specification links

- 4.8.1.1, 4.8.1.2, 4.8.1.3
- WS: 1.4, 3.3, 3.5, 3.6, 4.1
- MS: 1a, 1c

Starter activity

- **Purity; 5 minutes; page 186**

  Remind the student of work on elements, compounds and mixtures and their composition. The student could suggest which of these are pure substances. Establish the nature of a pure substance to a chemist.

Main activities

- **Pure substances and formulations; 20 minutes; page 187**

  Ask the student how melting and boiling points are used to identify pure substances. Discuss with the student how most of the substances we use (such as shampoo and washing powders) are complex mixtures. Explain that these mixtures are formulated products. The student can suggest other formulated products and complete the activity sheet.

- **Chromatography; 20 minutes; page 188**

  Explain that chromatography is a method that separates the pure substances in a mixture and helps identify them. Show the student how to interpret chromatograms and calculate R_f values. Investigating how paper chromatography can be used to separate and tell the difference between coloured substances is required practical 6, so it is likely that the student will have carried out chromatography experiments at school.

Plenary activity

- **Finding the question; 5 minutes**

  Tell the student the answer is 'formulations'. Ask them to suggest the question. You can repeat this with other answers, such as 'chromatography' and 'pure substance'.

Homework activity

- **Interpreting chromatograms; 60 minutes; page 189**

  This activity sheet is self-explanatory and requires the calculation of R_f values and the interpretation of experimental results.

Support ideas

- **Pure substances and formulations** The composition of fuels, cleaning agents, paints, alloys, fertilisers and foods provide more examples of formulations. The number of significant figures in an answer should be the same as the lowest number of significant figures in the measurements in the question.

Extension ideas

- **Pure substances and formulations** The student can investigate the melting points of impure substances.
- **Chromatography** The student could research the stationary phase and the mobile phase in gas chromatography.

Progress and observations

CHEMISTRY HIGHER

Starter activity: Purity

Learning objectives

- To define a pure substance
- To differentiate between the use of 'pure' in chemistry and in everyday language

Equipment

This orange juice is marketed as 'pure' juice. The producers mean that nothing has been added. It is simply the juice from oranges. But orange juice is a complex mixture of compounds in water.

1. **To a chemist, orange juice is not a pure substance. Explain why.**

   _____

   _____

2. **Write a definition of a pure substance in chemistry.**

   _____

   _____

3. **Look at the substances in the table. Tick the correct box or boxes for each substance.**

Substance	Described as pure by chemists	Could be described as pure by the general public
milk		
solid sodium chloride		
sea water		
petrol		
oxygen		
2 mol/dm³ hydrochloric acid		
black coffee		

CHEMISTRY HIGHER

Main activity: Pure substances and formulations

Learning objectives

- To know how melting points and boiling points are used to identify pure substances
- To know that formulations are made by mixing ingredients in carefully measured quantities

Equipment

- spare paper

Pure aspirin is a compound. Its melting point is 135 °C.

1. **Students have prepared samples of aspirin and measured its melting point. These are some of the student's results.**

Student	Anna	Megan	Jack	Dexter	Maya	Tom	Emma
Melting point (°C)	135	142	141	148	135	139	142

Which students have prepared a pure sample of aspirin? _____

2. **Dispersible aspirin tablets usually contain 300 mg of aspirin. Dispersible aspirin breaks up when added to water. Read the typical ingredients list for a dispersible aspirin tablet and answer the questions below on a separate piece of paper.**

Type of ingredient	Purpose	Ingredient
active ingredient	medicine	aspirin
bulking agents	bulk out the tablet and make it a suitable size	potato starch, lactose, talc and calcium carbonate
lubricant	stops the mixture sticking to the machinery during manufacture	sodium lauryl sulfate (a detergent)
sweeteners and flavours	improve the taste of the medicine	citric acid (the acid in lemons), lactose (a sugar)

a) An average aspirin tablet has a mass of 325 mg. What percentage of the tablet is active medicine?

b) The composition of each batch of dispersible aspirin is carefully checked before the batch leaves the factory. Why is this important?

c) Aspirin is a formulated product. What does this mean?

d) When a dispersible aspirin tablet is added to water, the citric acid reacts with calcium carbonate. Citric acid produces salts called citrates. Write a word equation for the reaction between citric acid and calcium carbonate.

e) Suggest how the reaction in d) helps break up the tablet.

f) Hard aspirin tablets are swallowed whole. Suggest how the formulation of a hard aspirin tablet is different from the formulation of a dispersible aspirin tablet.

CHEMISTRY HIGHER

Main activity: Chromatography

Time **20** mins

Learning objectives

- To explain how chromatography separates mixtures
- To interpret chromatograms
- To calculate R_f values

Equipment

Tom is carrying out an experiment to find out which inks are pure substances and which are mixtures. He has placed spots of each ink along a pencil line on the piece of chromatography paper and set up this apparatus.

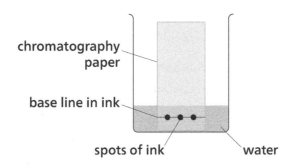

1. Name the stationary phase and the mobile phase in Tom's experiment.

   _____

2. Tom's experiment did not produce the expected results. Give two reasons why.

   _____

   _____

3. Ed carries out a similar experiment. This is Ed's chromatogram.

   a) Which inks are pure substances?

   _____

   b) Calculate the R_f values for each spot produced by ink D.

   _____

   _____

   c) Which two pure substances are present in ink D?

   _____

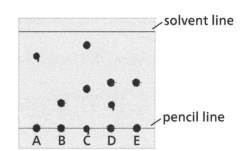

CHEMISTRY HIGHER

Homework activity: Interpreting chromatograms

Time **60** mins

Learning objectives

- To understand how chromatography separates mixtures
- To determine R_f values
- To know that different substances have different R_f values in different solvents

Equipment

- spare paper
- calculator

Becky is investigating the effect of different solvents on R_f values. She has made two chromatograms of a sample of brown food dye using water as one solvent and ethanol as the other solvent. The diagram shows her chromatograms.

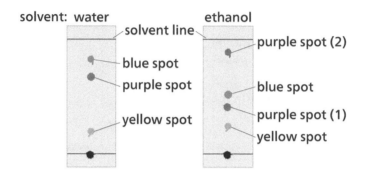

1. Complete the table by calculating the R_f value for each spot.

Solvent	Spot	R_f value
water	yellow	
	purple	
	blue	
ethanol	yellow	
	purple (1)	
	blue	
	purple (2)	

Now answer these questions on a separate piece of paper.

2. **What conclusion can Becky make about the effect of different solvents on the R_f values?**

3. **Suggest a reason why one purple spot was obtained using water as the solvent and two purple spots were obtained when using ethanol as the solvent.**

4. **What is the relationship between the distance moved by the coloured compound compared to the solvent and the R_f value?**

5. **Which coloured compound has the greatest attraction to the solvent when:**

   a) water is the solvent?

   b) ethanol is the solvent?

29 Answers

1. Orange juice contains more than one element or compound/it is a mixture.
2. A substance consisting of only one element or compound.
3. Substances pure to the chemist: solid sodium chloride, oxygen; all the substances in the table could be described as pure by the general public

Main activity: Pure substances and formulations

1. Anna and Maya
2. a) $\dfrac{300}{325} = 92.3\%$

   b) To ensure each tablet delivers the same amount of medicine and has the same properties
   c) A mixture whose ingredients are carefully measured
   d) calcium carbonate + citric acid → calcium citrate + carbon dioxide + water
   e) The carbon dioxide bubbles break up the ingredients.
   f) Sweeteners and flavours are not required; additives to make the tablet stick together (binders) are required

Main activity: Chromatography

1. Stationary phase: chromatography paper; mobile phase: water
2. Two of: a lid is needed; the base line should be drawn in pencil; the level of the solvent should be below the base line/ pencil line
3. a) A, B and E
   b) R_f values = 0.25 and 0.50
   c) B and E

Homework activity: Interpreting chromatograms

1. Allow slight variation in the R_f values, since it will be quite difficult to measure off the worksheet

Solvent	Spot	R_f value
water	yellow	0.19
	purple	0.68
	blue	0.84
ethanol	yellow	0.28
	purple (1)	0.45
	blue	0.55
	purple (2)	0.92

2. Compounds have different R_f values in different solvents.
3. The purple dye is not a pure substance. The two compounds in purple give different R_f values when ethanol is used as a solvent, but have the same R_f value when water is used as a solvent.
4. The greater the distance moved by the coloured compound, the higher the R_f value.
5. a) blue
   b) purple (2)

CHEMISTRY HIGHER

30 Chemical analysis: Flame tests and spectroscopy

Learning objectives

- To know how flame tests can be used to identify some metal ions
- To compare instrumental methods with chemical tests
- To interpret flame emission spectra

Specification links

- 4.8.3.1, 4.8.3.6, 4.8.3.7
- WS: 1.4, 2.2, 3.5

Starter activity

- **Instrumental methods; 5 minutes; page 192**

  Tell the student that the next two lessons cover different methods used to identify elements and compounds. Explain that this is part of the job of a forensic scientist and compare the equipment used in school labs with forensic labs.

Main activities

- **Flame tests; 20 minutes; page 193**

  Remind or tell the student of the purpose of flame tests and how to carry them out. Make sure they realise that it is the metal ions that produce the colour, not the metal atoms. The student has probably carried out flame tests in their school; they are part of required practical 7.

- **Flame emission spectroscopy; 20 minutes; page 194**

  Tell the student that flame emission spectroscopy is an example of an instrumental method of analysis. Discuss the fact that coloured flames produced by metal ions only contain certain wavelengths of light, and these can be viewed using a spectroscope. Explain that this is called a line spectrum and can be analysed to detect metal ions and their concentration. Ensure the student realises that different metal ions produce their own characteristic set of lines on a line spectrum.

Plenary activity

- **Assessing understanding; 5 minutes**

  Reverse roles. Ask the student to be the tutor and decide which questions they will set to test understanding of this lesson's content. They must provide the correct answers.

Homework activity

- **Problems with flame tests; 30 minutes; page 195**

  This activity compares the information provided by flame tests with that provided by flame emission spectroscopy.

Support ideas

- **Flame emission spectroscopy** You could ask the student to recall the spectrum of white light and the wavelengths that make up each colour in that spectrum, developing the idea of a line spectrum. The student could refer to their physics textbook to revise wavelengths of visible light. The reference sets of information may need explaining.

Extension ideas

- **Flame emission spectroscopy** The student can find out how a spectroscope works and research the line spectra of the noble gases.

Progress and observations

CHEMISTRY HIGHER

AQA

Starter activity: Instrumental methods

Time 5 mins

Learning objectives

- To know that instrumental methods can be used to detect elements and compounds
- To know the advantages of instrumental methods over test tube reactions to identify substances

Equipment

1. Forensic scientists use electrical instruments to identify elements and compounds. How does the equipment available in a forensic lab differ from the equipment in a typical school lab?

_____

_____

_____

2. Suggest problems forensic scientists could have using chemical tests instead of instrumental methods.

_____

_____

_____

_____

_____

CHEMISTRY HIGHER

Main activity: Flame tests

Time **20** mins

Learning objectives

- To know that flame tests can be used to identify metal ions
- To identify lithium ions, sodium ions, potassium ions, calcium ions and copper ions from flame test results

Equipment

1. Circle the correct ending to the sentence.

Flames tests are used to…

A. …identify metal atoms.

B. …identify metal ions.

C. …identify anions.

D. …identify non-metal ions.

2. The diagram shows the method used to carry out a flame test.

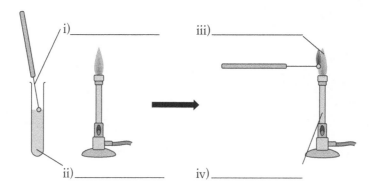

a) Label the diagram.

b) Write of list of bulleted points describing how to carry out a flame test.

_____

_____

_____

_____

3. Students have obtained these results from flame tests. Complete the table by identifying the metal ions.

Compound tested	Colour from flame test	Metal ions detected
V	green	
W	lilac	
X	crimson	
Y	orange-red	
Z	yellow	

CHEMISTRY HIGHER

Main activity: Flame emission spectroscopy

Learning objectives

- To know that flame emission spectroscopy is used to identify metal ions in solution
- To know how a line spectrum is obtained
- To interpret a line spectrum to identify unknown ions, given a reference set of line spectra
- To compare flame tests with flame emission spectroscopy

Equipment

The diagram shows a line emission spectrum of six metal ions in solution and one unknown metal ion. Each spectrum is measured in wavelengths (nm).

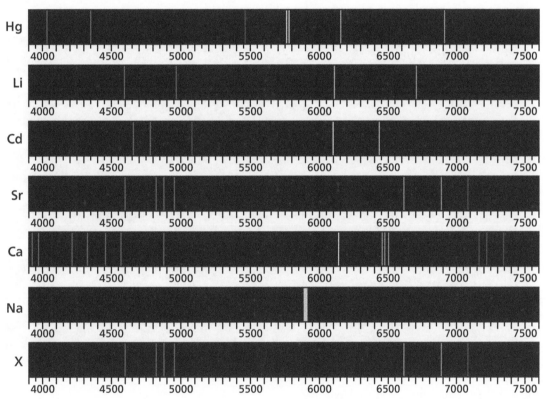

1. What colour do sodium ions produce in a flame test? _____

2. How does the line emission spectrum show this? _____

3. Predict the colour strontium ions produce in a flame test. _____

4. Use the line spectra to identify the metal ion X. _____

5. What is the advantage of a line spectrum over a flame test?

_____

6. Why do line emission spectra have a black background?

_____

CHEMISTRY HIGHER

Homework activity: Problems with flame tests

Learning objectives	Equipment
• To know that some metal ions in a mixture of metal ions can be masked in a flame test	none
• To compare flame emission spectroscopy with observation of laboratory flame tests to identify metal ions	

1. **Sam has carried out a flame test on an unknown metal compound (Z). He has obtained a yellow flame. Explain to your tutor the conclusion Sam can draw from the results.**

   _____

2. **These are line spectra of metal ions Z, plus others for reference.**

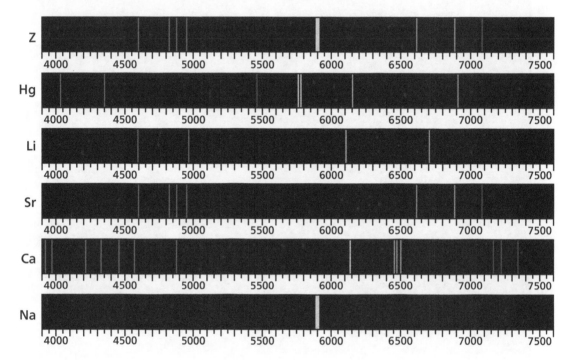

   a) Use the line spectra to identify the metal ions in Z.

   _____

   b) Explain why the results using line spectra are different to the results from the flame test.

   _____

   _____

   c) What advantage of line spectra over flame tests does this show?

   _____

30 Answers

Starter activity: Instrumental methods

1. Answer will depend on the student's school: schools with sixth forms may have spectroscopes to observe line spectra, but will not usually have the instrumentation to analyse these spectra.
2. Chemical tests: take longer (instrumental methods can be fully automated); may not be accurate because samples, reagents and/or glassware may be contaminated; rely on observation; may not be sensitive enough to detect small amounts; may not be suitable for small amounts of a sample

Main activity: Flame tests

1. B
2. a) i) Nichrome wire or flame test wire
      ii) Solution of metal ions
      iii) Blue flame
      iv) Bunsen burner
   b) Clean the flame test wire by dipping it in dilute hydrochloric acid and holding it in a blue Bunsen burner flame
      Dip the wire in a solution of the metal ions.
      Hold the wire in a blue Bunsen burner flame.
      Observe the colour of the flame.
3. V: copper
   W: potassium
   X: lithium
   Y: calcium
   Z: sodium

Main activity: Flame emission spectroscopy

1. yellow
2. There is a line at 5900
3. Red (strongest emission); accept lilac, purple
4. strontium
5. Line emission spectra do not rely on observation: they produce precise measurements
6. Light with these wavelengths is not emitted, so the background is black (black indicates the absence of light)

Homework activity: Problems with flame tests

1. Compound Z contains sodium ions.
2. a) Z contains a mixture of sodium ions and strontium ions.
   b) The colour produced by the sodium ions masked the colour produced by the strontium ions.
   c) Flame emission spectroscopy is more sensitive.

31 Chemical analysis: Chemical tests

Learning objectives

- To know how to identify common gases
- To know how to identify metal ions using sodium hydroxide
- To know the chemical tests for carbonates, halides and sulfates
- To use chemical tests to identify ions in a single unknown compound

Specification links

- 4.8.2.2, 4.8.2.3, 4.8.2.4, 4.8.3.2, 4.8.3.3, 4.8.3.4, 4.8.3.5
- WS: 2.2, 3.5

Starter activity

- **Identifying common gases; 5 minutes; page 198**

  With the exception of a test for chlorine, the student has probably covered the tests in this starter activity at Key Stage 3. You will need to describe the test for chlorine gas.

Main activities

- **Metal hydroxides; 25 minutes; page 199**

  Remind the student how flame tests and flame emission spectroscopy are used to identify metal ions. Explain that some metal hydroxides are insoluble and coloured, so we can also identify the metal ions by precipitating their hydroxides and matching the colour.

- **Carbonates, halides and sulfates; 15 minutes; page 200**

  Describe the tests used to detect carbonates, halides and sulfates and the positive results.

Plenary activity

- **A revision strategy; 5 minutes**

  The student can make up a mnemonic to help them to remember all or some of the chemical tests in this lesson.

Homework activity

- **Identifying an ionic compound; 60 minutes; page 201**

  This activity applies the tests covered in this lesson and flame tests covered in the previous lesson to the identification of an unknown ionic compound. This is required practical 7. You could remind the student of the need to prevent contamination of reagents and samples when carrying out chemical tests.

Support ideas

- **Metal hydroxides** Precipitation may need explaining using solubilities of ionic compounds. Show the student how a precipitate is shown with state symbols in an equation.
- **Carbonates, halides and sulfates** The chemical tests for halides and sulfates provide further opportunities for the student to practise writing ionic equations.

Extension ideas

- **Metal hydroxides** The student could suggest why potassium ions and other Group 1 ions cannot be detected using sodium hydroxide solution.
- **Carbonates, halides and sulfates** The student can suggest or find out why the tests for halides and for sulfates use acidified solutions.

Progress and observations

CHEMISTRY HIGHER

Starter activity: Identifying common gases

Learning objective	Equipment
• To describe the tests for hydrogen, oxygen, carbon dioxide and chlorine	none

1. **Complete the table by describing the test for each gas and the positive result.**

Gas	Identification test	Positive result
hydrogen		
oxygen		
carbon dioxide		
chlorine		

CHEMISTRY HIGHER

AQA

Main activity: Metal hydroxides

Time 25 mins

Learning objectives

- To know that sodium hydroxide can be used to identify some metal ions
- To identify copper ions, iron(II) ions, iron(III) ions from their hydroxides
- To distinguish aluminium(III) ions from calcium and magnesium ions using sodium hydroxide
- To write balanced equations for reactions to produce insoluble hydroxides

Equipment

- copy of the periodic table

1. **Sodium hydroxide can be used to identify some metal ions. Complete the table describing the reactions.**

Metal ions	Colour of precipitate when dilute sodium hydroxide solution is added	Observation when excess sodium hydroxide is added	Formula of hydroxide
copper(II)			
iron(II)			
iron(III)			
aluminium(III)			
calcium			
magnesium			

2. **Write balanced equations, including state symbols, for these reactions.**

   a) Copper sulfate solution reacting with sodium hydroxide solution

   _____

   b) Iron(III) chloride solution reacting with sodium hydroxide solution

   _____

   c) Iron(II) sulfate solution reacting with sodium hydroxide solution

   _____

3. **This is an ionic equation for the reaction between copper(II) ions and hydroxide ions:**

   $Cu^{2+}(aq) + 2OH^-(aq) \rightarrow Cu(OH)_2(s)$

   Write ionic equations for these reactions.

   a) Iron(II) ions with hydroxide ions _____

   b) Calcium ions with hydroxide ions _____

CHEMISTRY HIGHER

Main activity: Carbonates, halides and sulfates

Time 15 mins

Learning objectives	Equipment
• To know the reaction of carbonates with dilute acid • To know the reaction of halide solutions with silver nitrate solution in the presence of dilute nitric acid • To know the reaction of sulfate solutions with barium chloride solution in the presence of dilute hydrochloric acid	none

1. Add lines to link the boxes to show the pathways for the chemical tests and their positive results.

testing for carbonates	testing for bromides	testing for iodides	testing for chlorides	testing for sulfates

add dilute hydrochloric acid	add dilute nitric acid

add silver nitrate solution	add barium chloride solution	bubble gas through limewater

turns milky	white precipitate forms	cream precipitate forms	yellow precipitate forms

2. Name the precipitate formed in each test in question 1.

_____

_____

_____

_____

_____

CHEMISTRY HIGHER

Homework activity: Identifying an ionic compound

Time **60** mins

Learning objectives

- To describe chemical tests to identify an unknown ionic compound
- To describe a practical procedure to carry out chemical tests

Equipment

- copy of the periodic table

1. **You are provided with a solid sample of an unknown ionic compound. Describe how you would carry out tests to identify the metal ions (cations) and the non-metal ions (anions) in the compound. You must include step by step instructions.**

_____

_____

_____

_____

_____

_____

_____

2. **Students have carried out chemical tests to identify an unknown ionic compound. They have recorded these results.**

	Test	Result
A	Flame test	A green flame was produced
B	Add dilute sodium hydroxide to the solution	A blue precipitate formed
C	Add dilute hydrochloric acid to the solution	No reaction
D	Add dilute nitric acid, followed by silver nitrate solution	A cream precipitate formed
E	Add dilute hydrochloric acid, followed by barium chloride solution	No reaction

a) Name the ionic compound. _____

b) Write a balanced equation and an ionic equation for the reaction of the ionic compound with silver nitrate solution. Include state symbols.

_____

_____

31 Answers

Starter activity: Identifying common gases

1. hydrogen: add a burning splint; hydrogen burns with a squeaky pop
   oxygen: add a glowing splint; the splint relights
   carbon dioxide: bubble the gas through an aqueous solution of calcium hydroxide (limewater); the limewater turns milky/cloudy
   chlorine: add a piece of damp blue litmus paper; the litmus paper turns red and is then bleached white

Main activity: Metal hydroxides

1.

Metal ions	Colour of precipitate when dilute sodium hydroxide solution is added	Observation when excess sodium hydroxide is added	Formula of hydroxide
copper(II)	blue	no change	$Cu(OH)_2$
iron(II)	green	no change	$Fe(OH)_2$
iron(III)	brown	no change	$Fe(OH)_3$
aluminium(III)	white	precipitate dissolves	$Al(OH)_3$
calcium	white	no change	$Ca(OH)_2$
magnesium	white	no change	$Mg(OH)_2$

2. a) $CuSO_4(aq) + 2NaOH(aq) \rightarrow Cu(OH)_2(s) + Na_2SO_4(aq)$
   b) $FeCl_3(aq) + 3NaOH(aq) \rightarrow Fe(OH)_3(s) + 3NaCl(aq)$
   c) $FeSO_4(aq) + 2NaOH(aq) \rightarrow Fe(OH)_2(s) + Na_2SO_4(aq)$
3. a) $Fe^{2+}(aq) + 2OH^-(aq) \rightarrow Fe(OH)_2(s)$
   b) $Ca^{2+}(aq) + 2OH^-(aq) \rightarrow Ca(OH)_2(s)$

Main activity: Carbonates, halides and sulfates

1. Links should show the following:
   Testing for carbonates: add dilute hydrochloric acid; bubble gas through limewater; turns milky
   Testing for bromides: add dilute nitric acid; add silver nitrate solution; cream precipitate forms
   Testing for iodides: add dilute nitric acid; add silver nitrate solution; yellow precipitate forms
   Testing for chlorides: add dilute nitric acid; add silver nitrate solution; white precipitate forms
   Testing for sulfates: add dilute hydrochloric acid; add barium chloride solution; white precipitate forms
2. calcium carbonate; silver bromide; silver iodide; silver chloride; barium sulfate

Homework activity: Identifying an ionic compound

1. Make a solution using deionised water and divide the solution into five test tubes. (Note that four test tubes can be used if a flame test and one other test are carried out on the same test tube of solution.)
   Test tube 1: Clean a flame test wire, dip the wire into the solution and hold it in a blue Bunsen burner flame. Record the colour of the flame. (A damp wooden splint can be used instead of a flame test wire.)
   Test tube 2: Add dilute sodium hydroxide solution. Record the colour of any precipitate produced.
   Test tube 3: Add dilute hydrochloric acid. Collect any gas given off in a dropper and bubble through limewater. Record any changes.
   Test tube 4: Add dilute nitric acid followed by silver nitrate solution. Record the colour of any precipitate produced.
   Test tube 5: Add dilute hydrochloric acid followed by barium chloride solution. Record any precipitate produced.
2. a) copper bromide
   b) $CuBr_2(aq) + 2AgNO_3(aq) \rightarrow 2AgBr(s) + Cu(NO_3)_2(aq)$
      $Br^-(aq) + Ag^+(aq) \rightarrow AgBr(s)$

32 Chemistry of the atmosphere: The Earth's atmosphere

Learning objectives

- To know the proportions of gases in the atmosphere
- To interpret evidence and evaluate different theories about the Earth's early atmosphere
- To describe how early plants and algae increased the oxygen in the atmosphere and decreased the carbon dioxide
- To explain the formation of deposits of limestone, coal, crude oil and natural gas

Specification links

- 4.9.1.1, 4.9.1.2, 4.9.1.3, 4.9.1.4
- WS: 1.1, 1.2, 3.5, 3.7
- MS: 1a, 1c, 4a

Starter activity

- **Gases in the atmosphere; 5 minutes; page 204**

  The composition of the atmosphere is covered in Key Stage 3 science. Ask the student what they think the atmosphere consists of to gauge their existing knowledge. Establish the approximate percentage composition as nitrogen (80%), oxygen (20%), and small amounts of carbon dioxide, water vapour, argon and other noble gases. Explain that these proportions have been relatively stable for the past 200 million years.

Main activities

- **Investigating the percentage of oxygen in the atmosphere; 15 minutes; page 205**

  Discuss the experiment to measure the percentage of oxygen in air, including sources of error.

- **Evolution of the Earth's atmosphere; 25 minutes; page 206**

  Explain that the percentage of oxygen in the atmosphere has not always been at the current level. You can use the graph in the activity sheet to show the student how it has changed over the past one billion years. Discuss the possible reasons for the changes and how the Earth's atmosphere has evolved over the past 4.6 billion years. Emphasise that this is a theory to explain the facts we know and be aware that some students may have religious beliefs that contradict this theory.

Plenary activity

- **Find the question; 5 minutes**

  Give the student an answer to a question, such as 'carbon dioxide', 'volcanoes', 'water vapour' and ask them to make up the question.

Homework activity

- **Evaluating theories; 45 minutes; page 207**

  This activity requires the student to evaluate the theory given in the lesson. You could remind them where they have made hypotheses in experimental work and how this might lead to, or has led to, a theory.

Support ideas

- **Evolution of the Earth's atmosphere** The student can draw a time line mapping changes in the composition of the Earth's atmosphere. Photosynthesis and respiration may need more explanation; the student could refer to their biology textbook for more information.

Extension ideas

- **Evolution of the Earth's atmosphere** The student can describe an experiment to show that aquatic plants produce oxygen in sunlight, including how they would test the gas produced.
- **Evaluating theories** The student could investigate other theories about the early Earth's atmosphere.

Progress and observations

Starter activity: Gases in the atmosphere

Learning objectives

- To know the percentages of gases in the atmosphere
- To know that the composition of the atmosphere has been relatively stable for the past 200 million years

Equipment

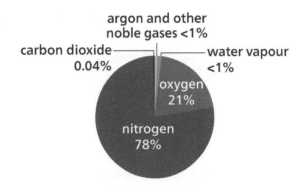

The pie chart shows the current composition, by volume, of the Earth's atmosphere.

1. List the gases in order of their abundance in the atmosphere.

_____

_____

2. Which gases in the air exist as molecules and which exist as atoms?

_____

_____

3. The percentage of one of the gases in the pie chart varies. Name the gas and explain why it varies.

_____

_____

TUTORS GUILD CHEMISTRY HIGHER

Main activity: Investigating the percentage of oxygen in the atmosphere

Time 15 mins

Learning objectives

- To know the proportions of gases in the atmosphere
- To interpret an experiment to measure the percentage of oxygen in the atmosphere

Equipment

The diagram shows the apparatus used in an experiment to measure the percentage of oxygen in the air.

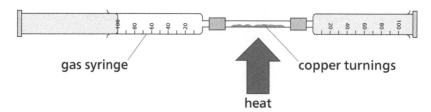

gas syringe   copper turnings

heat

1. **The copper turnings are heated and the air in the syringes is slowly passed backwards and forwards over the heated copper. The heating is stopped when the volume of gas in the syringes no longer changes.**

   a) How do the heated copper turnings remove oxygen from the air?

   _____

   b) Write a balanced equation for the reaction. _____

2. **What is left in the syringes when all the oxygen has been removed?**

   _____

3. **These are the results of the experiment.**

Initial volume of air/cm³	100
Final volume of air/cm³	83

   a) From these results, what is the percentage of oxygen in the air? _____

   b) Suggest why this result is less than figures given in textbooks for the percentage of oxygen in the air.

   _____

CHEMISTRY HIGHER

Main activity: Evolution of the Earth's atmosphere

Time 25 mins

Learning objectives

- To explain the Earth's early atmosphere
- To understand how carbon dioxide decreased in the atmosphere
- To understand how oxygen increased in the atmosphere
- To understand that the composition of the Earth's atmosphere has been fairly stable for 200 million years

Equipment

- spare paper

Answer the questions below on a separate sheet of paper.

1. **Scientists think the Earth is 4.6 billion years old. What do they think the Earth's atmosphere was like 3.6 billion years ago? Give reasons for your answer.**

2. **Why do scientists think the percentage of nitrogen changed from small amounts 3.5 billion years ago to 78% today?**

3. **The formation of the oceans had an effect on carbon dioxide levels in the atmosphere.**

   a) How did the oceans form?

   b) What happened to the carbon dioxide in the atmosphere when the oceans first formed?

   c) Where do we find this carbon dioxide today? Explain your answer.

4. **The graph shows how the percentage of oxygen in the atmosphere has changed.**

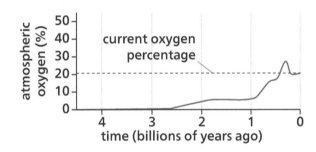

   a) Plants and algae evolved about 2.7 billion years ago. How did this affect the percentage of carbon dioxide in the atmosphere?

   b) Name and write a chemical equation for the reaction of plants and algae that changed the percentage of carbon dioxide in the atmosphere.

   c) Explain why the graph shows the percentage of oxygen in the atmosphere starting to increase about 2.7 billion years ago.

   d) Explain why animals could not evolve before 2.7 billion years ago.

5. **How do plants and animals keep the percentages of oxygen and carbon dioxide in the atmosphere fairly stable?**

CHEMISTRY HIGHER

AQA

Homework activity: Evaluating theories

Time **45** mins

Learning objectives

- To evaluate a theory about the Earth's early atmosphere
- To interpret evidence for a theory

Equipment

A hypothesis is a prediction aimed at explaining certain facts or observations. It is an educated guess, a suggested possible outcome. You have made hypotheses in your practical work.

Scientists carry out experiments to gather evidence. They can use this evidence to make conclusions. When there is enough valid evidence, they can develop theories to explain their observations.

This is an example:

- Make a hypothesis – more concentrated solutions have a faster rate of reaction
- Gather evidence – carry out experiments
- Develop a theory – the collision theory

1. The theory you have studied about the Earth's early atmosphere says it contained mostly carbon dioxide, with some water vapour and little or no oxygen. There were very small amounts of nitrogen, methane and ammonia.

   What is the evidence for this theory?

   _____

   _____

   _____

   _____

   _____

2. Some scientists say the evidence for this theory is poor. Why might they think that?

   _____

   _____

   _____

   _____

3. There have been many theories about the Earth's early atmosphere. Why do the theories keep changing?

   _____

4. It is possible that the theory in this lesson will become out of date and a new theory will develop. What will have to happen before a new theory develops?

   _____

   _____

5. Scientists think the composition of the atmosphere has been fairly stable for the past 200 million years, but there have been recent changes due to human activity. What are the recent changes?

   _____

   _____

32 Answers

Starter activity: Gases in the atmosphere

1. Most abundant: nitrogen; oxygen; argon and noble gases/water vapour; carbon dioxide
2. Molecules: nitrogen, oxygen, carbon dioxide, water; atoms: argon and other noble gases
3. Water vapour: amount depends on weather conditions and location; coastal areas have higher water content

Main activity: Investigating the percentage of oxygen in the atmosphere

1. a) Copper reacts with oxygen to form copper oxide.
   b) $2Cu(s) + O_2(g) \rightarrow 2CuO(s)$
2. Nitrogen, carbon dioxide, argon and other noble gases
3. a) 17%
   b) Possible reasons: not all oxygen reacted; there was insufficient copper present; the apparatus may have a small leak

Main activity: Evolution of the Earth's atmosphere

1. Mainly carbon dioxide and water vapour with small amounts of nitrogen, methane and ammonia. Volcanic activity produced the gases that made up the Earth's early atmosphere. By studying the composition of volcanic gases today, scientists assume early volcanoes produced the same gases.
2. Nitrogen is very unreactive and the amount increased over time.
3. a) Water vapour from the atmosphere condensed.
   b) Some carbon dioxide dissolved in the oceans; carbonates formed and were deposited on the sea bed.
   c) Limestone, chalk and marble rocks; these are deposits of calcium carbonate.
4. a) Decreased it
   b) Photosynthesis: $6CO_2(g) + 6H_2O(l) \rightarrow C_6H_{12}O_6(aq) + 6O_2(g)$
   c) Plants began to produce oxygen.
   d) Animals need oxygen for respiration, and oxygen was was not produced in significant amounts before then.
5. Plants use carbon dioxide and produce oxygen during photosynthesis, while animals and plants use oxygen and produce carbon dioxide during respiration. The rates of respiration and photosynthesis are about equal so the proportions of oxygen and carbon dioxide are balanced.

Homework activity: Evaluating theories

1. As the Earth cooled, scientists think there were many volcanoes. Volcanoes today give out carbon dioxide, with some ammonia, methane and nitrogen. Deposits of limestone and chalk are carbonates; they are sedimentary and must have formed at a time when there was a large percentage of carbon dioxide in the atmosphere. Studying the atmosphere of other planets provides similarities.
2. We cannot go back in time and provide direct evidence for the composition of the atmosphere 3–4 billion years ago. The theory is based on what volcanoes produce today; we do not know what volcanoes produced 3.5 billion years ago.
3. New evidence emerges which changes theories.
4. New evidence will have to emerge that doesn't fit the existing theory. A new theory will be developed from the new evidence.
5. The percentage of carbon dioxide is rising; pollutants are being added to the atmosphere.

33 Chemistry of the atmosphere: Greenhouse gases

Learning objectives

- To describe the greenhouse effect
- To describe activities which increase amounts of greenhouse gases in the atmosphere
- To evaluate the quality of evidence
- To describe the effects of global climate change
- To describe actions to reduce emissions of greenhouse gases

Specification links

- 4.9.2.1, 4.9.2.2, 4.9.2.3, 4.9.2.4
- WS: 1.3, 1.4, 1.5, 3.7
- MS: 1a, 1c, 3c, 4a

Starter activity

- **The greenhouse gases; 5 minutes; page 210**

  Ask the student to identify some greenhouse gases and the effect they have on global temperatures. (The role of carbon dioxide in climate change is covered in Key Stage 3 science.) Discuss changes in carbon dioxide concentration. You could compare these changes to the relative stability of the atmosphere over the past 200 million years.

Main activities

- **The greenhouse effect; 20 minutes; page 211**

  Discuss how greenhouse gases trap heat energy in the atmosphere. Ensure that the student understands that the gas molecules absorb the heat energy and trap it in the atmosphere, and that this happens throughout the atmosphere; the reflection of heat by a layer of greenhouse gases in the upper atmosphere is a common misconception. Explain the role of greenhouse gases in keeping the Earth at a temperature suitable for life.

- **Climate change; 20 minutes; page 212**

  Explain that some human activities increase amounts of greenhouse gases in the atmosphere (namely carbon dioxide and methane) and that many people think this increase in greenhouse gases is responsible for increasing global temperatures and climate change. Discuss the environmental implications of global climate change, such as rising sea levels, flooding, changes in habitats for plants and animals and potential problems for crops and food supplies. Explain why it is difficult to determine the quality of such evidence and misrepresentation of it.

Plenary activity

- **Changes; 5 minutes**

  Swap roles with the student and ask them to devise three questions (plus answers) to summarise this lesson's content. Possible questions are: describe the greenhouse effect in terms of long and short wave radiation in the Earth's atmosphere; name three possible outcomes of global climate change; why is it important that people are informed about global climate change?

Homework activity

- **Carbon footprint; 60 minutes; page 213**

  Explain to the student that the carbon footprint is the total amount of carbon dioxide and other greenhouse gases emitted over the life cycle of a product. Full instructions are provided on the activity sheet.

Support ideas

- **The greenhouse effect** The student may need reminding of calculations involving gas volume, as in lesson 16.
- **Climate change** The student may need help in understanding that valid evidence should be repeatable and precise and it is difficult to control variables in factors affecting climate change.

Extension ideas

- **Carbon footprint** The student can investigate life cycle assessments in preparation for lesson 36. The student can use the Levi's website to read about methods used to reduce their carbon footprint and make their product more sustainable.

Progress and observations

CHEMISTRY HIGHER

Starter activity: The greenhouse gases

Time **5** mins

Learning objectives

- To name the greenhouse gases
- To interpret graphs showing recent changes in carbon dioxide concentration

Equipment

- calculator

1. What is a greenhouse gas?

_____

_____

2. Name three gases in the atmosphere that act as greenhouse gases.

_____

3. The graph shows carbon dioxide concentrations in the atmosphere since 2012, at Mauna Loa in Hawaii.

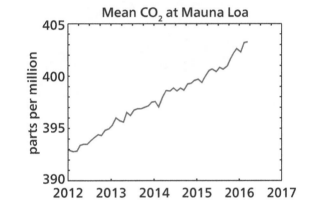

a) What is 400 parts per million as a percentage? _____

b) By how many parts per million did the carbon dioxide concentration change between 2012 and 2016?

_____

c) Before the industrial revolution in the 1800s, carbon dioxide made up 0.028% of the atmosphere. What is this in parts per million?

_____

CHEMISTRY HIGHER

TUTORS' GUILD

Main activity: The greenhouse effect

Time 20 mins

Learning objectives

- To know that greenhouse gases maintain the temperature on Earth at a level suitable for life
- To explain the greenhouse effect in terms of long and short wavelengths of radiation interacting with matter

Equipment

1. **Use the diagram to explain the greenhouse effect. Your answer should include the words long wave, short wave, and radiation.**

   _____

   _____

   _____

   _____

2. **The average temperature on Earth is 15 °C. Scientists estimate that without water vapour, carbon dioxide and methane in the atmosphere, the average temperature would be −18 °C.**

   a) Explain why the Earth would be cooler without greenhouse gases.

   _____

   _____

   b) How would the diagram have to change to show an atmosphere with no greenhouse gases?

   _____

   _____

AQA

CHEMISTRY HIGHER

Main activity: Climate change

Learning objectives

- To name human activities which increase amounts of greenhouse gases in the atmosphere
- To know that increases in amounts of greenhouse gases in the atmosphere may cause global climate change
- To describe some effects of climate change
- To evaluate the quality of evidence

Equipment

The graph shows average global temperatures since 1860.

1. By how much has the average temperature increased between 1880 and 2010?

_____

2. How does this graph compare with the change shown in the graph in the starter activity?

_____

_____

_____

global average temperature (°C) 5 year average

14.6
14.5
14.4
14.3
14.2
14.1
14.0
13.9
13.8
13.7
13.6
13.5

1860 1880 1900 1920 1940 1960 1980 2000

year

3. Name two human activities that increase the amount of the following gases in the atmosphere:

a) carbon dioxide _____ b) methane _____

4. Describe to your tutor the four effects of global climate change.

5. Scientists generally agree about how greenhouse gases work in the atmosphere, but not everyone agrees that human activity – which increases amounts of carbon dioxide and methane in the atmosphere – is causing average temperatures to rise or leading to climate change.

Why is it difficult to provide good quality evidence that humans are causing climate change? Discuss with your tutor.

6. Read this extract from a newspaper report:

> Scientists have measured an average global temperature rise of 0.5 °C over the past 35 years. This rise is thought to be responsible for the increase in heat waves, drought, flooding and damage to crops and coral reefs. Scientists are predicting that a 2.0 °C rise in average global temperatures will cause a more dangerous change in climate. They are warning that some low lying countries may be wiped out altogether.

a) Name one fact in this report that is certain.

_____

b) Name two uncertain pieces of information in this report and explain why they have uncertainties.

_____

c) Why is it important that newspapers publish this information?

_____

CHEMISTRY HIGHER

Homework activity: Carbon footprint

Time 60 mins

Learning objectives

- To describe the carbon footprint of a product and how it can be reduced
- To describe actions to reduce emissions of carbon dioxide and methane
- To explain why action may be limited

Equipment

- calculator

The carbon footprint is the total amount of carbon dioxide and other greenhouse gases emitted over the full life cycle of a product. The carbon footprint can be reduced by reducing emissions of carbon dioxide and methane.

A typical pair of denim jeans produces 33.4 kg of carbon dioxide over its lifetime. This is from harvesting the cotton, through to disposal of the jeans, and includes manufacture and care such as washing.

An average T-shirt produces 6.0 kg of carbon dioxide over its lifetime.

1. **1 mol of gas occupies 24 dm³ at room temperature and pressure. Calculate the volume of carbon dioxide produced over the lifetime of:**

   a) a pair of jeans _____

   b) a T-shirt. _____

2. **Suggest how jeans manufacturers can reduce the carbon footprint of a pair of jeans.**

   _____

   _____

3. **How can the owner of the jeans reduce the carbon footprint?**

   _____

   _____

4. **Some clothing manufacturers are not very willing to reduce their carbon footprint. Suggest why.**

   _____

   _____

   _____

33 Answers

Starter activity: The greenhouse gases

1. A gas in the atmosphere that absorbs long wave radiation and helps to maintain temperatures on Earth that are high enough to support life
2. Carbon dioxide, methane, water vapour
3. a) 0.04%
   b) 10 ppm
   c) 280 ppm

Main activity: The greenhouse effect

1. The answer should include the following points:
   - radiation from the Sun reaching Earth is short wave radiation
   - short wave radiation passes through the Earth's atmosphere; some is absorbed by the Earth
   - longer wave radiation is emitted from the Earth
   - some longer wave radiation escapes the atmosphere, some is absorbed by molecules of greenhouse gases
2. a) Greenhouse gases in the atmosphere absorb heat energy and radiate it back to the Earth's surface. Without greenhouse gases, this heat energy would escape the atmosphere and the Earth would be cooler.
   b) The diagram would show all longer wave radiation escaping the atmosphere.

Main activity: Climate change

1. 1.1/1.2 °C
2. Both show an increase in the dependent variable.
3. a) For example, burning fossil fuels and clearing forests
   b) For example, rearing cattle for the meat industry and gas emitted from landfill deposits
4. For example, rising sea levels, melting ice, changes in habitat for some species, creation of desert areas
5. There are many variables, such as volcanic activity and particulate matter in the atmosphere, that are difficult to control; the Earth's climate has changed many times in the past
6. a) An average global temperature rise of 0.5 °C over the past 35 years
   b) The 0.5 °C rise is thought to cause the increase in heat waves etc. – this is uncertain because there may be other causes, such as natural global cycles and volcanic activity.
   A rise of 2.0 °C may cause more dangerous climate change – this is uncertain because we do not know if a 2.0 °C rise will have this effect, as there is no direct evidence.
   c) So that people/governments can prepare for the effects of climate change, such as developing new crops, flood defences, etc.

Homework activity: Carbon footprint

1. a) $\dfrac{33400\,g}{44\,g} \times 24\,dm^3 = 18218\,dm^3$
   b) $\dfrac{6000\,g}{44\,g} \times 24\,dm^3 = 3273\,dm^3$
2. Use alternative energy sources to farm the cotton, power the manufacturing process and power the retail process (delivery)
3. Wash the jeans less frequently and/or at a lower temperature; recycle the jeans when they are too old to wear
4. It can be expensive to make changes to processes to lower carbon footprint

34 Chemistry of the atmosphere: Atmospheric pollutants

Learning objectives

- To describe how atmospheric pollutants are produced by burning fuels
- To predict the products of combustion of a fuel given its composition and conditions of burning
- To describe and explain the problems caused by pollutants in the atmosphere

Specification links

- 4.9.3.1, 4.9.3.2
- WS: 1.4, 1.5
- MS: 4a

Starter activity

- **Combustion of fuels; 5 minutes; page 216**

  Remind the student of the work covered on alkanes and hydrocarbons in lesson 26.

Main activities

- **Pollutants from fuels; 20 minutes; page 217**

  Explain that incomplete combustion occurs if there is insufficient oxygen present and identify the products of incomplete combustion. Tell the student that, apart from containing carbon and/or hydrogen, many fuels also contain sulfur. Explain how sulfur dioxide forms during combustion. Discuss the production of nitrogen oxides from oxygen and nitrogen in the atmosphere at the high temperatures reached in vehicle engines. Check that the student realises vehicles are not the only source of atmospheric pollutants.

- **Effects of pollutants; 20 minutes; page 218**

  Discuss the toxic nature of carbon monoxide, including its reaction with haemoglobin. Explain why oxides of nitrogen, sulfur dioxide and particulates are damaging to health. You could refer back to the size of particles covered in lesson 12. Discuss global dimming and its possible outcomes.

Plenary activity

- **True or false; 5 minutes**

  Give the student a number of statements, such as 'particles of carbon in the atmosphere contribute to global dimming', which they can identify as true or false. Other suitable statements are: 'carbon dioxide is a product of incomplete combustion'; 'oxides of nitrogen are produced from impurities in the hydrocarbon fuel' and 'sulfur dioxide forms acid rain'.

Homework activity

- **Acid rain; 60 minutes; page 219**

  Full instructions are provided on the activity sheet. Encourage the student to provide detailed answers, rather than short phrases such as: 'damages buildings'.

Support ideas

- **Pollutants from fuels** The student may need extra help with equations for complete and incomplete combustion.
- **Effects of pollutants** Explain that there are several oxides of nitrogen with different formulae. The term 'oxides of nitrogen' is usually used to describe NO and NO_2.

Extension ideas

- **Effects of pollutants** The student could research the limits on emissions required for MOT tests, or find out how catalytic converters work.

Progress and observations

CHEMISTRY HIGHER

Starter activity: Combustion of fuels

Learning objectives	Equipment
• To know that burning fossil fuels is a source of atmospheric pollutants • To revise hydrocarbon fuels and complete combustion	none

The combustion of fuels is a major source of atmospheric pollution. The exhaust fumes from cars contain the products of combustion of the fuel used.

Circle the letter next to the correct ending to each sentence.

1. Petrol and diesel fuels contain mainly…

A. alkenes.

B. octane.

C. alcohols.

D. hydrocarbons.

2. When petrol and diesel combust in a vehicle engine, the fuel reacts with…

A. oxygen.

B. antioxidants.

C. nitrogen oxides.

D. carbon monoxide.

3. If complete combustion could take place in a car engine, the exhaust fumes would contain…

A. oxides of nitrogen only.

B. particles of carbon and water.

C. carbon dioxide and water.

D. carbon monoxide and water.

CHEMISTRY HIGHER

Main activity: Pollutants from fuels

Learning objectives

- To know that carbon monoxide and particles of carbon are produced as products of incomplete combustion of hydrocarbon fuels
- To know that sulfur dioxide is produced from impurities in hydrocarbon fuels
- To explain how oxides of nitrogen are produced by burning fuels

Equipment

1. Complete the table by describing how the products and pollutants form and by giving an equation for the reaction.

Pollutant	How it forms	Chemical equation
carbon dioxide		Write an equation to show its formation from octane.
carbon monoxide		Write an equation to show its formation from octane.
carbon particles (soot)		Write an equation to show its formation from octane.
water		Write an equation to show its formation from octane.
sulfur dioxide		Write an equation for the formation of sulfur dioxide.
oxides of nitrogen		Write an equation for the formation of NO.

CHEMISTRY HIGHER

Main activity: Effects of pollutants

Time 20 mins

Learning objectives

- To know the toxic effects of carbon monoxide
- To know the health effects of sulfur dioxide, oxides of nitrogen and particulates
- To explain global dimming

Equipment

Smog is a major problem in some cities.

It is caused by the pollutants released into the atmosphere when fuels are burned and contains carbon monoxide, oxides of nitrogen, sulfur dioxide and particulates, as well as unburned hydrocarbons. Each of these affects our health.

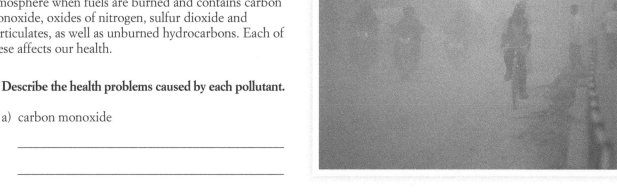

1. **Describe the health problems caused by each pollutant.**

   a) carbon monoxide

   _____

   _____

   _____

   b) oxides of nitrogen and sulfur dioxide

   _____

   _____

   c) particulates

   _____

   _____

2. **Every ten years, 2% less sunlight reaches the Earth's surface. Scientists think this is due to particles in the atmosphere from burning fuels. It is called global dimming.**

   a) Why do particles in the atmosphere affect the amount of sunlight reaching the Earth's surface?

   _____

   _____

   b) Scientists think that global dimming may have lessened the effects of global warming. Governments around the world are introducing regulations to limit particle emissions. How might this affect global warming?

   _____

   _____

AQA

CHEMISTRY HIGHER

Homework activity: Acid rain

Time **60** mins

Learning objectives	Equipment

Learning objectives

- To describe how emissions of sulfur dioxide and oxides of nitrogen cause acid rain
- To explain how industries have reacted to reduce acid rain

Equipment

1. Explain how pollutants from burning fuels cause acid rain.

_____

_____

_____

2. What effect does acid rain have on:

a) buildings? _____

_____

b) habitats and wildlife?

_____

_____

_____

3. The graph shows quantities of acid rain emissions from different sources between 1990 and 2007 in the UK.

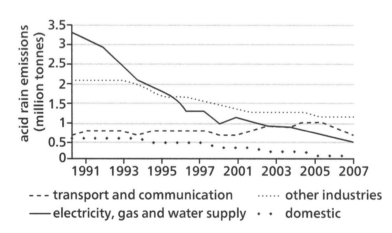

--- transport and communication   ⋯⋯ other industries
—— electricity, gas and water supply   ·· domestic

Describe the overall trend in acid rain emissions between 1990 and 2007.

_____

4. These are two strategies aimed at reducing acid rain emissions:

a) treating waste gases from power stations with powdered calcium carbonate; calcium sulfate and carbon dioxide are the products. Complete the equation for the reaction.

$2SO_2(g) + 2CaCO_3(s) + O_2(g) \rightarrow$ _____ + _____

b) fitting catalytic converters to car exhausts; these remove oxides of nitrogen from exhaust gases. Complete the equation for the reaction. The products are carbon dioxide and nitrogen.

$2CO(g) + 2NO(g) \rightarrow$ _____ + _____

Starter activity: Combustion of fuels

1. D
2. A
3. C

Main activity: Pollutants from fuels

1.

Pollutant	How it forms	Chemical equation
carbon dioxide	from complete combustion of hydrocarbons	$2C_8H_{18} + 25O_2 \rightarrow 16CO_2 + 18H_2O$
carbon monoxide	from incomplete combustion of hydrocarbons	$2C_8H_{18} + 17O_2 \rightarrow 16CO + 18H_2O$
carbon particles (soot)	from incomplete combustion of hydrocarbons	$2C_8H_{18} + 9O_2 \rightarrow 16C + 18H_2O$
water	from complete combustion of hydrocarbons	$2C_8H_{18} + 25O_2 \rightarrow 16CO_2 + 18H_2O$ $2C_8H_{18} + 17H_2O \rightarrow 16CO + 18H_2O$ $2C_8H_{18} + 9O_2 \rightarrow 16C + 18H_2O$
sulfur dioxide	from the combustion of sulfur	$S + O_2 \rightarrow SO_2$
oxides of nitrogen	from nitrogen and oxygen in the air at high temperatures in engines	$N_2 + O_2 \rightarrow 2NO$

Main activity: Effects of pollutants

1. a) Carbon monoxide reacts with haemoglobin in red blood cells to produce carboxyhaemoglobin. The reaction is irreversible and carboxyhaemoglobin cannot carry oxygen around the body.
   b) Both cause respiratory problems.
   c) Particulates can pass into the lungs (PM_{10}) and alveoli ($PM_{2.5}$) and cause respiratory problems.
2. a) Sunlight hits the particles and is reflected back into space.
   b) Global warming may increase as particulates are reduced.

Homework activity: Acid rain

1. Sulfur dioxide and oxides of nitrogen dissolve in rainwater to produce an acid solution, which lowers the pH of rain.
2. a) Buildings made from limestone and marble (calcium carbonate) react with the acid rain and are eroded.
   b) Leaf surfaces are damaged, resulting in plants having difficulty exchanging gases. The pH of lakes decreases, changing the habitat for plants and animals. Many plants and animals can tolerate only a small pH range.
3. Emissions have decreased.
4. a) $2SO_2(g) + 2CaCO_3(s) + O_2(g) \rightarrow 2CaSO_4(s) + 2CO_2(g)$
   b) $2CO(g) + 2NO(g) \rightarrow 2CO_2(g) + N_2(g)$

CHEMISTRY HIGHER

35 Using resources: Using the Earth's resources

Learning objectives

- To understand the role of chemistry in sustainable development
- To know the difference between pure water and potable water
- To describe the differences in the treatment of groundwater, salty water and waste water to produce potable water
- To evaluate different methods of mining copper

Specification links

- 4.10.1.1, 4.10.1.2, 4.10.1.3, 4.10.1.4
- WS: 1.4, 1.5, 2.2, 3.5

Starter activities

- **Pure water and potable water; 5 minutes; page 222**

  Use the activity sheet to discuss the differences between potable and pure water with the student. The student can make notes and answer the questions verbally.

Main activities

- **Producing potable water; 20 minutes; page 223**

  Discuss the different sources of potable water and the treatment required, explaining the substances that need to be removed. Explain that water is a natural resource and, along with other natural resources, provides us with foods, timber, some clothing and fuels. Explain that we also use finite resources by processing them into energy and materials. Ask the student to suggest how chemistry plays a role in making sure these processes are sustainable. You could use the diagram on the activity sheet to support the discussion. Encourage the student to use scientific language and present information in a logical manner.

- **Phytomining and bioleaching; 20 minutes; page 224**

  Explain why we now need to mine low grade ores to extract copper. Remind the student that copper is a finite resource. Discuss the traditional methods of mining and extracting copper and compare this with bioleaching and phytomining. You could revise displacement reactions and electrolysis here if time allows.

Plenary activity

- **Sustainable development; 5 minutes**

  Tell the student that chemistry plays an important role in sustainable development. The student can give examples of the role of chemistry from the lesson, such as treating waste water and developing less intrusive mining methods.

Homework activity

- **Analysing and purifying water samples; 60 minutes; page 225**

  Analysis and purification of water samples from different sources is required practical 8. In this activity sheet, the student will draw conclusions from given results and predict other results.

Support ideas

- **Phytomining and bioleaching** The student can identify finite and renewable resources from a given list. The student can refer to lessons 17 and 20 to recap displacement reactions and electrolysis.

Extension ideas

- **Producing potable water** The student can find out how ion exchange resins purify water.
- **Phytomining and bioleaching** The student could research the Chilean copper industry: 10% of the copper produced in Chile is mined by bioleaching.

Progress and observations

CHEMISTRY HIGHER

Starter activity: Pure water and potable water

Learning objectives

- To understand the term potable
- To distinguish between pure water and potable water
- To identify finite and renewable resources

Equipment

This is a label from a bottle of natural mineral water.

TYPICAL ANALYSIS (mg/l)	
CALCIUM	54
MAGNESIUM	20
POTASSIUM	3
SODIUM	20
BICARBONATE	240
CHLORIDE	40
SULPHATE	15
NITRATE	<0.2
IRON	0
ALUMINIUM	0

The water is, of course, safe to drink. Discuss these questions with your tutor.

1. **Is the mineral water pure water?**

2. **What is pure water to a chemist?**

3. **Water that is safe to drink is called potable water. What is the difference between pure water and potable water?**

4. **How could you tell whether a sample of water was pure?**

5. **What properties do you think potable water should have?**

6. **Where does potable water in the UK come from?**

7. **The mineral water comes in a plastic bottle. Are the following things renewable resources or finite resources?**

   a) the plastic bottle

   b) the mineral water

CHEMISTRY HIGHER

Main activity: Producing potable water

Learning objectives

- To describe the differences in the treatment of groundwater, sea water and waste water to produce potable water
- To give reasons for the steps used to produce potable water

Equipment

- spare paper

Look at the diagram. It shows three routes to producing potable water.

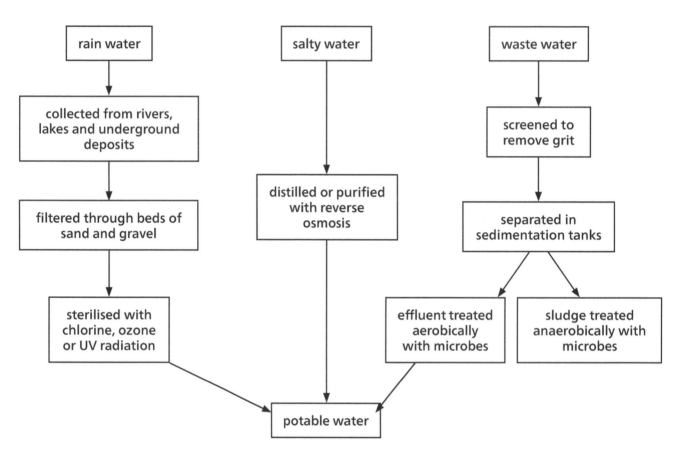

On a separate piece of paper, compare the different methods used to produce potable water under these headings. Give reasons for your answers.

1. **How easy is it?**

2. **How quick is it?**

3. **How expensive is it?**

4. **In some areas, water is extracted from rivers and treated to produce potable water. River water is a natural resource. If we extract too much water from the river, the river may dry up. What role does chemistry play in making this supply sustainable?**

 **CHEMISTRY HIGHER**

 AQA

Main activity: Phytomining and bioleaching

Time **20** mins

Learning objectives

- To know about the processes of phytomining and bioleaching
- To compare phytomining and bioleaching with traditional methods of mining and extracting copper

Equipment

These are three methods used to mine copper.

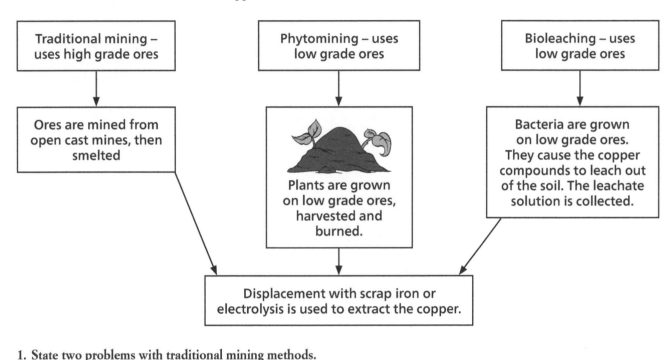

| Traditional mining – uses high grade ores | Phytomining – uses low grade ores | Bioleaching – uses low grade ores |

Ores are mined from open cast mines, then smelted

Plants are grown on low grade ores, harvested and burned.

Bacteria are grown on low grade ores. They cause the copper compounds to leach out of the soil. The leachate solution is collected.

Displacement with scrap iron or electrolysis is used to extract the copper.

1. State two problems with traditional mining methods.

_____

_____

2. What properties do the plants used for phytomining need?

_____

_____

3. Complete the table to compare the three methods. Explain your predictions to your tutor.

	Traditional mining and smelting	Phytomining	Bioleaching
Pollution			
Other environmental problems			
Time required			

Homework activity: Analysing and purifying water samples

Time **60** mins

Learning objectives

- To know that pure water can be obtained by distillation
- To know that flame tests can be used to identify metal ions
- To know that chemical tests can be used to identify non-metal ions

Equipment

Three ground water samples have been collected from the site of an old copper mine. Sulfuric acid had been used to extract the copper. Chemical tests were carried out on the water samples. The pH was measured. These are the tests and results.

Water sample	pH of water sample	Addition of sodium hydroxide solution	Addition of dilute nitric acid and silver nitrate solution	Addition of dilute hydrochloric acid and barium chloride solution
A	4	blue precipitate formed	no reaction	white precipitate formed
B	6	green precipitate formed	white precipitate formed	white precipitate formed
C	2	blue precipitate formed	no reaction	white precipitate formed

1. Identify the ions detected in samples A, B and C.

_____

_____

2. How could you use flame tests to confirm the metal ions present in samples A and C?

_____

_____

3. Sample A was distilled and chemical tests carried out on the contents of the distillation flask and the distillate. Complete the table to predict the results.

Water sample A	pH of water sample	Addition of sodium hydroxide solution	Addition of dilute nitric acid and silver nitrate solution	Addition of dilute hydrochloric acid and barium chloride solution
Distillation flask				
Distillate				

35 Answers

Starter activity: Pure water and potable water

1. No (it contains minerals as well as H_2O)
2. Pure water contains only water molecules.
3. Pure water contains only water molecules; potable water may contain dissolved solids.
4. The boiling point should be 100 °C.
5. Levels of solutes not damaging to health; no microbes
6. Ground, rivers, lakes, reservoirs
7. a) Finite resources
   b) Finite resources

Main activity: Producing potable water

1. Rain water: relatively simple process; salty water: distillation or separation by reverse osmosis are more complicated processes; waste water: requires removal of contaminants, a more complicated process
2. Rain water: relatively quick; salty water and waste water: time consuming processes
3. Rain water: cheapest method once system is in place; salty water: expensive, because energy is needed to change water to water vapour; waste water: moderately expensive due to running costs of sewage treatment works
4. Clean water is extracted from waste water and returned to the water system.

Main activity: Phytomining and bioleaching

1. Traditional mining and smelting cause many environmental problems (sulfur dioxide emissions, land removal); high grade ores are running out
2. Need to be large and fast growing; need to accumulate copper compounds
3.

	Traditional mining and smelting	Phytomining	Bioleaching
Pollution	Produces sulfur dioxide	Limited pollution; carbon dioxide absorbed in photosynthesis is released when plants are burned.	Leachate solution may contaminate surrounding areas and waterways.
Other environmental problems	Land removal; produces a lot of waste rock	Dependent on good growing conditions	Can produce toxic chemicals
Time required	Relatively quick	Requires a growing season	A slow process, up to two years

Homework activity: Analysing and purifying water samples

1. A: H^+, Cu^{2+}, SO_4^{2-}
   B: H^+, Fe^{2+}, Cl^-, SO_4^{2-}
   C: H^+, Cu^{2+}, SO_4^{2-}
   The distillation flask contains the ions present in the original sample and will give the same results. The distillate is pure water, so is pH7 and will not form precipitates in the other chemical tests.
2. Samples A and C should produce a green flame.
3.

Water sample A	pH of water sample	Addition of sodium hydroxide solution	Addition of dilute nitric acid and silver nitrate solution	Addition of dilute hydrochloric acid and barium chloride solution
Distillation flask	1–4	blue precipitate forms	no reaction	white precipitate forms
Distillate	7	no reaction	no reaction	no reaction

CHEMISTRY HIGHER

36 Using resources: Life cycle assessments and recycling

Learning objectives

- To understand life cycle assessments
- To carry out simple life cycle assessments to compare two products
- To understand the need to reduce, reuse and recycle to preserve limited resources
- To evaluate ways of reducing the use of limited resources

Specification links

- 4.10.2.1, 4.10.2.2
- WS: 1.3, 1.4, 1.5, 3.5
- MS: 1a

Starter activities

- **Limited and renewable resources; 5 minutes; page 228**

  Explain that many products we rely on are manufactured from limited and finite resources and use energy from limited resources in the manufacturing process. Explain that not all finite resources are limited, for example water.

Main activities

- **Life cycle assessments; 20 minutes; page 229**

  Remind the student how carbon footprints measure the amount of greenhouse gases emitted over the lifetime of a product. Discuss the other ways a product has an environmental impact over its lifetime, such as water consumption and disposal in landfill. Explain the life cycle assessments of paper and plastic bags on the activity sheet and the difference between subjective and objective information. Question 3 can be marked as a level of response question.

- **Reducing the use of resources; 20 minutes; page 230**

  Explain how this can be achieved through reduction of use, reuse and recycling. Use examples of reusing and recycling glass and recycling metals to illustrate this idea.

Plenary activity

- **Media interpretations; 5 minutes**

  Discuss with the student how life cycle assessments can be misleading when only selected parts are used. They can suggest how a newspaper headline such as: 'paper bags use up more fossil fuel than polythene bags' might be misleading.

Homework activity

- **Ceramic or disposable coffee cups?; 60 minutes; page 231**

  The student is asked to write life cycle assessments for ceramic and disposable coffee cups. This is a subjective exercise requiring comparative statements.

Support ideas

- **Life cycle assessments** The student can refer back to lesson 33 to recap carbon footprints.
- **Ceramic or disposable coffee cups?** Value judgements are included in the homework activity and may need explaining.

Extension ideas

- **Life cycle assessments** The student can write a life cycle assessment for a smartphone.
- **Reducing the use of resources** The student can find out why and how copper is recycled.

Progress and observations

CHEMISTRY HIGHER

Starter activity: Limited and renewable resources

Learning objectives	Equipment

- To identify products manufactured from finite resources
- To identify products manufactured from limited resources

Look at this list of products.

- a loaf of bread
- a poly(ethene) bag
- a wooden shed
- cotton material
- a car body
- bioethanol in fuel
- a smartphone
- a leather bag
- a glass bottle

1. Which of the products in the list are manufactured from finite resources?

_____

_____

2. Which of the products you identified in question 1 are made from limited resources?

_____

_____

3. What term is used to describe products that are not made from finite resources?

_____

4. Which of the products in the list may be manufactured using energy from fossil fuels?

_____

_____

CHEMISTRY HIGHER

Main activity: Life cycle assessments

Learning objectives

- To understand why life cycle assessments are carried out
- To differentiate between subjective and objective data
- To compare life cycle assessments of paper and plastic bags

Equipment

- calculator

Paper or plastic?

This life cycle assessment compares a paper carrier bag with a plastic carrier bag. These figures are for one bag, used once.

	Paper bag	Plastic bag
Raw materials	wood	crude oil, gas
Energy to make one bag	2600 kJ	760 kJ
Solid waste	33.9 g	14.9 g
Total emissions to the atmosphere	0.08 kg	0.04 kg
Volume of water used	4546 dm³	264 dm³

1. These are some stages in a life cycle assessment:

   - extraction of raw materials and processing
   - manufacturing and packaging
   - use
   - disposal

   What details are missing from the table which could influence whether paper or plastic bags are used?

   _____

   _____

2. Which information in the table is objective?

   _____

3. Supermarkets and other retailers are reducing the use of plastic bags by charging for them. There is currently no charge for paper bags. Use the information in the table to evaluate the decision to charge for plastic bags but not for paper bags.

   _____

   _____

   _____

   _____

   _____

   _____

   _____

   _____

   _____

[6 marks]

CHEMISTRY HIGHER

Main activity: Reducing the use of resources

Learning objectives

- To know that reduction in use, reuse and recycling of materials reduce the use of limited resources
- To know that glass bottles can be reused or recycled
- To know that metals can be recycled

Equipment

---

1. A, B and C are three actions that reduce the use of resources. Which is a reduction in use, which is reuse and which is recycling?

A. taking old clothes to a charity shop _____

B. using less shampoo to wash your hair _____

C. making a denim bag out of an old pair of denim jeans _____

---

2. The diagrams below show how glass containers, such as bottles, are produced and recycled.

a) Sand, soda ash and limestone are finite resources, but they are not limited. What does 'finite but not limited' mean?

_____

_____

_____

_____

glass production

mixing → melting → shaping → glass containers

- sand
- soda ash
- limestone
- other chemicals

glass furnace (approx 1500 °C)

molten glass blowing

b) Why does it make good economic and environmental sense to recycle glass bottles?

_____

_____

_____

_____

glass recycling

collection of used glass → sorting by colour → washing (remove impurities) → crushing and melting → moulding into new products

c) Glass bottles can also be reused. They are collected, washed and used again. What properties does glass have to make glass bottles suitable for reuse?

_____

_____

---

3. Metals can be recycled by melting and recasting into different products. How is scrap steel recycled to make new steel?

_____

_____

CHEMISTRY HIGHER

Homework activity: Ceramic or disposable coffee cups?

Time **60** mins

Learning objectives

- To produce and compare life cycle assessments for ceramic and disposable coffee cups
- To make value judgements

Equipment

- spare paper

The ceramic cup is made from clay. It can be used up to 500 times, but needs to be washed.

The disposable cup is made from paper lined with poly(ethene). Paper lined with poly(ethene) cannot easily be recycled. It is designed to be used once and thrown away.

1. **On a separate piece of paper, write life cycle assessments to compare the ceramic cup and disposable cup. The table below provides an outline for your assessments. Your information will be subjective (it will not include figures). Try to make good judgements, called value judgements.**

	Ceramic coffee cup	Disposable coffee cup
Raw materials		
Extraction of raw materials and processing		
Manufacturing of cups		
Transport throughout the life cycle		
Use (washing etc.)		
Disposal		

Starter activity: Limited and renewable resources

1. Poly(ethene) bag, car body, smartphone, glass bottle
2. Poly(ethene) bag, car body, smartphone
3. renewable
4. All use energy, possibly from fossil fuels.

Main activity: Life cycle assessments

1. How the bag is used; how many times it is used; how the bag is disposed of (recycled or landfill)
2. All except the raw materials
3. Student's own answers. This is a level of response question. Marks can be awarded as follows:
   5–6 marks: detailed answer including information from the table and consideration of how the bag is used; contains calculations; answer is logical and includes scientific language; some conclusions are made and justified
   3–4 marks: answer includes some relevant points based on information from the table and use; some conclusions are made
   1–2 marks: some relevant points are made using information from the table; no conclusions are made

Main activity: Reducing the use of resources

1. A: reuse; B: reduction in use; C: recycling
2. a) They are resources which will run out in the end, but we have abundant supplies now.
   b) Making glass uses a lot of energy, often from limited resources/fossil fuels; recycling reduces waste in landfill
   c) Glass is unreactive, so it does not react with the contents of the bottle. Glass can also be cleaned and sterilised at a high temperature.
3. Scrap steel is added to molten iron from the blast furnace to make new steel.

Homework activity: Ceramic or disposable coffee cups?

1. Possible answers include the following.
   Ceramic coffee cups:
   - made from clay, which has to be fired at high temperature
   - transport uses fossil fuels
   - can be reused many times
   - have to be washed before reuse – washing uses energy from fossil fuels
   - end up in landfill/cannot be recycled

   Disposable coffee cups:
   - made from crude oil and wood; fractional distillation and cracking of crude oil are required, and processing of wood to make paper uses energy
   - transport uses fossil fuel
   - regular deliveries required for coffee outlets
   - end up in landfill/cannot be recycled

37 Using resources: Materials

Learning objectives

- To understand methods used to prevent corrosion
- To know the composition and uses of some alloys
- To compare the physical properties of clay, glass, ceramics, polymers, composites and metals

Specification links

- 4.10.3.1, 4.10.3.2, 4.10.3.3
- WS: 1.4, 2.2, 3.5
- MS: 4a

Starter activities

- **Alloys; 5 minutes; page 234**

  The relative hardness of alloys was covered in lesson 11. This activity revises these ideas. Explain that this lesson covers other materials we commonly use.

Main activities

- **Corrosion; 20 minutes; page 235**

  Discuss the conditions needed for the corrosion of metals and the essential features of experiments to investigate conditions required for corrosion (e.g. controlling variables). Ensure the student is using the terms 'rusting' and 'corrosion' correctly. Explain methods used to prevent corrosion, including sacrificial protection. Question 3 can be answered verbally.

- **Ceramics, polymers and composites; 20 minutes; page 236**

  Explain that the materials we commonly use must have appropriate properties for their function. You can illustrate this by referring to the different types of polymer, such as HD and LD poly(ethene) and thermosoftening and thermosetting polymers. Soda lime glass and borosilicate glass are also good examples. Explain how composites combine two materials to give the required properties. Questions 2 and 3 can be answered verbally.

Plenary activity

- **The role of chemistry; 5 minutes**

  Tell the student that chemistry has played a vital role in developing the materials discussed in this lesson. Ask the student to use the content of the lesson to provide examples of the role it has played

Homework activity

- **Gold alloys and others; 60 minutes; page 237**

  Remind the student that an alloy is a mixture of a metal with one or more other elements.

Support ideas

- **Corrosion** Explain the role of the reactivity series in deciding which metals can prevent rusting of iron by sacrificial protection.
- **Ceramics, polymers and composites** The student can refer back to lesson 29 to explain polymerisation and the structure of poly(ethene).

Extension ideas

- **Ceramics, polymers and composites** The student can research the composition of different composites, such as reinforced steel.
- **Gold alloys and others** The student could investigate the composition of silver alloys, such as sterling silver, and their uses.

Progress and observations

Starter activity: Alloys

Learning objectives

- To revise the structure of an alloy
- To explain why alloys are harder than pure metals
- To know the composition of brass and bronze

Equipment

The diagram shows the structure of an alloy.

Circle the letter next to the correct answer for each question.

1. Which is the best definition for an alloy?

   A. a compound of two metals

   B. a mixture of a metal and one or more other elements

   C. a mixture of two metals

   D. a mixture of different sized particles

2. Why are alloys harder than the pure metal?

   A. They are mixed with harder metals.

   B. The different sized metal atoms enable the layers to slide over each other.

   C. The different sized particles prevent the layers of metal atoms sliding over each other.

   D. The cross links between the atoms stop the layers sliding.

3. What is the composition of brass?

   A. copper and tin

   B. tin and zinc

   C. copper and iron

   D. copper and zinc

4. What is the composition of bronze?

   A. copper and tin

   B. tin and zinc

   C. copper and iron

   D. copper and zinc

CHEMISTRY HIGHER

Main activity: Corrosion

Learning objectives

- To interpret results of investigations into methods of preventing rusting
- To describe an experiment to show the conditions needed for rusting

Equipment

- pencil

1. **Some students are planning an investigation of the conditions required for rusting. This is their hypothesis: 'Both air and water are required for iron to rust.' They set up three test tubes with different conditions. Each test tube contains an iron nail.**

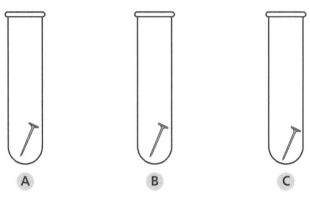

A   B   C

a) Complete the diagram to show the contents of each test tube. You can add an extra test tube if needed.

b) What are the conditions in each test tube?

_____

_____

_____

c) Predict the results. _____

_____

2. **The experiment shown is investigating sacrificial protection.**

a) Explain the results.

_____

_____

_____

_____

_____

X   Y   Z

magnesium strip

iron nail   tin strip

wire

water

slightly rusty   very rusty   not rusty

b) Describe two other methods of preventing rusting.

_____

_____

3. **Explain why aluminium doesn't appear to corrode even though it is a reactive metal.**

_____

_____

CHEMISTRY HIGHER

Main activity: Ceramics, polymers and composites

Learning objectives	Equipment
• To know how glass, ceramics and composites are made	none
• To explain the properties of high density and low density poly(ethene)	
• To explain the properties of thermosetting and thermosoftening polymers	

1. Complete the table to show how each material is made.

Material	How is it made?
soda lime glass	
borosilicate glass	
clay ceramics	
composites	

2. These diagrams show different types of poly(ethene). They have different properties. Use the diagrams to explain why.

A
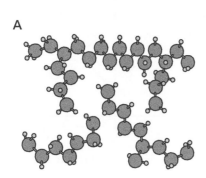

B
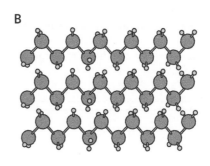

3. These diagrams show different polymer structures with different properties. The lines represent long polymer chains. Discuss the following questions with your tutor.

C
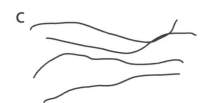

D

a) What do we call each type of polymer?

b) Explain their different properties.

TUTORS' GUILD CHEMISTRY HIGHER

Homework activity: Gold alloys and others

Time 60 mins

Learning objectives

- To know how gold alloys are used in jewellery
- To know the composition and properties of some steels
- To interpret and evaluate the composition of alloys

Equipment

1. The table shows information on gold alloys used to make jewellery.

	Carat	Composition
Yellow gold	24	gold
Red gold	18	gold, copper
White gold	18	gold, platinum
White gold	9	gold, silver

a) Which type of gold is a pure substance? _____

b) Which metal is responsible for the red colour in a gold alloy? _____

c) What is the percentage of copper in red gold? _____

d) What is the percentage of gold in 9 carat gold? _____

2. Steel is an alloy of iron and carbon, with other metals added. The graph shows how the percentage of carbon in steel affects its hardness.

a) What is the relationship between the percentage of carbon in steel and its hardness?

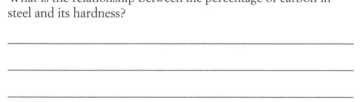

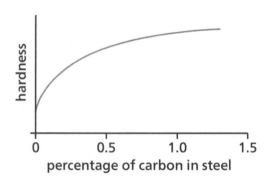

b) Low carbon steels are generally more useful than high carbon steels. Explain why.

_____

_____

c) Stainless steel contains a maximum of 0.08% carbon. What other metals are added to make it hard and corrosion resistant?

_____

37 Answers

Starter activity: Alloys

1. B
2. C
3. D
4. A

Main activity: Corrosion

1 a) Diagrams need to show:
  • one test tube with water and air/oxygen – e.g. nail in water, test tube not sealed
  • one test tube with water but no air – e.g. nail in boiled water with a layer of oil on top
  • one test tube with air/oxygen but no water – e.g. nail in sealed test tube with drying agent/calcium chloride
  b) Air/oxygen and water; water only (no air/oxygen); oxygen only (no water)
  c) Only the nail in the test tube with both air/oxygen and water should rust.
2. a) X: rusts because air and water are present
    Y: rusts because iron is more reactive than tin
    Z: does not rust because magnesium is more reactive than iron
  b) For example: painting, coating with a layer of oil/grease
3. A protective layer of aluminium oxide forms on the surface, protecting aluminium from further corrosion.

Main activity: Ceramics, polymers and composites

1. Soda lime glass: heating sand, sodium carbonate and limestone together
    Borosilicate glass: heating boron trioxide and sand together
    Clay ceramics: heating clay
    Composites: mixing fibres or fragments in a matrix or binder
2. A is low density poly(ethene). It has side branches which lower the density and melting point.
    B is high density poly(ethene). It has a crystalline structure, which gives it a higher density and higher melting point.
3. a) C: thermosoftening (thermoplastic)
      D: thermosetting
  b) The chains in thermosoftening polymers can slide over each other so the material softens as it is heated. The chains in thermosetting polymers are held rigid by the cross links so the material does not soften when heated.

Homework activity: Gold alloys and others

1. a) Yellow gold/24 carat gold
  b) copper
  c) 25%
  d) 37.5%
2. a) The hardness increases as the percentage of carbon increases.
  b) They can be shaped more easily because they are softer.
  c) Chromium and nickel

CHEMISTRY HIGHER

38 Using resources: Ammonia and fertilisers

Learning objectives

- To understand the Haber process
- To explain the reaction conditions used in the Haber process
- To know the composition of NPK fertilisers
- To know how fertilisers are produced

Specification links

- 4.10.4.1, 4.10.4.2
- WS: 1.4, 3.3
- MS: 1a, 1c, 3b, 3c, 4a

Starter activities

- **The importance of ammonia; 5 minutes; page 240**

  Briefly discuss the graph in the activity with the student and establish the importance of fertilisers in food production. Explain the role of ammonia as a source of nitrogen in fertiliser and the formula of the ammonium ion.

Main activities

- **The Haber process; 20 minutes; page 241**

  Remind the student of the lesson on equilibria and the effects of changing conditions. The homework activity in lesson 25 covered the effects of changing conditions in the reaction $N_2 + 3H_2 \leftrightharpoons 2NH_3$. Describe the features of the Haber process, including sources of raw materials and the separation of ammonia. Question 2 can be treated as a level of response question.

- **NPK fertilisers; 20 minutes; page 242**

  Explain that most fertilisers contain nitrogen for healthy leaves, phosphorus for healthy root systems and flowers and potassium for general growth. Show the student how the percentage of each element is shown in the NPK rating. Discuss how NPK fertilisers are produced, the source of each element and the compound that goes into the bag of fertiliser.

Plenary activity

- **Laboratory and industrial methods; 5 minutes**

  Ask the student to compare the method used in the homework activity to prepare a fertiliser ingredient with the industrial preparation. They can identify one similarity and one difference.

  If time allows, discuss the student's revision plans: their revision timetable, how they are revising and which areas need extra attention.

Homework activity

- **Preparing a fertiliser; 60 minutes; page 243**

  This is a synoptic activity based on the preparation of ammonium sulfate and involves several calculations.

  A pH probe is included in the method; the student may not be familiar with pH probes and they may need some explanation.

Support ideas

- **The Haber process** The student can refer back to lessons 24 and 25 to revise chemical equilibria and the effects of changing reaction conditions.

Extension ideas

- **The Haber process** The student can find out about the successful but tragic life of Fritz Haber.
- **NPK fertilisers** The student could identify the reactants needed to produce other ammonium salts, such as ammonium chloride.

Progress and observations

CHEMISTRY HIGHER

Starter activity: The importance of ammonia

Time 5 mins

Learning objectives	Equipment

- To explain the need to use fertilisers to feed the world's increasing population
- To know the role of ammonia in fertiliser production
- To write formulae for ammonium salts

The graph shows the changes in the world's population since 1950, and predicted changes up to 2050.

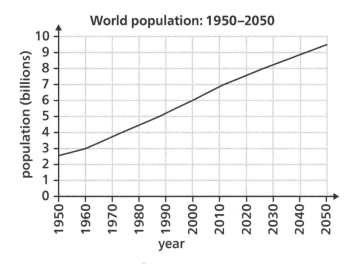

We just about grow enough food to feed the world today. Some scientists estimate that fertilisers account for up to 50% of the food crops farmers produce at present.

1. By how much is it estimated that the world's population will increase between 2020 and 2050?

_____

2. Most fertilisers provide nitrogen, phosphorus and potassium for plants. What role does ammonia play in this?

_____

3. Ammonia is a gas at room temperature. Ammonium salts such as ammonium sulfate are used in fertilisers. Ammonia is NH_3. The ammonium ion is NH_4^+. Write formulae for:

a) ammonium sulfate _____

b) ammonium chloride _____

c) ammonium carbonate. _____

CHEMISTRY HIGHER

AQA

Main activity: The Haber process

Time **20** mins

Learning objectives

- To know the sources of raw materials for the Haber process
- To describe the Haber process
- To explain the conditions used in the Haber process

Equipment

- spare paper

1. **The diagram shows the Haber process to make ammonia.**

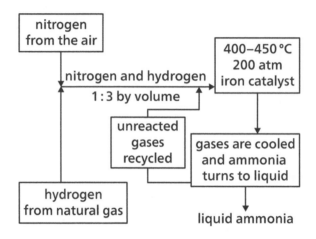

Explain:

a) why nitrogen and hydrogen are mixed in a 1:3 ratio

_____

_____

b) why it is necessary to recycle unreacted gases

_____

_____

c) why an iron catalyst is used

_____

_____

d) why ammonia can be separated from the unreacted gases by cooling.

_____

_____

2. **On a separate piece of paper, write a short passage to explain why manufacturers use a temperature of 400°C–450°C, a pressure of 200 atmospheres and an iron catalyst during the Haber process.**

   The reaction to produce ammonia is exothermic. You should comment on the effect of each condition on the position of the equilibrium.

CHEMISTRY HIGHER

Main activity: NPK fertilisers

Time **20** mins

Learning objectives

- To calculate masses of nitrogen, phosphorus and potassium in NPK fertilisers
- To describe how NPK fertilisers are produced

Equipment

- calculator

The diagram shows a 5 kg bag of NPK fertiliser. The numbers show the percentage of each element in the fertiliser, and refer, reading from left to right, to nitrogen, phosphorus and potassium.

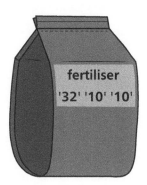

fertiliser
'32' '10' '10'

1. **Complete the table.**

Element provided by fertiliser	nitrogen	phosphorus	potassium
Mass/kg of each element in the 5 kg bag of fertiliser above			
Compound in fertiliser providing the element	ammonium sulfate	calcium phosphate	potassium chloride
Source of each compound			

2. **Why does phosphate rock have to be treated before it can be used in a fertiliser?**

_____

_____

_____

AQA

CHEMISTRY HIGHER

Homework activity: Preparing a fertiliser

Time **60** mins

Learning objectives	Equipment

- To know how to prepare an ammonium salt
- To carry out concentration calculations
- To convert moles to masses
- To calculate reacting amounts from balanced equations
- To calculate percentage yield and atom economy

- calculator

Students are preparing a sample of ammonium sulfate from ammonia solution and sulfuric acid.

This is their method:

- Fill a burette with $1\,mol/dm^3$ sulfuric acid. Record the initial volume.
- Measure $20\,cm^3$ ammonia solution into a conical flask.
- Add a pH probe.
- Swirl the ammonia solution in the conical flask. While swirling, add sulfuric acid to the ammonia solution, $1\,cm^3$ at a time, until the pH starts to fall. Then add ammonia drop by drop until the pH is 7. Record the final volume of sulfuric acid.
- Pour the solution into an evaporating basin and evaporate to half its original volume.
- Leave the solution to crystallise.

The equation for the reaction is: $2NH_3(aq) + H_2SO_4(aq) \rightarrow (NH_4)_2SO_4(aq)$

1. What is present in the flask when the pH is 7?

_____

2. $12.0\,cm^3$ of $2\,mol/dm^3$ sulfuric acid were used to react with the ammonia solution. How many moles of sulfuric acid is this?

_____

3. What is the maximum number of moles of ammonium sulfate that could be made? _____

4. What is the theoretical yield of ammonium sulfate in grams? _____

5. The students weighed their ammonium sulfate. They produced 2.08 g. What is the percentage yield?

_____

6. What is the atom economy of the reaction?

_____

Starter activity: The importance of ammonia

1. About 2 billion
2. Ammonia provides nitrogen.
3. a) $(NH_4)_2SO_4$
   b) NH_4Cl
   c) $(NH_4)_2CO_3$

Main activity: The Haber process

1. a) Ammonia is NH_3; one nitrogen atom combines with three hydrogens atoms; moles of different gases occupy the same volume
   b) The reaction to produce ammonia is reversible, so nitrogen and hydrogen are present at equilibrium.
   c) To increase the rate of reaction; to reach equilibrium more quickly
   d) Ammonia has a higher boiling point than nitrogen and hydrogen, so it liquefies before nitrogen and hydrogen when cooled.
2. A low temperature gives a higher yield of ammonia since the forward reaction is exothermic. However, a low temperature also gives a slow rate of reaction, so it takes a long time to reach equilibrium. A high pressure gives a higher yield of ammonia: four moles of reactants give two moles of products, so a higher pressure shifts the equilibrium to the right. However, it is expensive to maintain a high pressure. A compromise temperature and pressure are used to balance yield and cost, and a catalyst is used to decrease the time taken to reach equilibrium.
   If treated as a level of response question: 5–6 marks: A logical explanation including the effects of pressure and temperature on the yield of ammonia leading to the justification of compromise conditions.
   3–4 marks: Some correct explanations of the effects of temperature and/or pressure on the yield of ammonia. An explanation of reasons for using compromise conditions is attempted.
   1–2 marks: Some valid points are made, but no clear logical explanation of conditions used is given.

Main activity: NPK fertilisers

1. Mass of nitrogen: 1.6 kg; mass of phosphorus: 0.5 kg; mass of potassium: 0.5 kg
   source:
   - Ammonium sulfate: ammonia is reacted with sulfuric acid
   - Calcium phosphate: phosphate rock is mined and reacted with sulfuric acid or nitric acid to produce soluble phosphate salts
   - Potassium chloride: mining
2. Phosphate rocks are insoluble. They must be converted into soluble salts so that phosphorus can be absorbed by plant roots.

Homework activity: Preparing a fertiliser

1. Ammonium sulfate solution
2. 0.024 mol
3. 0.024 mol
4. 3.168 g (3.17 g to 2 decimal places)
5. 66%
6. 100%

Glossary

Acid rain
Typical acid rain has a pH of 4 or below (normal rain has a pH of 5.5)

Activation energy
The energy needed to start a reaction; the energy needed to break bonds

Actual yield
The amount of product obtained during a practical procedure

Addition polymerisation
Many small molecules (monomers) join to make one very long molecule (polymer)

Alcohols
A homologous series with a –OH functional group

Alkali
A soluble base, such as sodium hydroxide

Alkali metal
A metal in Group 1

Alkanes
A family or homologous series of hydrocarbons with the general formula C_nH_{2n+2}

Alkenes
A homologous series with a C = C functional group, and the general formula C_nH_{2n}.

Alloy
A metal with another element added

Alpha particle
Positively charged particle; a helium nucleus

Amino acid
The monomer of a protein

Ammonium salt
A salt containing the positive ion NH_4^+

Anhydrous
A salt that does not contain water of crystallisation

Anode
The positive electrode

A successful collision
A collision that results in a reaction

Atom
The smallest part of an element that can exist

Atom economy
A measure of the amount of starting materials that ends up as useful products, calculated by: the relative formula mass of the desired product from the equation divided by the sum of relative formula masses of all the reactants from the equation, multiplied by 100

Atomic number
The number of protons in an atom

Atomic weight
An old measurement used to compare the mass of atoms; we now use relative atomic mass

Avogadro constant
The number of particles in one mole of a substance; Avogadro constant = 6.02×10^{23}

Battery
Two or more cells connected in series

Bioleaching
A method used to extract metals from low grade ores by growing bacteria which produce a leachate solution containing copper compounds

Bond energy
The energy needed to break bonds, usually given in kJ/mol

Collision theory
A theory describing how particles collide and react

Carbon nanotube
A cylindrical fullerene

Carboxylic acids
A homologous series with a –C(=O)OH functional group

Catalyst
Substance that changes the rate of a reaction but is not used up in the reaction

Catalytic cracking
A method used to crack hydrocarbons using a zeolite catalyst

Cathode
The negative electrode

Ceramic
A material made from clay

Chromatogram
The results of a chromatography experiment

Chromatography
Technique for separating the soluble components of a mixture, such as food dye or ink

Climate change
A change in global weather patterns

Complete combustion
Reaction of a hydrocarbon with excess oxygen producing carbon diode and water

Composite
A material consisting of reinforcing fibres or fragments in a matrix or binder

Compound
A substance containing two or more different types of element

Concentrated acid
An acid solution containing high amounts of acid

Concentration
The amount of a solute dissolved in a given volume of solvent

Condensation polymerisation
Many small molecules (monomers) join to make one very long molecule (polymer), eliminating a small molecule at each link

CHEMISTRY HIGHER

Glossary

Control variables
Variables that have to be kept constant in an investigation, as they can affect the outcome

Corrosion
The destruction of a material by chemical reactions with substances in the environment

Covalent bond
A chemical bond between non-metals in which electrons are shared

Cracking
Breaking longer alkanes into shorter, more useful, alkane and alkene molecules

Crude oil
The remains of biomass formed millions of years ago

Crystallisation
Separation of a soluble solid from a solution by evaporating the solvent

Delocalised electrons
Electrons that are free to move throughout a structure

Dilute acid
An acid solution containing little acid

Displacement reaction
Reaction in which one atom or group of atoms is displaced by another more reactive one

DNA (deoxyribonucleic acid)
A large molecule containing two polymer chains in the form of a double helix which encodes genetic instructions

Dot and cross diagram
A representation of a chemical bond showing how electrons are arranged

Double covalent bond
Two pairs of electrons shared between two atoms

Earth's early atmosphere
The atmosphere that existed on Earth for the first billion years

Electrolyte
A solution that conducts electricity

Electrode
Rods of metal or graphite used to conduct electricity through a solution

Electrolysis
Passing an electric current through a solution

Electron
Negatively charge subatomic particle, located in electron shells

Electronic structure
The arrangement of electrons in an atom

Element
A substance containing one type of atom only

Empirical formula
A formula showing the type and ratio of atoms

Endothermic reaction
A reaction in which energy is transferred from the surroundings to the reactants

Energy level or electron shell
Area in an atom where an electron may be located

Equilibrium
The stage in a reversible reaction when the forward and reverse reactions are occurring at the same rate

Ester
The product of reacting an alcohol with a carboxylic acid (water is also a product).

Exothermic reaction
A reaction in which energy is transferred to the surroundings

Filtration
Using a filter for separation of a liquid from an insoluble solid

Finite resource
A resource present in limited amounts on Earth

Flame emission spectroscopy
An instrumental method used to identify metal ions in solution

Flame test
A method used to identify metal ions in solution using a Bunsen burner

Formulation
A mixture containing components in measured amounts

Forward reaction
The reaction from left to right in the equation of a reversible reaction

Fraction
A product from fractional distillation containing compounds with similar boiling points

Fractional distillation
Separation of a mixture of liquids with different boiling points into different components (fractions) by evaporation and condensation

Fullerene
A hollow carbon molecule in which each carbon atom is covalently bonded to three other carbon atoms, forming spheres or tube shapes

Gas volume
One mole of gas occupies $24\,dm^3$ at room temperature and pressure

General formula
A formula in which numbers of atoms can be substituted to give the molecular formula

Giant covalent structure
A large covalently bonded structure such as diamond or silicon dioxide

Glossary

Global dimming
The reflection of sunlight back into space by particulate matter in the atmosphere

Graphene
A single layer of graphite one atom thick, with atoms arranged in a honeycomb shape

Greenhouse effect
Greenhouse gases absorb some long wave radiation in the atmosphere and prevent it from escaping the atmosphere. This maintains the temperature at a level suitable for life.

Greenhouse gas
A gas that absorbs long wave radiation in the atmosphere; for example, carbon dioxide, methane or water vapour

Group
A vertical column in the periodic table containing elements with similar properties

Haber process
The industrial method used to produce ammonia from hydrogen and nitrogen gas

Halides
Ionic compounds containing negative Group 7 ions

Halogen
An element in Group 7

Homologous series
A family of chemicals with the same general formula

Hydrated
A salt containing water of crystallisation

Hydrogen fuel cell
A cell using the oxidation of hydrogen to produce water

Incomplete combustion
Combustion producing water and carbon monoxide and/or carbon

Intermolecular forces
The weak attraction between adjacent molecules

Ion
A charged particle; an atom that has lost or gained electrons

Ionic bond
Strong electrostatic attraction between oppositely charged ions which forms between a metal and non-metal

Ionic lattice
The giant structure of an ionic compound

Isotopes
Atoms of the same element which have the same atomic number, but different mass numbers; they have the same number of protons, but different numbers of neutrons

Le Chatelier's principle
If a system is at equilibrium and a change is made to any of the conditions, then the system responds to counteract the change

Life cycle assessment
An assessment of the environmental impact of a product from extraction of its raw materials to its disposal

Limited resource
A finite resource of which there are limited amounts on Earth

Limiting reactant
A reactant that is completely used up in a reaction while another reactant is in excess

Line emission spectrum (plural spectra)
A chart showing the wavelengths of light emitted by metal ions in solution when they emit energy

Mass number
The number of protons plus neutrons in an atom

Mathematical requirements
A list of mathematical skills students will be required to demonstrate in GCSE chemistry assessment

Mean rate of reaction
Quantity of reactant used or product formed divided by time

Mendeleev
Dmitri Mendeleev was a Russian chemist who arranged the elements in a periodic table that evolved into the periodic table we use today.

Metal
An element that is shiny when polished, conducts heat and electricity well, and is malleable and flexible. Metals often have high melting points and react to form positive ions.

Metallic bond
A bond between metal atoms in which positive metal ions are attracted to delocalised electrons

Metal oxide
A compound containing a metal and oxygen

Mixture
A mixture consists of two or more elements or compounds which are not chemically combined together.

mol/dm³
A unit used to measure concentration

Mole
The amount of a substance containing 6.02×10^{23} particles

Monomer
The small molecules that link up to make a polymer

Nanometre (nm)
One billionth of a metre, $1\,nm = 10^{-9}\,m$

Nanoparticles
Particles with diameters between $1\,nm$ and $100\,nm$

Nanoscience
The study of particles between $1\,nm$ and $100\,nm$

Neutralisation
A reaction between an acid and an alkali or a base (such as a metal oxide, metal hydroxide or metal carbonate) to produce neutral products, a salt and water

CHEMISTRY HIGHER

Glossary

Neutron
A neutral subatomic particle, located in the nucleus

Noble gas
An element in Group 0

Non-metal
An element that is not shiny, does not conduct heat or electricity well, and does not form a positive ion when it reacts

Non-rechargeable battery
A battery with a limited life as the chemicals are used up

NPK fertiliser
A fertiliser providing nitrogen, phosphorus and potassium

Nuclear model
The current atomic model; negatively charged electrons orbit a central positively charged nucleus

Nucleus
Located in the centre of an atom and consisting of protons and neutrons (hydrogen has one proton only)

Oxidation
The gain of oxygen; the loss of electrons

Particle theory
A theory modelling particles as solid, inelastic spheres with no forces of attraction between particles

Particulates
Small solid particles in the atmosphere

Percentage yield
The mass of product actually made divided by the maximum theoretical mass of product, multiplied by 100

Period
A horizontal row in the periodic table

Phosphate rock
Any rock containing phosphorus

Photosynthesis
Reaction in the green parts of plants between carbon dioxide and water in the presence of light to produce glucose and oxygen

pH scale
A scale from 1 to 14 measuring the acidity or alkalinity of a solution

Phytomining
A method used to extract metals from low grade ores by growing, harvesting and burning plants that accumulate the metal

Plum pudding model
Atomic model consisting of negatively charged spheres in a cloud of positive charge

Polymer
Large molecule with a regular repeating unit

Phosphate rock
Any rock containing phosphorus

Photosynthesis
Reaction in the green parts of plants between carbon dioxide and water in the presence of light to produce glucose and oxygen

pH scale
A scale from 1 to 14 measuring the acidity or alkalinity of a solution

Phytomining
A method used to extract metals from low grade ores by growing, harvesting and burning plants that accumulate the metal

Plum pudding model
Atomic model consisting of negatively charged spheres in a cloud of positive charge

Polymer
Large molecule with a regular repeating unit

Polypeptide
A section of a protein molecule

Position of equilibrium
Both reactants and products are present in concentrations that do not change; the rate of the forward reaction is the same as the rate of the reverse reaction

Positive ion
An atom that has lost one or more electrons

Potable water
Water that is suitable for drinking

Precipitate
An insoluble substance formed in a chemical reaction between two solutions

Proton
A positively charged subatomic particle, located in the nucleus

Pure substance
A single element or compound

Rate of reaction
How fast a reaction occurs

Reaction pathway
A series of chemical reactions used to make a particular product

Reaction profile
A diagram showing the relative energies of reactants and products in a reaction, including the activation energy

Redox reaction
A reaction in which one substance is oxidised and another is reduced

Rechargeable battery
A battery which can be recharged by reversing the chemical reactions by applying an electric current

Recycling
Processing discarded products into new products

Reduction
The loss of oxygen; the gain of electrons

CHEMISTRY HIGHER

Glossary

Relative atomic mass
The average mass of all naturally occurring isotopes of an element, taking abundance into consideration

Relative formula mass (M_r)
The sum of the relative atomic masses of all the atoms in a formula

Respiration
The reaction between glucose and oxygen; energy is released and carbon dioxide and water are produced

Reverse reaction
The reaction from right to left in the equation of a reversible reaction

Reversible reaction
A reaction that can proceed in both directions

R_f value
The distance moved by a substance divided by the distance moved by the solvent

Rusting
The reaction of iron with air/oxygen and water

Simple cell
A chemical reaction designed to produce an electric current which consists of two different metals in an electrolyte connected in a circuit

Simple distillation
Separation of a liquid from a solution by evaporation and condensation

Single covalent bond
One pair of electrons shared between two atoms

Spectroscope
An instrument to observe line emission spectra

States of matter
How a substance exists; as a solid, liquid or gas

State symbols
Abbreviations used in chemical equations to show whether the substance is a solid (s), liquid (l), gas (g) or in solution (aq)

Steam cracking
A method used to crack hydrocarbons by heating under pressure in the absence of air

Strong acid
An acid that is completely ionised in solution

Surface area to volume ratio
The total surface area of an object divided by its volume

The law of conservation of mass
No atoms are lost or gained in a chemical reaction

Theoretical yield
The maximum calculated amount of a product that could be formed from a given amount of reactants

Theory
A scientific idea to explain observations backed up by evidence

The range (of a set of measurements)
The difference between the highest and lowest measurement

The reactivity series
A list of metals in order of their reactivity/tendency to form positive ions

Titration
A practical procedure involving a burette and pipette, used to determine exact reacting volumes of solutions

Transition metal
A metal located in the block of elements between Groups 2 and 3 in the periodic table

Triple covalent bond
Three pairs of electrons shared between two atoms

Uncertainty Viscosity
The thickness of a liquid; low viscosity is very runny, high viscosity is thick

Weak acid
An acid that is partially ionised in solution

Working scientifically
This is a list of all the activities scientists do. It is assessed throughout the GCSE chemistry papers.

THE PERIODIC TABLE OF ELEMENTS

Group

Key

| relative atomic mass |
| **atomic symbol** |
| name |
| atomic (proton) number |

1		
H		
Hydrogen		
1		

1	2											3	4	5	6	7	0
																	4 **He** Helium 2
7 **Li** Lithium 3	9 **Be** Beryllium 4											11 **B** Boron 5	12 **C** Carbon 6	14 **N** Nitrogen 7	16 **O** Oxygen 8	19 **F** Fluorine 9	20 **Ne** Neon 10
23 **Na** Sodium 11	24 **Mg** Magnesium 12											27 **Al** Aluminium 13	28 **Si** Silicon 14	31 **P** Phosphorus 15	32 **S** Sulfur 16	35.5 **Cl** Chlorine 17	40 **Ar** Argon 18
39 **K** Potassium 19	40 **Ca** Calcium 20	45 **Sc** Scandium 21	48 **Ti** Titanium 22	51 **V** Vanadium 23	52 **Cr** Chromium 24	55 **Mn** Manganese 25	56 **Fe** Iron 26	59 **Co** Cobalt 27	59 **Ni** Nickel 28	64 **Cu** Copper 29	65 **Zn** Zinc 30	70 **Ga** Gallium 31	73 **Ge** Germanium 32	75 **As** Arsenic 33	79 **Se** Selenium 34	80 **Br** Bromine 35	84 **Kr** Krypton 36
85 **Rb** Rubidium 37	88 **Sr** Strontium 38	89 **Y** Yttrium 39	91 **Zr** Zirconium 40	93 **Nb** Niobium 41	96 **Mo** Molybdenum 42	98 **Tc** Technetium 43	101 **Ru** Ruthenium 44	103 **Rh** Rhodium 45	106 **Pd** Palladium 46	108 **Ag** Silver 47	112 **Cd** Cadmium 48	115 **In** Indium 49	119 **Sn** Tin 50	122 **Sb** Antimony 51	128 **Te** Tellurium 52	127 **I** Iodine 53	131 **Xe** Xenon 54
133 **Cs** Caesium 55	137 **Ba** Barium 56	139 **La*** Lanthanum 57	178 **Hf** Hafnium 72	181 **Ta** Tantalum 73	184 **W** Tungsten 74	186 **Re** Rhenium 75	190 **Os** Osmium 76	192 **Ir** Iridium 77	195 **Pt** Platinum 78	197 **Au** Gold 79	201 **Hg** Mercury 80	204 **Tl** Thallium 81	207 **Pb** Lead 82	209 **Bi** Bismuth 83	210 **Po** Polonium 84	210 **At** Astatine 85	222 **Rn** Radon 86
223 **Fr** Francium 87	226 **Ra** Radium 88	227 **Ac*** Actinium 89	261 **Rf** Rutherfordium 104	262 **Db** Dubnium 105	266 **Sg** Seaborgium 106	264 **Bh** Bohrium 107	277 **Hs** Hassium 108	268 **Mt** Meitnerium 109	271 **Ds** Darmstadtium 110	272 **Rg** Roentgenium 111	285 **Cn** Copernicium 112	286 **Uut** Ununtrium 112	289 **Fl** Flerovium 112	289 **Uup** Ununpentium 112	293 **Lv** Livermorium 112	294 **Uus** Ununseptium 112	294 **Uuo** Ununoctium 112

* The Lanthanides (atomic numbers 58 – 71 and the Actinides (atomic numbers 90 – 103) have been omitted.
Relative atomic masses for Cu and Cl have not been rounded to the nearest whole number.

Revise mapping guide

Pearson's *Revise* series provides simple, clear support to students preparing for their GCSE (9 -1) exams. Parents may ask you if you know of any independent study resources that they can work through with their child, or you may wish to provide such resources yourself.

We have provided below a mapping guide for each lesson in this pack to a corresponding page in the *Revise* series, to make such recommendations easier for you. See page 5 for a list of recommended titles for students studying AQA GCSE (9 -1) Chemistry. The Revision Guides and Revision Workbooks for each level correspond page-for-page, so the page references are the same for both.

	Lesson	*Revise* AQA GCSE (9–1) Chemistry Higher Revision Guide Page
1	**Diagnostic Lesson**	
2	**Atoms, elements, compounds and mixtures**	Elements, mixtures and compounds **1**; Filtration, crystallisation and chromatography **2**; Distillation **3**
3	**The development of the atomic model and relative electrical charges**	Historical models of the atom **4**; Particles in an atom **5**; Atomic structure and isotopes **6**
4	**Atomic mass, relative atomic mass and electronic structure**	Atomic structure and isotopes **6**; Electronic structure **7**
5	**The periodic table and its development**	Development of the periodic table **8**; The modern periodic table **9**
6	**Groups of elements**	Group 0 **10**; Group 1 **11**; Group 7 **12**
7	**Properties of transition metals**	Group 1 **11**; Transition metals **13**
8	**Ionic bonding and compounds**	Ionic bonding **17**; Giant ionic lattices **18**
9	**Covalent bonding and metallic bonding**	Covalent bonding **19**; Small molecules **20**; Polymer molecules **21**; Metallic bonding **24**; Giant metallic structures and alloys **25**
10	**The particle theory and properties of small molecules**	Chemical equations **14**; Small molecules **20**; The three states of matter **26**
11	**Structure and properties**	Polymer molecules **21**; Diamond and graphite **22**; Graphene and fullerenes **23**; Metallic bonding **24**; Giant metallic structures and alloys **25**
12	**Particle size and nanoparticles**	Nanoscience **27**
13	**Chemical equations and measurements**	Chemical equations **14**; Relative formula mass **29**
14	**Moles, equations and concentrations**	Moles **30**; Balanced equations, moles and masses **31**; Reacting masses **32**
15	**Percentage yield and atom economy**	Reaction yields **38**; Atom economy **39**
16	**Concentrations and gas volumes**	Concentration of a solution **34**; Core practical - Titration **35**; Titration calculations **36**; Reactions with gases **37**
17	**Metals, oxidation and reduction**	Reactivity series **41**; Oxidation **42**; Reduction and metal reaction **43**
18	**Acids and salts**	Reactions of acids **44**; Core practical – Salt preparation **45**
19	**Acids and pH**	Core practical – Titration **35**; Titration calculations **36**; The pH scale **46**

Revise mapping guide

Published by Pearson Education Limited, 80 Strand, London, WC2R 0RL.

www.pearsonschools.co.uk

Text © Pearson Education Limited 2018
Series consultant: Margaret Reeve
Edited by Elektra Media Ltd
Designed by Andrew Magee
Typeset by Elektra Media Ltd
Produced by Elektra Media Ltd
Original illustrations © Pearson Education Limited 2018
Illustrated by Elektra Media Ltd
Cover design by Andrew Magee

The right of Lyn Nicholls to be identified as author of this work has been asserted by her in accordance with the
Copyright, Designs and Patents Act 1988.

First published 2018

20 19 18 17
10 9 8 7 6 5 4 3 2 1

British Library Cataloguing in Publication Data
A catalogue record for this book is available from the British Library

ISBN 9781292201269

Printed in the United Kingdom by Ashford Colour Press Ltd

Acknowledgements
We would like to thank Tutora for its invaluable help in the development and trialling of this course.

The authors and publisher would like to thank the following individuals and organisations for their kind permission to
reproduce copyright material.

Photographs
(Key: b-bottom; c-centre; l-left; r-right; t-top)

123RF: Molekuul 180, Nick Bell 183, V S Anandha Krishna 213, Steven Cukrov 231r; **Alamy Stock Photo:** Science
History Images: 045, Mikael Karlsson 192, Skanda Gautam/ZUMA Wire 218; **Science Photo Library:** Andrew Lambert
Photography 054; **Shutterstock:** Orlando_Stocker 216, Edyta Pawlowska 231l

All other images © Pearson Education

Notes from the publisher
Pearson has robust editorial processes, including answer and fact checks, to ensure the accuracy of the content in
this publication, and every effort is made to ensure this publication is free of errors. We are, however, only human,
and occasionally errors do occur. Pearson is not liable for any misunderstandings that arise as a result of errors in this
publication, but it is our priority to ensure that the content is accurate. If you spot an error, please do contact us at
resourcescorrections@pearson.com so we can make sure it is corrected.